# ADVENTURES IN PORKLAND

# Adventures in
# PORKLAND

## HOW WASHINGTON WASTES YOUR MONEY AND WHY THEY WON'T STOP

## BRIAN KELLY

TIMES 𝕿 BOOKS

RANDOM HOUSE

This work was originally published in hardcover and in slightly different
form by Villard Books, a division of Random House, Inc., in 1992.

Library of Congress Cataloging-in-Publication Data

Kelly, Brian
Adventures in Porkland: how Washington wastes your money
and why they won't stop/Brian Kelly.
p.    cm.
ISBN 0-8129-2313-8
1. Budget—United States.    2. Waste in government spending—United
States.    3. Patronage, Political—United States.    I. Title.
HJ2052.K45    1992
336.3'9'0973—dc20                                              92-53649

Manufactured in the United States of America on acid-free paper
9  8  7  6  5  4  3  2
First Edition

ILLUSTRATIONS BY PAT OLIPHANT
BOOK DESIGN BY JO ANNE METSCH

*To Daniel and Laura,*
*who'll have to pay for all this someday.*

"A government which robs Peter to pay Paul can always depend on the support of Paul."
—George Bernard Shaw

"Who stole the tarts?"
—Lewis Carroll,
*Alice's Adventures in Wonderland*

# CONTENTS

# PREFACE TO THE PAPERBACK EDITION

W HEN I STARTED WRITING THIS BOOK GEORGE BUSH WAS
unbeatable, and Bill Clinton was just one more unknown politician
among a small rabble of Democratic candidates willing to lay themselves on the altar of sacrifice. Hard as it is to believe, Ross Perot
didn't exist in political terms. By the time the presidential campaign really got moving there was also a $3.5 trillion government
deficit and a federal budget that was spurting bright red ink like
blood from a punctured artery at a rate of more than $200 billion a
year. As a result of these spending numbers, a very queasy feeling
was developing in the stomachs of many Americans, a sense that
our democratic system, long cherished as one of mankind's greatest
accomplishments, was seriously out of whack and absolutely in-
capable of finding a way to bring itself back into balance.

There were several reasons for this fiscal insanity, one of which
was the object of my immediate interest: the time-honored but
little understood practice of pork-barrel politics in which favored
members of the United States Congress get to apportion vast
chunks of the general public's money for the amusement of a very

specific public—namely, anyone who can do the congressman some good. But as of this writing a few short years later, I can safely conclude: Some things change. Of course, other things stay the same.

*Adventures in Porkland* is about a year in the life of the taxpayers' money. It is a window into one of the many ways that politicians in Washington spend the dollars pulled every week from the paychecks of those who earn them. Many people think pork is the essence of at least one theory of politics—the one that says all politics is local. This philosophy holds that the elected official's job is to take care of the folks back home, in a Washington that is a marketplace of competing factions where the strong, swift, and clever will usually prevail. Pork is the politics of self-interest, and— let's be realistic about this—it's human nature. Pork is a free lunch. It's spending other people's money. It's checks without balances, school without teachers, highways without traffic cops, law without prisons. It is, in short, the sort of thing most of us probably couldn't stop ourselves from doing if left unsupervised.

The instinct to pork barrel will not soon go away. Many of the people I wrote about are still involved in the game, and the conditions are much the same. But since the 1992 election, some factors are not the same and lead me to think that, remarkable as this statement is, reform of the atrocities catalogued herein is, just maybe, possible.

Of course this pipe dream would not for an instant cause me to reconsider any of the brutally harsh judgments I've rendered on people and process here. *Porkland* says nasty things as it tries to make prominent members of our national leadership look foolish, craven, shallow, and cynical. My resolve to stay this course rests, first, on the certainty that all the foolish, craven, shallow cynicism I portray did indeed happen, and second, on the suspicion that despite a shaft of sunlight breaking through the clouds, we could backslide very quickly into the abyss if we don't pay attention.

This book was written not for politicians—or political scientists, political consultants, political chat-show hosts—but for voters. *Porkland* provides a snapshot that shows how politicians will do what they think they must to survive as amoral actors in a free-market political system where you get only what you can take. The controlling ethic is dictated by the voters. If the dentist in Dubuque, the student in Fayetteville, the homemaker in Macon,

want change, they need only demand it. If they don't, they get the
government they deserve.

As I write this right now, in the middle of August 1993, with Bill
Clinton trying to figure out where to go on vacation, Congress
harmlessly in recess, and most decent folk tucking into a great big
salad in the backyard, Americans seem to want change. They want
it because they have read books like *Porkland*, listened to our
eccentric national economics teacher Professor Perot, followed the
increasingly sophisticated discussion of the budget in the media,
and realized how screwed up things are. The result has been (hold
on, Tim Leary) a change of consciousness. Many, many voters have
come to the conclusion that government spending matters, the
national debt matters, wasted money matters.

A new appreciation of the evils of pork is only a part of that
change. But it is a significant part because of pork's role as a leading
indicator. If you can cut the pork, you can start cutting other, more
costly programs. Pork is obvious waste—it's not the easiest thing to
eliminate, but once you know it exists, it's hard not to want to.
When you get a look at a good piece of pork, you'll want to say,
"Huh? I'm working for Uncle Sam until May of each year so we can
buy some shady congressman his own personal amusement park
railroad?" (True story. See Chapter 6.) Pork is little silly things and
big silly things: forestry money for the city of Chicago, army forts
whose last job was to fight the war of 1812, the restoration of
William McKinley's mother-in-law's home, superhighways in
towns with no stoplights, farm subsidies intended to bail us out of
the Great Depression. Great fodder for journalists to make fun of
and impossible to get rid of—or so went the perennial Washington
wisdom.

But by the summer of 1992 something was afoot. The presidential campaign, spurred in large part by Perot, became a debate on
the economy in general and government overspending in particular. Who could have imagined, a half dozen years ago, a talk-show
host like Larry King devoting whole programs to deficit reduction
and featuring Perot and his charts? Soon everyone had charts and
people were appreciating the stakes. The budget began to play a
role in congressional elections, where it would have been ignored
a few years earlier. A law to balance the budget seemed all but sure
to pass Congress, until the mighty spending champion Senator
Robert Byrd drained off key votes with an arm-twisting marathon,
capped by an eight-hour floor speech, lest anyone doubt he was

serious. Once-sacred pork-barrel programs such as the manned space station and the superconducting supercollider were suddenly fighting for their lives and only narrowly surviving. It was as if the forces of nature on Capitol Hill were suddenly slipping out of balance.

Just how far things had gone became almost comically apparent in late summer when a desperate George Bush—impaled on his own economic inaction—began to flutter like a used-car salesman as he tried to dole out pork projects in key electoral states, such as Florida, Michigan, Texas, and California. Ya wanna new airbase? A contract to build obsolete tanks? A half-assed helicopter? You got it! No problem! It's on me! This was not a new ploy, presidents having found it necessary for generations. But the reaction was new. Polls showed the voters were repulsed by the transparent cynicism, even in the states where he'd made the promises. Sure, nobody in Dallas was going to turn down a new jet airplane contract, but elsewhere in the Lone Star State voters were shaking their heads in disgust.

Clinton mostly had the good sense to keep his mouth shut in matters of pork. He promised to keep alive a few isolated boondoggles—the space station among them—but otherwise played the role of diligent New Democrat, unbeholden to the spendsters in that *other* Democratic party. In one memorable speech, vice presidential candidate Al Gore went so far as to tell Connecticut submarine workers that the spending party was over.

When the voting was over, Clinton had won with an anemic plurality, assured in large part because of the healthy dissident vote scored by Perot. The Texas titan's nearly 20 percent said something about the voters' dawning grasp of money and politics. Clinton clearly wasn't listening, because pork almost did him in before he got started. When he offered the outlines of his economic plan, the first doggie out of the chute was a so-called stimulus plan of some $30 billion for a variety of projects that were supposed to create jobs and kick the economy out of its doldrums. Republican Senate Minority Leader Bob Dole, on the other hand, seems to have heard the Peronistas loud and clear. He called the stimulus package a greasy piece of pork intended to pay off a handful of urban mayors who had helped Clinton win the election. It didn't help the White House that some of the projects to be funded were swimming pools, tennis courts, car parks, and high-priced summer jobs. Economists of every political stripe came to virtually unani-

mous agreement that, call it pork or call it poultry, it would do little
or nothing for the economy.

And then there was the bad form of it: I have this plan to balance
the budget and put our fiscal house in order, Clinton said, with
tough choices and spending cuts and new taxes—but first we're
going to give away a bunch of money. In Clinton's defense, this
argument had worked many times in the past. As an intent student
of politics, he knew it was quite reasonable to underestimate the
attention span of the American voter.

Reading the mood of the country, Dole, a man who was not
known to be averse to dipping into the trough when it suited him,
turned "pork" into a dirty word and orchestrated a Republican
assault that essentially consisted of shouting it to every talk show,
newscast, and Rotary Club in the country. Whenever Clinton said
"jobs," the Republicans cried "pork." Jobs. Pork. Jobs! Pork!

Pork won. Try as hard as he could, Clinton could not round up
the votes to pass the stimulus package. He failed most stunningly
at his own immensely cynical ploy: When senators went home for
Easter recess, the White House planted bald stories in swing states
such as Pennsylvania and New York to the effect that the relevant
senator—Al D'Amato, Arlen Specter, whoever—was thwarting the
president in his attempt to bring goodies to the state. Still, it didn't
take. People didn't want the stuff. They saw it for the bundle of
cheap geegaws that it was and said, with as clear articulation as has
been heard in a long time, Fix the damn deficit before you start
fooling around with these sideshows.

Clinton was shell-shocked. Defeated, crippled. A has-been before he was a been. "Another Failed Presidency Already?" asked a
wry story in *The Washington Post*. All because of pork.

Clinton hadn't noticed that Congress—which is, despite the general perception, a body that represents the thinking of people who
vote and is extremely sensitive to their changes of mood—was a
different place. There were 110 freshmen, a good number elected
on some kind of reform, chase-out-the-rascals platform. Some of
the old bulls were gone, most notably Jamie Whitten, the secretive
southerner who dominated the House Appropriations Committee
until he tried the patience of even his fondest coconspirators by
refusing to step down when they gently pointed out that he was in
his eighties and too infirm to continue serving. Among other power-
houses of the money committees, Republican Joe McDade was
under indictment, and it was rumored that Dan Rostenkowski was

facing the likelihood of indictment; House Public Works chairman
Robert Roe retired; Senator Quentin Burdick was dead, and others
had been hobbled by age and ethics investigations. The most immediate casualty was Robert Byrd, who had led the charge on
Clinton's stimulus package and been handed a humiliating defeat.
There was talk of a new day, an end to some of the more virulent
pork practices.

Of course, as I said earlier, while some things change, others
don't. Consider the fact that the first choice for committee assignments among those 110 freshmen was Public Works, traditionally
a trove of federal fat earmarkable to a cooperative congressman's
district. The House leadership, ever willing to go along with a
young member who'd like to get along, expanded the committee
and put twenty-eight new members on it. Asked about his new
calling in life, John Mica, a Florida Republican, sounded like a sly
old pro when he told *The Washington Post* that he wanted on to get
a shot at Clinton's promised stimulus package. A fiscal conservative, he still wanted Uncle Sugar to buy a new highway for prosperous Orlando. Might that rightly be called pork, the *Post* asked?
No, sir, said Mica. Because foreign tourists visit Disney World, it's
"not merely a Florida project. I view it as a project of national
importance."

The public's hunger for pork had not disappeared entirely, either. After all, even the cleverest congressman cannot think up all
these spending schemes on his own; there's a whole lot of people
out there with outstretched hands. Few said it better than the
Reverend Paul S. Tipton, president of the Association of Jesuit
Colleges and Universities. Commenting on the recent huge increases in academic pork (one of the areas in which pork has been
growing of late), he told *The Chronicle of Higher Education*, "It is
the classic American way. The congressman goes to Congress to
help his district out. The people inside the Beltway like to criticize.
But, frankly, that is why these guys and ladies are elected—to help
a local university—that is what they do. I am personally quite
supportive of it."

So it was a wiser Bill Clinton who plotted his strategy to get his
budget and tax bill through the House and Senate, which he succeeded in doing with exactly no votes to spare. The Deal was as
enigmatic as Clinton, appearing to be all things to all people. On
the one hand, there was some deficit reduction based on slashed
programs; on the other hand, he seemed to be promising pork as

fast as he could to get the thing passed. He caved on going after most farm subsidies, for instance, and let the space station go through. But the defense budget finally got some meaningful trims and the supercollider appeared near terminal trouble. The Clinton plan targeted a lot of the smaller but hugely annoying pork projects for extinction—though that's been said before.

More significant than the outcome was the debate, which was all based on the premise that cuts are necessary. The winners were those who kept their pet projects intact, without seeing any expansion. The ratio became the litmus test: taxes to cuts. Originally Clinton seemed willing to sign on to the notion of two dollars in cuts for every dollar in new taxes. Eventually it became more like one dollar to one dollar, the lowest ratio that was acceptable. But the battle was being fought on the cutters' turf. The plan almost sank not because there wasn't enough spending but because there weren't enough cuts.

He's a slippery one, that Clinton. But at least he knows the new reality: The deficit matters to a lot of voters—probably enough to throw him out in 1996. Clinton's political inclinations are mysterious. Is he a New Democrat? An Old Democrat? Or, more likely, a Lyndon Johnson pragmatist who shows great skill at wielding the power of presidency? But whereas Johnson's mandate was social change, the thing now staring Clinton in the face is the budget deficit. He's gotten his tax increase, so now the debate is all on the question: Is enough spending being cut? The pressure will come from there.

Pork—whether symbolically destructive but relatively cheap projects such as Steamtown USA or big-dollar giveaways such as farm subsidies—will be a battleground. These are some of the tough calls Clinton keeps talking about. The moderate Democrats are on the verge of wielding a huge influence over both the House and Senate. During the budget battle, Republicans mostly sat on their hands and carped, refusing to come up with enough specifics and in the process squandering a good deal of moral authority. The swing votes were those Dems in the middle. Five or ten more pork-hating Democrats elected in 1994 could control the House, one or two more, the Senate.

Not that slashing pork and curbing the pork mentality will solve all our problems. But we've seen evidence that it's a start. And it's mighty good for the soul. Change is possible. The Clinton package may ease the deficit but won't end it; the reductions still come mostly from taxes on the rich and from defense. Spreading the burden further and deciding just what the federal government ought to be doing with its time and money will be the politics of at least the rest of the decade. There will be more summits, more deals, more frustration, more Perot, more backsliding. More sneaking in of a project here or there. But more potential for change than at any time in the twenty years I've followed Washington.

As I looked at the new edition of *Porkland* I thought about the subtitle. Given my new optimism, was it hyperbole to say "How Washington Wastes Your Money and Why They Won't Stop"? No, I decided. I'm willing to concede that they *can* stop. But they still *won't*—unless the voters make them.

—Brian Kelly
  Washington, D.C.
  August 1993

# INTRODUCTION

# BUBBLE, BUBBLE, TOIL AND TROUBLE

I HADN'T GIVEN LAWRENCE WELK MUCH THOUGHT IN THE PAST twenty-five years or so. Not since my grandmother would switch the dial to Channel 7 on Saturday nights and settle in for an hour of ruthlessly wholesome entertainment by the man they called "The Champagne Music Maker."

"And ah-one, and ah-two . . ." he began each week as the tinny hum of accordion music squeezed its way through the speakers of the Dumont console television set. "Wunnerful! Wunnerful!" the king of middlebrow melodies would say when the song ended, proudly admiring his musicianship and that of his severely barbered orchestra. Then, while soap bubbles floated from a hidden machine, he'd bow in the direction of his singers and dancers—including the Lovely Norma Zimmer and snaky Bobby Burgess—who looked back with the sort of glazed grin I later came to associate with the followers of Reverend Moon.

Even at the age of eight or nine I knew something was odd here. Nobody could be that cheerful, especially while pounding out polkas that made me feel like I was trapped at the children's table of

an endless wedding. Besides, how could you trust someone who
had an accent like Colonel Klink on *Hogan's Heroes*?

Like a bad dream, the sound of that too-happy accordion floated
back into my brain not long ago. It was in the fall of 1990, in—of all
places—the U.S. House of Representatives. The lawmakers were
in the midst of an agonizing, months-long debate about why the
country was going broke and how to fix it.

"And ah-one, and ah-two, and ah-five hundred thousand dollars!" shouted Silvio Conte, the acerbic congressman from Massachusetts who took great pleasure in nettling his fellow members for
their attempts to sneak strange spending items into the many bills
that became law each year. He'd just discovered another one:
somebody had slipped into the farm bill a $500,000 grant to make
a memorial out of Lawrence Welk's boyhood farm in Strasburg,
North Dakota. Tucked in amid instructions to the government on
how to spend many billions of dollars on everything from peanut-
growing subsidies to Russian wheat sales was an order to create a
national monument honoring a man who is, without question, the
most famous son of Strasburg, North Dakota, but arguably no more
famous than Mitch Miller, Les Brown and His Band of Renown, or
Doc Severinsen, and certainly less famous than Ed Sullivan—none
of whom have government-financed memorials.

"What will they do for an encore?" Conte thundered at his colleagues with mock outrage—because no matter how insane the
intended appropriation, he never took his admonishments too seriously. "Earmark funds to renovate Guy Lombardo's speedboat?
Or restore Artie Shaw's wedding tuxedo?"

Several less colorful congressmen expressed similar concerns.
They worried, for instance, that at a time when the federal government was spending about $300 billion more than it was taking
in each year, when the government had just reopened after shutting down for a few days because Congress and the White House
couldn't agree on a new budget, when cuts were being made in all
sorts of spending programs and taxes raised on everything from
gasoline to beer, when polls showed that Americans were beginning to think that Washington really was a madhouse run by a
bunch of blow-dried lunatics and that the whole system was truly
in danger of collapsing, that in such an environment, giving tax
dollars to something called Welk Heritage Inc. to make a tourist
attraction out of the mud-walled birthplace of a decidedly second-
rate entertainer seemed at best wasteful and at worst a terrible

message to send to the world about the seriousness with which Congress took its responsibilities.

The bill passed overwhelmingly.

When I first heard about it a few days later from a friend who works on Capitol Hill, I laughed. Those zany congressmen, I thought, at it again. Another silly stunt by the gentlemen and ladies who represent democracy at its finest. Certainly the item was fodder for the kind of guys who shout back at their television sets, the ones who yell, "You corrupt bastard!" every time they see a favorite senator or cabinet member on the news. And I don't for a moment underestimate how many TV shouters are out there rising from the Herculon-covered couches of America on any given day and screaming back that memorable slogan of impotent rage from the movie *Network*, "I'm mad as hell, and I'm not going to take it anymore!" Americans have become a nation boiling with barely contained rage over so many subjects. But of course in this case they *were* going to take it because that's the way the system works, and as those of us who write about politics for a living know, the minor outrages of Congress are only one more part of that system. Just politics as usual. We know that something like wasting money—even a half-million dollars—on a Welk monument is merely an amusing tidbit for a slow news day, one that sets right-wing goldbugs and Ralph Nader alumni to wailing but is nothing to get worked up about for an ordinary, sophisticated person. We know, after all, that Congress's shifty little deals aren't the sort of things that *really* matter like, say, the federal budget deficit *really* matters or mortgage interest rates or unemployment *really* matter. Don't we?

But the Welk story brought back that vague discomfort I used to feel while fidgeting on my grandmother's scratchy chairs waiting for the show to end. For days I couldn't get the sound of accordion music out of my head, nor the image of Welk's demonic grin. I knew that nobody was going to make me watch his show again, so what was bothering me?

Then I mentioned the anecdote to a magazine editor I know, and he asked one of those dumb questions that only good editors can ask.

"So how'd it get in there?"

"What?"

"The paragraph that says that the federal government has to spend a half-million dollars to build a monument to Lawrence Welk."

"Well, you know, it's probably part of some program that some congressman who likes accordion music wanted," I said unconvincingly. He looked at me, unconvinced.

"I mean, who exactly wanted this goofy boondoggle? And how the hell'd he get Congress to pass it? These things don't just happen by magic, do they?"

I didn't know. Though I'd never covered Congress full time, I'd written about it often, but usually as part of some grand issue: nuclear weapons, the environment, foreign relations—the sort of grave topics one hears thrashed out on a weekly basis by the tense-jawed panelists of *Meet the Press*. These are Big Issues that require one to attend background briefings and subcommittee hearings and seek out the thousands of eager staffers who are more than willing to explain their boss's position on whatever the subject at hand. This is Important Work, the nation's business, even. Here is the reason scores of pantingly ambitious former high school class presidents flock to Washington each year seeking a foot in the door of the Ultimate Senior Prom Committee, and the reason endless waves of slyly ambitious former high school newspaper editors break their behinds on statehouse beats across America so they can eventually earn a crack at the story behind the Big Senior Prom Scandal. This was most of what I knew about Congress.

But in the years that I'd been editing *Regardie's*, a Washington business magazine whose journalistic mission is to ferret out the triangle of money, power and greed that defines the capital of the free world, I had come to think that there might actually be two Congresses working away beneath the Capitol dome. There is the "Gas Congress" and the "Money Congress." I began to realize that even though the front-page stories come from the Gas Men, the real power is with the money. The Gas Congress, the one most people know, talks endlessly about a lot of bullshit and occasionally does something good, like the Civil Rights Act or the original Clean Air Bill, the defeat of a particularly evil Supreme Court nominee or a hearing that raps the knuckles of some Wall Street pirate. The Money Congress, on the other hand, is a cold-blooded business run by a handful of people who deal with incredibly boring numbers and spend incredible amounts of money. After all, the ultimate power of Congress is the ability to take money out of people's pockets. The Constitution says so.

The most dangerous place to stand in Washington is between some of the more prominent members of the Gas Congress—Ted

Kennedy, Bob Dole, Joe Biden, Alan Simpson, Tom Foley, Newt Gingrich—and a television camera. You're sure to be trampled. The Money Congress, led by people like Robert Byrd, Dan Rostenkowski, Robert Roe and Jamie Whitten and followed by a couple dozen folks you'd never hear of unless you voted for them, prefer that the press and the public keep their distance.

The Lawrence Welk memorial was surely the handiwork of the Money Congress. That much I could guess. But if I wanted to find out how it had come to be, to answer that simple question, "How'd it get in there?" I was going to have to learn about a complicated new world. With the melody of "The Beer Barrel Polka" sawing through my brain, I was about to be pulled into the same sort of rabbit hole that swallowed Lewis Carroll's Alice, a wonderland where nothing is as it seems, a world of odd people and customs where words don't mean what they say, where money isn't money and spending means saving; a place where all decisions are made in the bright sunshine of public scrutiny except for any decisions that truly matter; a place where hundreds of thousands of words are spoken and copied and lovingly stored away each day as if each one is so precious that its loss alone could begin to unravel the delicate cloth of democracy and yet where there is never any record of the most important discussions; a place where men who have the greatest contempt for each other call one another "my distinguished and learned colleague for whom I have only the deepest respect." After all my years of listening to hot air escape from the magnificent marbled halls of the Capitol, Lawrence Welk was the beginning of a grown-up's education into one of the most baffling conundrums of American life: how the U.S. government really spends our money.

# ADVENTURES IN PORKLAND

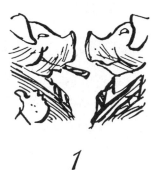

## 1

# ROLL OUT THE
# BARREL

**S**OMEHOW THE MAGNIFICENCE OF CAPITOL HILL ON A SUNNY day makes money seem a trivial issue. The muscular dome of the Capitol, ringed by white columns and braced by the ersatz but majestic neo-Greco-Roman facades of the House and Senate chambers, juts from a grassy garden of manicured trees and bursting flowers designed by Frederick Law Olmsted. "We have built no national temples but the Capitol," Congressman Rufus Choate remarked more than 150 years ago, and he's still mostly right. Residents of Washington should periodically get down on their knees and thank the taxpayers of America for maintaining this showplace at the head of the equally impressive greensward known as the Mall—just as they should thank them for all the free museums, the well-tended monuments, the National Zoo, the magnificent Rock Creek Park, and the world's cleanest subway system. Admittedly the District of Columbia, at least those parts where drug dealers aren't engaged in open warfare during the evening hours, is a trove of taxpayer largesse that helps to create a wonderfully tidy, livable city and explains to a large extent why when congressmen and bureaucrats move to Washington, they often perform all manner of unspeakable acts in order to stay. But the best asset of the city, its focal point, is still the Capitol, looking westward across the Mall past the squat, massive structures that contain the bureaucracy, beyond the elegant but slight White House and on out to the whole of America spreading before it for three thousand miles. A person would be hard pressed, or hard hearted, to stand in the shadow of this most powerful symbol and argue that it wasn't worth every penny that's ever been spent on it. The cost of what takes place inside is another story.

You'd hardly guess that in the main building and nine others surrounding it, all linked by underground passageways and a subway system, is a throbbing daytime city of 25,000 of the most cravenly ambitious people a body would care to meet—and that's not counting the senators and congressmen. The Hill, as it's known to all who worship and fear it in Washington, has swelled to an enormous bureaucracy of its own, a complex mess of fiefdoms otherwise known as committees and subcommittees, run by battalions of staffers, all moving at double speed and some even working on your behalf. They talk as fast as Wall Street bond traders and would sell you out just as quickly. They talk in their own shorthand— "Where's your boss on HR twelve-fifty?" "You mean the caucus amendment?" "Yeah, as amended." "Dunno. Haven't figured out what to tell him yet."—but unlike many other parts of this government, they do talk.

So it didn't take a detective to figure out who was behind the movement to elevate Lawrence Welk to sainthood. A curious person just had to ask a few of the right staffers. It turned out that in all of Congress there was only one man with the means and the motive. They call him "Q.B."

"Oh, that's Q.B.'s deal all the way," a Senate staffer said, after the usual grant of anonymity. As a rule, you cannot ask a Hill staffer his opinion on the weather without a firm agreement that you'll only quote him as "a Hill staffer."

"I think he was pals with Welk or something," the staffer continued. "Anyway, if Q.B. wants it, he gets it. He's one of the barons. Anything else?" End of conversation.

If Lawrence Welk is the most famous citizen of North Dakota, Quentin Burdick, the senior senator of the Prairie State, is second. At the age of eighty-three, this hunched and dozing old gentleman appears to be in need of constant medical assistance. At committee hearings, his aides continually whisper into his ear; rumor has it they're reminding him to breathe. If you saw him on a bus, you'd give him your seat, then move away in case he collapsed. If you saw him on a park bench, you might call an ambulance, or at least give him a quarter.

But in Congress his ancient body is surrounded by a force field, sort of like those that bestowed magical powers on medieval gnomes. He's the by-product of a democracy that decrees that a man can never be too old or feeble to hold office, unless the people who put him there say so. And the last time anyone checked, the voters of North Dakota said he was just fine with them. Why shouldn't they? Burdick epitomizes the aging lion with only the interests of his constituents at heart—along with his own, of course. The son of a congressman, he spent twenty years trying to get himself elected to something, and when he finally won his own congressional seat in 1958, he wasn't about to put it at risk. They grow wheat in North Dakota, so wheat prices must be supported. They house nuclear missiles in North Dakota, so the Pentagon must be supported. No need to get much more complicated than that, unless of course you add in a bunch of questionable dams, highway crossings and research grants to study wheat weevils, all of which add up to North Dakotans paying a total of about $2 billion in federal taxes but getting close to $3 billion in federal spending back. You'd keep the crafty old gnome in office, too.

By virtue of his seniority, and nothing else, he heads a key subcommittee: the one that oversees farm spending for the Senate Appropriations Committee. The appropriators—sometimes called the Barons of Capitol Hill, sometimes the College of Cardinals—are the ones who actually write the bills that tell how the government will spend its tax money. What Burdick did in the case of Welk was simply to put a paragraph into the several-hundred-page agriculture appropriations bill—a bill that spends $52.2 billion—to set aside $500,000 for the Welk project.

The paragraph said: "The Strasburg Economic Development Corp. and Welk Heritage Inc. in North Dakota are restoring Lawrence Welk's birthplace to promote tourism, create jobs and create businesses which do not currently exist. This appropriation includes $500,000 to assist in this effort."

No discussion. No argument from other committee members. It's the way things are done. In every spending bill, the big dogs get at least a handful of projects for their home districts, and this was one of Burdick's bones.

Actually, it's called pork. Or, more properly, pork barreling. And Burdick is viewed by his colleagues as a decent, though not stellar, pork barreler. Loosely defined, pork is the money of everyone being spent for the pleasure of a few. It's federal dollars going to a local area for strictly local purposes. "Pork is money that a congressman or senator tries to get for his own district but wouldn't dream of trying to get for anyone else's," was how one former congressman explained it. Or, in the words of Professor Alan Schick of the University of Maryland, "Pork is spending with a Zip code attached to it." This much you could find out from a high school civics text; pork barrel is right there alongside those other great terms like logroll, bicameral, gerrymander, filibuster and lame duck. The conventional wisdom is that pork is usually penny-ante projects worth a few million dollars each—a post office here, a highway crossing there, maybe a bridge now and then. Most Americans think of pork about as often as they've thought about Lawrence Welk in the last twenty years. And true, the North Dakota museum fits the classic definition and thus seems harmless. But the subject gets much more complicated.

"Pork is what Congress is all about," explained a White House aide who follows the maneuverings of that body with keen professional interest. "It's the politics of self-interest. If you're a congressman and you want to get reelected—and you do because it's a pretty great job despite all the whining you hear from them—then you give things to the people who can vote for you. In return they keep electing you. The hell with what it means for the rest of the country. All congressmen would score pork if they had the power. But the big guys eat first, then toss leftover scraps to those they favor. And because everyone wants it, a sort of balance of terror emerges where no one will challenge the porkers because they want theirs someday. You'd be making a mistake if you thought of this as petty. There's big stakes here. You have to take a deal like Welk and multiply it by many, many similar deals before you can get an idea of what's going on."

"Pork *is* politics," explained Tony Coelho, a former congressman from California and a man with a finely honed sense of the chemistry between money and power. "There may be a congressional district that elects its representative and doesn't expect pork, but I don't know of one. American politics is very basic, it's very bottom line. It's 'What can you deliver?' When I was a congressman, people didn't want to know about some nationwide program helping out Arkansas. They wanted to know 'What have you done for California?' Usually, that comes down to pork. Something you can show them that you did for them. When I headed the Democratic Congressional Campaign Committee, I used to coach guys in how to get pork. It's how you win. It's the system. And I'll say straight out, I don't think it's bad."

Certainly pork is as old as politics. Probably the senators of Athens made bathhouse deals over whose district would get the new temple and who'd get the shipyard. In the American system of government, the pursuit of pork gives action to Tip O'Neill's favorite phrase, "All politics is local." No morsel found in the halls of Congress is too small for a representative to bring home with that same sense of pride as a dog returning to his master with a fresh-killed rat between his teeth. From the first Congress of the United States, pork became a staple of politics mostly because of how the system was set up. Those wonderful old women-hating slave owners who ran the country wanted a Congress of competing local interests and they wanted congressmen who, because of their two-year terms, would be acutely attentive to the folks back home in Saltlick, Virginia, Bootstrap, Georgia or wherever. The standard of a politician's worth quickly became "What have you done for me lately?" And what he had better do was bring home the bacon. The Senate, incidentally, was supposed to be a chamber of gentlemen who were above that sort of thing, but some would argue that gradually they've become the worst practitioners.

The actual phrase "pork barrel" comes from the pre–Civil War custom of doling out slabs of salt pork from a big barrel to the field slaves who crowded around and clamored for their share. An unknown pundit made the analogy to congressmen charging to get their piece of the few big spending bills that moved through Congress in those days. By the 1870s, the phrase was in common usage, though it wasn't immortalized until 1919, when, in an essay in the *National Municipal Review*, one C. C. Maxey, wrote, "Members of Congress, in the stampede to get local appropriation items into the omnibus rivers-and-harbors bills, behaved so much like . . . slaves rushing the pork barrel that these bills were facetiously styled pork-barrel bills." At the time, most federal spending for local projects was found in the Rivers and Harbors Bill, everything from canals and dams to harbor dredging and piers; there were no federal highways or railways, for instance, or much of a defense industry. In later years, as the government vastly expanded the areas in which it would spend money, the term "pork" took on its own omnibus meaning.

But whatever you called it, many lawmakers—the great and the minor—considered the pursuit of parochial spending part of their daily chores. When the first Congress approved a plan to build a lighthouse at the mouth of the Chesapeake Bay, suddenly everyone had to have a lighthouse. As Congressman Clarence Cannon liked to recall fondly, justifying his own pork raids many years later, "During the American Revolution, George Washington used to call out for 'beef, beef, beef,' but the Continental Congress called out for 'pork, pork, pork.' "

Thus the concept of one nation under greed was born.

As early as 1799, Congressman John Randolph, a decidedly more cynical and less accomplished man than his Virginia brethren such as Jefferson, Madison and Monroe, could savor "That most delicious of all privileges—spending other people's money." Jefferson noticed the same instinct and considered it a flaw in the system he'd helped to create, an unbridled invitation to let human nature run free right there on the very floor of the institution that was supposed to represent the perfectibility of man. "The same prudence which in private life could forbid our paying our own money for unexplained projects forbids it in the dispensation of the public moneys," he said, though no doubt by this point some freshman congressman was remarking to his benchmate, "Who's that old red-haired guy and what's he ever done, anyway?"

The game was brought to a new level under President Andrew "To the Victor Belong the Spoils" Jackson, who scanned the federal treasury with the gaze of a pirate and devised his own rudimentary plan to redistribute wealth away from places like Boston and toward places like Tennessee, where he happened to be from. "Ever since Andrew Jackson put us into the business of using federal money for 'internal improvements,' " Congressman Dick Armey said recently, "the most influential members of Congress have naturally sought to ensure that their home districts are more internally improved than others."

Not that Jackson could help himself to the Treasury. He was opposed by the likes of Daniel Webster of Boston, supposedly one of the country's greatest statesmen, who nonetheless was intent on getting all he could for his own constituents. He was particularly adamant about maintaining tariffs that supported the region's factory-owning plutocrats at the expense of everyone else in the country. Webster was also an early master of the sort of extremely narrow pork that today we call bribery. He received retainers from the Second National Bank and in turn supported the renewal of its charter. He also took cash and phony loans from the British bankers at the powerful House of Baring and supported them in, among other causes, a treaty to map the U.S.-Canada border that was distinctly unfavorable to the U.S. But the Barings showed they were wise to his ways, and perhaps the future ways of Congress, when one wrote, "The only way to do with Mr. Webster is not to give him credit . . . because he has no sense of what is right in money affairs."

Pork soon became an entrenched part of the process, as did unrestrained spending. By 1877 the House stripped power from the appropriations subcommittee that handled water projects because of its "excessive economy mindedness," in the words of historian Richard Fenno. The committee didn't get that prime turf back until 1920, when it had decided to be more cooperative and start spending like sailors on shore leave. A similar revolt took place in the mid-1950s, when the committee momentarily lost its senses once more and tried to take a hard look at how it spent money. Such a nod to frugality by the appropriators has never again been repeated.

But over the years, this sort of behavior has done more than most to earn Congress scorn as well as to cement in the public mind the deliciously derisive image favored by editorial cartoonists of porcine figures in suits and ties slopping at a trough labeled "taxes." In his turn-of-the-century Washington memoir *The Education of Henry Adams*, the author writes of a conversation with a cabinet secretary who tells him the facts of capital life: "You can't use tact with a congressman! A congressman is a hog! You must take a stick and hit him on the snout."

That pork barreling distorted the nation's business was apparent to Teddy Roosevelt, among others, who wrote, "Our magnificent river system, with all its superb possibilities for public usefulness, was dealt with by the National Government not as a unit, but as a disconnected series of pork-barrel problems, whose only real interest was in their effect on the re-election of a congressman here and there."

At virtually the same moment, President Calvin Coolidge, the

amiable, disconnected Ronald Reagan of his day, was futilely scold-
ing Congress: "Nothing is easier than spending the public's money.
It does not appear to belong to anybody. The temptation is overwhelming to bestow it on somebody." And then he took a nap.

As pork became an established function of the Congress and the
barrel became deeper, the pursuit mutated into exotic forms. For
some it was a test of competition, even manhood. "Every time
those damn Yankees get a hambone, I'm going to get a hog," vowed
John Nance Garner, the earthy Texan who served as Speaker of the
House in the early 1930s. L. Mendel Rivers, who controlled military spending, had stuffed so many bases and shipyards into his
district of Charleston, South Carolina, that Carl Vinson once
taunted him, "Mendel, if you put anything else down there in your
district, it's gonna sink." He did, and it didn't.

Mike Kirwan, who headed the pork-rich Appropriations Subcommittee on Public Works until the mid-1960s, refined the notion
of a brotherhood of pork by testing his fellow appropriators' loyalty.
He'd long wanted to build a canal from his hometown of Youngs-
town, Ohio, to Lake Erie, a project most everyone outside his
district thought was crazy. But when "Iron Mike" was looking
down the barrel of a tough reelection campaign one year, his pro-
tégés called on everyone who'd ever benefited from his largesse
and rallied them with the cry "Let's build this ditch for Mike!"

There followed a remarkable succession of sixty-four speeches
whose "lofty language," according to columnist Jack Anderson,
"sounded like a funeral service." But Kirwan was very much alive
and holding tight to the power to grant pork-barrel projects coveted by each of the sixty-four. While quoting the tributes, Anderson noted that giants of the Congress such as Carl Albert wanted a
$13 million water project, Edward Boland wanted $16 million for
Cape Cod seashore development, Al Ullman wanted $6 million for
a damn, Hale Boggs wanted a cemetery. And on and on. At one
point, Ullman remarked, "Mike Kirwan is made of the stuff that
built America." Everyone in the room knew that that stuff was
other people's money. Kirwan's ditch was approved in an unre-
corded voice vote.

Kenneth Gray, an old-boy Appropriations member from southern Illinois, became legendary in the 1950s for a painfully frank
speech on the floor of the House in which he said he was facing stiff
competition back home and pleaded for a few tidbits of pork. He
got them, along with some disdainful scowls. Even when Congress

was a looser place, pork was lumped into the same furtive category as relationships with mistresses and lobbyists.

Pork also became a sort of high-test grease for accomplishing major initiatives, a seamy means to noble ends. Senator Albert Gore, Sr., of Tennessee tells the story of why his first Senate opponent, Kenneth McKellars, was so formidable. During World War II, President Franklin Roosevelt called the leaders of Congress to the White House for a secret meeting about the need to beat the Nazis to the development of an atomic bomb. The fate of the country was at stake, Roosevelt said gravely; petty concerns would have to be put aside and red tape cut to get a bomb facility built quickly. All the leaders pledged their total support, until he came to McKellars, who chaired the Appropriations Committee.

"Mr. President, I agree that the future of our civilization may depend upon the success of this project. Where in Tennessee are we going to build it?"

It was built—quickly—in Oak Ridge, Tennessee.

A similar power play accounts for the fact that while virtually all of the National Aeronautics and Space Administration space flights are launched from Cape Canaveral in Florida, the mission control center is in Houston. Those with cynical minds naturally assume it was because of Lyndon Johnson, who was Senate majority leader during the years the project was being approved and a man who'd carved a hog or two. But a search for pork often reveals more devious methods. Jack Valenti, a top aide to Johnson, said that it wasn't Johnson's deal at all. "That was Albert Thomas all the way," Valenti said, referring to a longtime congressman from Houston. "I'd have liked to have Johnson take credit for it, but Albert was the one who had the real power there. He headed the appropriations subcommittee that funded NASA." But the people in Houston knew all along, because Thomas surely reminded them.

Pork has also come to play a role in passing major bills with sweeping national impact. In this way, it's long been a first cousin of logrolling, which is best described as the "you scratch my back, I'll scratch yours" theory of legislation. As part of such deal making, those trying to pass a given bill will sweeten it by adding dozens and sometimes hundreds of items of interest to individual members. In the slang of the Hill, you can often "roll a bill by porking it up." Phil Burton, the late California congressman who was strongly proenvironment, was so intent on passing a bill in the late 1970s to designate parts of California a national preserve that he put new federal parks and monuments into hundreds of congressional districts. "We called it the Park Barrel Bill," a former staffer explained. "Who could oppose it?"

Russell Long, who headed the Senate Finance Committee while it accomplished several major rewrites of the tax law, refined the technique of doling out "tax pork," narrow loopholes that often would benefit only a few of a senator's constituents, in return for his support. Dan Rostenkowski took the art to a new level, sliding in billions of dollars of special favors in order to muscle the 1986 tax reform bill, which many view as a major improvement in tax fairness, out of his Ways and Means Committee. Lyndon Johnson is said to have doled out pork in liberal doses to win passage of the 1964 Civil Rights Bill. Pork as necessary evil.

But sometimes the outcome had nothing to do with the greater good. Bob Kerr, the corpulent Oklahoma senator who headed the Public Works and Transportation Committee, went to the pork barrel constantly to buy support for the interests of his beloved oil industry, which in turn had helped make him one of the wealthiest men in the Senate. Kerr was known to close the door and ask a colleague to name his price: a dam, a tunnel, a reservoir in return for a vote. Then, too, he kept quite a bit for himself. Jack Anderson estimated that by the early 1960s, $3 billion in NASA installations had found their way to Oklahoma and Texas while so many dams and waterways were cut into Kerr's home state that one congressman remarked, "You'll soon be able to cross Oklahoma without touching dry land."

Still, despite all the hoary old political storytelling passed on to eager generations of ambitious young pols over Irish whiskys beside the fire, pork barreling is neither old nor quaint. The game has been played with deadly earnest in recent years. Ronald Reagan, one of the most successful vetoers ever and a man who usually got what he wanted from Congress, almost got his head handed to him when he vetoed the 1987 highway bill because it contained a relatively modest $2 billion in pork projects. Republicans and conservative Democrats deserted him in droves, including his own House Minority Leader, Bob Michel, a known pork lover. He was overridden in one of his biggest legislative defeats and quickly backed off his hostile posture, lest he repeat the mistake of Jimmy Carter ten years earlier.

As his first major legislative initiative, Carter, who had been elected on his outsider credentials, tried to take an outsider stand

and gut the water projects bill. As governor of Georgia, he'd had great success blunting many environmentally insane public works projects such as useless dams that flooded thousands of acres of forest. But then, all of Carter's presidency was premised on revisiting his Georgia statehouse successes, and as the crafty pros of the Hill put it, "That dog weren't gonna hunt up heah."

"The road can be smooth or the road can be rough," said Senator Robert Byrd, then the Democratic leader, in one of the more portentous warnings ever to emanate from America's Mount Olympus. And the road was indeed rough as Carter's people played out a comedy of errors but unflinchingly stuck to their script. Congress reacted with a fury that left even Republican Silvio Conte complaining that the rules had changed to "You scratch my back or I'll stab yours." The lead-butted Carter actually hung tough enough to win some of what he wanted, but he lost the war. His relations with Congress were crippled, and, some have argued, his presidency was doomed from that point on. Typical of the animosity, Speaker Tip O'Neill began to refer to Hamilton Jordan, Carter's chief of staff, as "Hannibal Jerkin." From then on, even the summer interns knew that that dog called Jimmy couldn't hunt in a henhouse.

David Stockman got a similar education a few years later. The man tapped to implement Ronald Reagan's promised revolution in tax and budget policies, Stockman made a quick mistake that would plague the economy for many years: he caved in to a Congress that would let him cut taxes, but wouldn't let him cut spending. The key to making Reagan's plan work was to do both at the same time.

In his memoir, *The Triumph of Politics*, he recalls a meeting in Tip O'Neill's office with the likes of Jim Wright, Dan Rostenkowski and Carl Perkins. "I stared out at the faces of the Politburo of the Welfare State," the most imposing of whom was O'Neill, who "with his massive corpulence and scarlet, varicose nose, was a Hogarthian embodiment of the superstate he had labored so long to maintain." Stockman laid out many of the programs he said would have to be trimmed, things like the Appalachian Regional Commission with its expensive road projects, the Economic Development Administration and its poorly managed handouts to businesses, funds for sewers and local highways and, in a second phase, the bulging entitlement programs such as Social Security, Medicare and federal pensions. The old foxes toyed for a while with the zealous young conservative, agreeing that it was a "new day" and "changes had to be made." O'Neill concluded affably, "We don't agree with everything, but this young fellow sure knows what he's talking about." Stockman took it as a compliment—although O'Neill surely meant it as a warning to his colleagues—and left the meeting feeling good.

As time went on, the Politburo took Stockman apart like a quota-deficient tractor commissar from Minsk, beating him on most of his attempts to cut the programs they had so carefully assembled. But it wasn't just the usual suspects who were attacking.

"I was shocked to find that the Democrats were getting so much Republican help in their efforts to keep the pork barrel flowing," he wrote. Although he managed to hold spending flat for two years, he eventually lost the support of the White House as well and watched in frustration as the Reagan Revolution turned into a lopsided tax giveaway that, coupled with giant defense budgets, sent the deficit soaring.

The lesson taught over and over was that pork is not to be trifled with, or at least not by someone who hasn't lined up his ducks very carefully. But is it nonetheless trifling? Is pork a mere eccentricity of the process of democracy, or is it ruining the process? Oddly, little is written in defense of pork and not much more about its broader effects. The common conclusion has been that it is a slimy but harmless practice. Yet there is some argument that pork barreling has long been distorting the way government spends money. William Safire quotes Paul Douglas, a clean-government Illinois senator who had a pretty firm grip on the reality of thirty years ago, as saying, "As groups win their battle for special expenditures, they lose the more important war for general economy. . . . They are like drunkards who shout for temperance in the intervals between cocktails."

Whether or not pork demeans the process, it certainly demeans any individual who has a higher calling in mind. As an obscure senator, Henry Fountain Ashurst of Arizona, moaned to his constituents in the early part of the century, "You send me to Washington to represent you in the senate. But you do not send me there because you are interested in grave questions of national or international policy. When I come back to Arizona . . . you ask me: 'What about my pension?' or 'What about that job for my son?' I am not in Washington as a statesman. I am there as a very well paid messenger boy doing your errands. My chief occupation is going around with a forked stick picking up little fragments of patronage for my constituents."

But few in the Washington establishment of elected officials, bureaucrats, journalists and academics have ever seemed to treat pork very seriously. It's become an accepted and unchallenged part of the system—which is not to say unnoticed. The meager literature of pork also shows that as long as there's been pork, there've been pork hunters. Some, like Drew Pearson and his successor Jack Anderson, made a standing gag of taking sardonic pokes at the latest outrage. Senator William Proxmire used to hand out his monthly Golden Fleece Award. But it was all treated as minor meat in a town full of roast beef. Any journalist looking for a quick, catchy story has known for generations that one characteristic of pork is that it abhors the light of publicity; once it's out in the open, it looks pretty silly. To this day, each year a few nuggets are so laughable, so greasy, so offensive that they strike the fancy of the media and the public and provoke cries of outrage and ridicule. And then are quickly forgotten.

In just the past few years, Congress has funded studies on the sexual habits of Japanese quail and how long it takes to cook breakfast eggs. A $7 million grant went to study jet lag and a half-million dollars to build a ten-story replica of the Pyramid of Cheops and an 800-foot model of the Great Wall of China in Bedford, Indiana. Scientists have been given the taxpayers' take to examine why people fall in love, the causes of rudeness, cheating and lying on tennis courts, better ways to can mackerel and the likelihood of Belgian endive growing in Massachusetts. The citizens of Idaho got a Bavarian-style gondola for one of their many ski resorts, and Israelis on the West Bank of Israel got $3.5 million for two Orthodox religious schools and a teacher training facility—a gift that only happened to be in direct opposition to U.S. foreign policy, which doesn't recognize the West Bank.

Thus the Lawrence Welk Museum was merely this year's entry in the long, grand tradition of those pork-barrel projects that go a little too far. Predictably, once the deal came to light, the dogs of scorn descended on the Hill, led by none other than George Bush, who called it a "pork-barrel bonanza" and used it to tee off a tough speech about Congress's waste and ineptitude. Now admittedly this is a man who throughout his presidency has been kinder to the Russian parliament than to his own Congress, but consider that even North Dakota's leading newspaper, *The Fargo Forum*, found itself unable to swallow the Welk freebie. "At a time when the farm bill's food and nutrition programs face the budget ax," the paper wrote, "the money for fixing up a few rundown buildings and constructing a motel is an egregious misappropriation. . . . If the Welk legacy is as important as the people of Strasburg seem to think, restoration of his home should be financed by private donations. If the bandleader's fans are as numerous and dedicated as the promoters of the Welk homestead tourist attraction say, raising private dollars should be no problem."

Even Welk, who was living in syndication-check splendor in Southern California, couldn't stomach it. His daughter told the press, "We were astonished and I must say embarrassed." His frugal German soul must have been sturming.

There was one good argument mounted in defense of the museum. Strasburg resident Fred Martin, with the sort of understated rural wisdom that made America great, told the Associated Press, "If there's money to throw away, we might as well have it."

But Senator Quentin Burdick, who suddenly found himself in the unusual position of having to defend his action, couldn't get away with anything so simple and true.

"It's not for Mr. Welk or anything like that," he tried. "It's to promote tourism generally, attract new business and create new jobs. It's an economic development program." Soon the cause would be world peace. He sounded like a ten-year-old piling whopper upon whopper as he tried to explain why he didn't have his homework done.

His press secretary tried to blunt the damage. "Anybody who has been to Strasburg can see that they can use some help," Jean Broadshaug said, adding that Burdick wouldn't answer any more questions on the matter. And yes, she had a point. In fact, the whole state is sort of like America's little corner of Russia. Its population hasn't grown since World War I and had been suffering from a three-year drought and wheat prices at two dollars a bushel. But a reasonable person might wonder if this automatically means that we should have the federal government pay the Disney Corporation to turn the entire state into the Czar World theme park. After all, lots of places in the country could use some help, but then those places don't have Q.B. on their payroll.

The specific idea formed by the Welk Heritage committee was to finish restoring the bandmaster's sod-walled birthplace and then to build a museum and a bed-and-breakfast lodge to celebrate the Volga Germans, that is, Germans who had migrated to Russia and then to North Dakota, presumably because they found the barren, windblasted land similar to the steppes, but without the pogroms. Not that Welk would know much about it. He hit the road as soon as he could. At seventeen he talked his father into buying him a $400 accordion if he'd agree to work the farm until he was twenty-one. Though he wasn't even the best accordion player in Strasburg, when the magic date arrived, he made tracks to the metropolis of Yankton, South Dakota, where he started his first band in 1924.

The heritage committee had raised some private funds, mostly from Welk's foundation, and they were already working on restoring the house, but they decided to see if Burdick could help with their vision to make the place a tourist mecca. He found some money tucked away in the Farmer's Home Administration, an agency set up to provide low-interest mortgages for the rural poor that has turned into its own sort of boondoggle with more than $50 billion in uncollectable loans. Burdick's subcommittee oversees the agency.

Sneaking a few bucks from a favored program is the sort of thing Burdick does all the time. And that he'd gotten his hand slapped by the media didn't change anything. Even after the uproar, his office told the North Dakota papers that he expected the money would start flowing to Strasburg within a few weeks. But something was different about this one. In a rare blast of courage, several members of Congress said they weren't going to let it lie. Apparently stung more by the outside reaction than the specific project, several younger members who took the institution seriously vowed to find a way to slash out the Welk project.

Their attitude was in keeping with the mood of Capitol Hill in the fall of 1990. There were angry forces swirling about, and many congressmen felt surly as they were forced to vote for a series of tax increases, which were among the largest in history, at the same time they were watching pet programs get thinned by the budget diet (to speak in terms of whacking spending with a budget ax, as some politicians did, was ludicrous; binges followed by modest diets was a better way to explain federal spending). Welk was merely one final irritant, just a small part of one of the great money tussles in recent years, a battle that involved hundreds of billions of dollars and, some would say, the foundation of the U.S. economy. And at the heart of the fight was pork.

# 2

# THE HOUSE THAT
# PORK BUILT

THE LAWRENCE WELK MUSEUM WAS THE CHILD OF A FRANKEN-
stein monster called the Fiscal 1991 Budget Summit Accord, sometimes simply referred to as the Omnibus Budget Reconciliation
Act, or, most ominously, OBRA, as in cobra. Basically it was the
deal cut between the White House and Congress on how to spend
the government's money for the year that ended on September 30,
1991. It was a big, bloody mess of an agreement that managed to
burn and pillage all kinds of interests—not the least being the
American taxpayer—while making a few people very happy. The
negotiations were a rancorous affair that threatened for a time to
sink both George Bush and the Congress. In large part the deal was
saved by thousands of Welk-like projects, costing billions of dollars
and handed over wholesale from the White House to Congress. It
was the deal that pork made.

The budget deal, for anyone who tried to unravel it, was also a
graduate-level introduction to the principles of Washington accounting. Here was something hailed as a deficit-reduction package that nonetheless boosted taxes, increased spending and raised

the deficit. Watching the sleight of hand passing before your eyes was like watching a three-card monte dealer plying his trade in Times Square. How'd he do that? the ten-year-olds in from the suburbs wonder. Anyone watching the budget deal unfold would be wondering the same thing.

In the fall of 1990, a lot of people thought the country was coming apart. Polls showed consumer confidence heading south faster than jobs from the Rust Belt, Bush's popularity plunging and Congress all but written off as a workable institution. "Is it any wonder that the people of this nation view us as the only insane asylum in the world operated by its own inmates?" Iowa Congressman Jim Ross Lightfoot screeched on the House floor. For Washington creatures, the *good news* was that the country was moving toward a war in the Persian Gulf that somewhat distracted the man on the street from the really awful matters at home, including the fact that the economy was slipping into a recession. But despite all this, the immediate cause for what the pollsters discovered was a deep sense of despair were the actions of a group of middle-aged white men who'd been closeted in a mess hall at Andrews Air Force Base outside Washington for much of the summer.

The idea was to have a budget summit between the leaders of Congress and Bush's top money henchmen: Budget Director Richard Darman, Chief of Staff John Sununu and Treasury Secretary Nicholas Brady. Put everybody into a room far from the normal theaters of Washington; secure them from the prying eyes of lobbyists and other special-interest groups; remove them from the rabble of Congress; and arrange them in what, by Washington standards, was meant to be an intimate gathering: about two dozen principals at the table and maybe a couple of hundred staffers milling around a cavernous room. In this relaxed setting, how could they help but hammer out a deal unsullied by the grubbiness of politics?

At least that was the theory. The reality was that the matter on the table at Andrews defined the very essence of politics: If you control the money, you control everything.

But as everyone in that room knew, the single greatest political problem facing the U.S. government, then and now, is that there isn't enough money. Either more has to come in (meaning, raise taxes), or we've got to realize that we expect government to do too much for us and we better ask it to do less (meaning, cut spending). Until something changes one way or the other, you have political deadlock. And, it doesn't take the chairman of the Federal Reserve Board to tell you, a negative bank balance. Thus the federal budget deficit. So the point of Andrews, indeed any summit, was that you can try to make that fattening red behemoth of a deficit seem as benign as possible, but the beast will have to be heard.

A few words here about the deficit, which becomes an inescapable, looming character in any journey into the world of pork. One quickly learns disturbing things about the deficit.

It's enormous.

Common sense says it's dangerous to the health of the country.

And no one cares.

Almost all politicians, after reading their polls, view the deficit as an abstract issue that the average voter can't grasp. Although hundreds of billions and even trillions of dollars of red ink are involved in the various parts of the deficit, politicians have concluded that Joe Six-pack, Bubba, Harry Homeowner and all the permutations of the middle-American schlepper don't see how it affects their day-to-day life.

All of which may answer the question of why there was *political* tension at Andrews—as in "Who's going to get the upper hand in this negotiation and come out looking good?"—but no sense of urgency about the *substance* of what was being debated. Actually, the fiscal 1991 budget deal was just one more chapter in a ten-year-old drama that's got many years left to run. Before this deal was even finished, the seasoned veterans were sure that by 1993, after the presidential election, there would be yet another new summit to undo the old summit and perhaps even make some genuine reforms. Perhaps.

But at Andrews, what everyone mostly did was eat and argue, eat and posture, eat and stall. As the level of antagonism increased, the military chefs laid out more and more elaborate buffets with roasts and casseroles and make-your-own-sundae bars. Congressmen complained that the fattening food was killing them. Of course, they could have said no, but Congress isn't that kind of place. And judging from the increasingly portly spans of Darman and Sununu, neither is the White House.

Along with their girth, Darman and Sununu brought to the table combined SAT scores approaching a perfect 3,200 and IQs said to be at the genius level. Just ask them. As the negotiations went on, the two squat right-hand men of George Bush even began to resemble each other in an eerie way, wearing the same shapeless dark gray suits with too-short pants and strutting into the room chests forward like a couple of pigeons laying claim to a park bench.

But they weren't there for the same reason. Darman was the cleverer-than-thou architect of the summit who had vast experience in budget gamesmanship. He played a key role in the Reagan Revolution during which he and David Stockman were the two accountants-from-hell who presided over the botched plan to cut taxes and cut spending (it didn't quite work out that way) that pumped the current deficit to its astoundingly bloated size. In a famous scene in Stockman's memoir, he and Darman realize what a fiasco they're creating and Darman says, "I don't know which is worse: winning now and fixing up the budget mess later or losing now and facing a political mess immediately." After a pause, he concludes, "We win it now. We fix it later." Almost a decade later, Darman was still trying to fix it. Some said his motive was ego; others said it was genuine public service; still others, guilt.

Sununu was simply a pathological bully. For reasons only his analyst knew for sure, he lived in order to be nasty to someone. The former governor of New Hampshire had bailed Bush out in that crucial primary in 1988 and earned the president's gratitude for his toughness and obstinacy. Now he was the baddest of the bad cops that Bush has always kept around to handle unpleasant chores. That the beady-eyed onetime nuclear physics professor was at the summit in the first place made some congressmen deeply suspicious of Bush's motives. They saw Sununu as a sort of political officer keeping watch on Darman, the way the KGB used to attach a man to army units to make sure the Red line was being toed.

Off to the side was the gaunt, patrician Brady, who acted like a befuddled priest at a hookers' convention. He was proxy for the noblesse oblige side of Bush, watching in uncomprehending amazement as these grubby little politicians whacked and jibed at each other.

But in the end, the grubbiest of all was Sununu, who couldn't keep his natural boorishness in check. He reflected his boss's contempt for Congress, but like any overly ambitious toady he took it too far. He treated the congressional leaders across the table— serious people like Richard Gephardt, Leon Panetta and James Sasser—as though they were countermen at McDonald's waiting to take his order. Often while one was speaking, he would converse loudly with Darman, sometimes laughing, sometimes interrupting with his view of the situation. "He tends to let you know how smart he is," said one participant. Week after week, he'd lean back in his chair and blithely dismiss the various proposals made by the Democrats.

Then one day, he had his feet propped on the conference table as he scanned the latest Democratic proposal, quickly tossing it back with a curt "That's garbage."

At that moment, Senator Robert Byrd stood up.

There were perhaps two hundred people in the spacious officers' mess hall, and usually the noise level was quite high as staffers mumbled to one another and scurried around the room. When Byrd rose, everyone stopped.

"With all due respect," he began in his overly formal manner, his defiantly pointy chin and pomaded ripple of white hair giving him the look of a deranged rooster, "anyone who worked for the *staff* of Senator Robert Byrd would never be so impertinent."

Sununu, for once, listened.

"I've worked with the *staffs* of eight presidents, and I've never seen such discourtesy. I am sure this president would be disturbed to see how the Senate of the United States was being treated by his *staff*," Byrd said, drawing out the word *sta-yaff* with his West Virginia hill country accent so no one could mistake the point at hand.

On any given day, Byrd matched Sununu tit for tat in distasteful characteristics. Byrd saw Sununu's arrogance and raised him with pompousness; where Sununu was rude, Byrd was numbingly long-winded; if Sununu brusquely suffered no fools, Byrd stupefied them with pedantic lectures about the true lessons to be learned from the Peloponnesian wars. But while Sununu was then enjoying the temporary favor of his patron in the White House, Byrd was an elected official with a secure seat and a well-tended power base among Senate colleagues who didn't necessarily like him but respected and feared him. Byrd held all the high cards, and he knew it.

He went on to ream Sununu and to remind the president's men that he was one senator who wasn't about to be ignored.

"You may fail to pass this budget *with* my support, but you *certainly* won't pass it without me."

Darman, who saw his plan teetering on the edge of failure—which would mean a harsh political blow to Bush and who-knew-what fate for Darman himself—also saw an opportunity. He knew the Hill, and he knew Byrd's power as the chairman of the Appropriations Committee. "If you know the Senate, you know that anyone who crosses Byrd is a fool," a White House staffer explained succinctly. Darman has many unfortunate characteristics, ranging from deviousness to hypocrisy, but foolishness is not among them.

In the previous budget deals, Darman had been careful to "accommodate" Byrd by not opposing his favored projects. In 1989, for instance, when the White House was trying to pass a supplemental budget that sent aid to the Nicaraguan contras, Byrd mentioned that a government telescope in West Virginia had been blown down in a windstorm. Darman quickly inserted a $75 million provision to replace it. The bill passed with a relative minimum of other waste, and Darman later told friends, "That was the cheapest $75 million telescope the federal government ever bought."

He knew that this year, Byrd was obsessed with getting more money for those areas his committee controlled, the so-called "domestic discretionary" spending accounts, which make up most of the government's business except for defense and the entitlement programs such as Social Security and Medicaid. Domestic discretionary is also the account from which most of the pork emerges. Darman knew that Byrd had lectured his summit colleagues about the need for more spending in these areas, one night keeping them in their seats after dinner while he brought out charts and graphs to illustrate a passionate hour-long speech.

"I know what it is to be the runt pig," Byrd had told them, harking back to his days slopping hogs in the coal holler, "to find it hard to get up to the trough to stay alive."

Domestic spending, the runt pig of the budget, had been starved during the Reagan years, he said, forced to take cuts while other programs grew. He reminded them that the power of Congress had also been curtailed because domestic spending was the place where members could make decisions, instead of the programs like Social Security, where spending was mandated. But what he meant was that the ability to distribute pork, to do favors, to reward the powerful and punish the recalcitrant was being hampered. And then he let this powerful assemblage know that they were all in the game together.

"I look in the drawer of my desk in the Appropriations Committee and I find 215 requests from the distinguished senator from Oregon, Mr. Hatfield," he said, nodding in his direction. "All of them good projects, mind you. I find 267 requests from Mr. Domenici, the very accomplished senator from New Mexico . . ."

He went around the room and with flawless memory cited dozens of projects sought by everyone there, Democrats and Republicans alike, for in Byrd's Appropriations Committee, money, not partisanship, rules. ("At times like these," recalled former Congressman Bill Frenzel, who sat through Byrd's lecture, "you can't tell a Republican from a Democrat. When they're salivating over a new bridge project, the same amount of drool hits the tarmac.")

"These are all necessary projects," Byrd went on, launching into one of his patented soliloquies, "but I don't see how we can accommodate them without more funds. We've got to invest in America.

"I happen to believe that this country still has the spirit to which de Tocqueville referred over 150 years ago when he said, 'The incredible American believes that if something has not yet been accomplished, it is because he has not yet attempted it.'

"Samson took the jawbone of an ass and killed a thousand Philistines. The early American took an ax, a Bible, a rifle and a bag of seeds, and he hewed the forests, blazed the trails and crossed the mountains to the prairies from sea to shining sea, and he built a nation.

"Moses struck the rock at Horeb with his rod, and the water gushed forth. The incredible American struck the rock of our natural resources, and we have exceeded all other countries in the production of steel, coal, chemicals and glass.

"Elijah, when he came to the Jordan with his son, Elisha, tossed his mantle on the waters of the Jordan, and the waters parted and the two crossed over Jordan on dry land. The incredible American built shining, massive bridges that glimmer in the sun, that span the Mississippi, the Missouri, the many great rivers of this country."

In his florid, romanticized lecture he managed to cite, from memory, the words of Daniel Webster, Lycurgus the Lawgiver, various Old Testament tales, and the poet J. G. Holland, as well as a breathtaking array of budget numbers, and in one tour de force passage, to rattle off, in order, the names of thirty-nine American presidents—". . . Garfield, Arthur, Cleveland, Benjamin Harrison, Cleveland again . . ."—and their contribution to the accumulated budget deficit, which wasn't much. The whole problem, in his view, lay with the last two presidents, and the numbers on his charts made a pretty good case.

"Pericles, one of the greatest of Athenians, said to his countrymen, 'Set your eyes upon the greatness of your country and re-member that her greatness was won by men with courage, with a knowledge of their duty, and with a sense of honor in action.'

"In this time of trouble, America needs men. America needs politicians—statesmen who have courage and a knowledge of their duty."

But what America really needed, Byrd was saying between the lines, was more money to spend on the projects he wanted. States-manship was not the issue here. His ultimate point was that, fig-ured his way, domestic spending had been shortchanged for a decade and whether you called it pork or investment in America, it was only a small part of the budget problem. "This little runt puppy has been on the operating table for ten years under the knife, yet there are those who want to cut on it more."

For the moment, his logic was unassailable.

Darman knew all this. He knew what was on Byrd's mind. So right after Byrd's poleaxing of Sununu, he approached him.

"Can I have a minute, Senator?"

What came next was a week-long poker game between two smart men playing with other people's money.

It was quickly established that pork was much of what Byrd wanted, and Darman didn't mind. He's no hard-liner when it comes to spending, and those who know him say that in his most candid moments, he even agrees with Byrd's analysis that the domestic accounts have suffered. The only question was how much Byrd would get.

In the end it was a lot. In what was supposed to be one of the tightest budgets in history, he got immediate increases of more than 10 percent for the $200 billion in spending his committee controlled and further increases over the five-year life of the deal that would total an extra $200 billion. Darman paid a very high price, financially and politically, as conservatives began to see him as some sort of Marxist in their midst.

But Byrd wanted more. He wanted to kill the Gramm-Rudman-Hollings budget law before it killed him. The "old" budget reform law, dating to 1985, Gramm-Rudman set specific targets for the deficit and, if Congress and the president couldn't meet them, mandated an automatic across-the-board cut—called a sequester. But many programs were exempt from the sequester, including so-called entitlement spending such as Social Security. So what was left to cut was most of the domestic discretionary spending programs under Byrd's jurisdiction. Unquestionably, he was getting squeezed hard by Gramm-Rudman.

Darman didn't have a problem with relieving the pressure. Gramm-Rudman, though it was slowly reducing the deficit, was becoming a pain for the White House as well. Darman was going to have to sequester about $100 billion in spending, and that wouldn't make anyone happy. "Darman believes in government," a former top White House aide said. "He believes in letting it work as smoothly as you can. He's got no stomach for cutting things and upsetting the process." Besides, Darman had his own plan, and Byrd could make it happen.

Darman, a man who makes Niccolò Machiavelli seem simple and direct, wanted a change in the budget process that would essentially set strict limits, or caps, on all categories of federal spending. Once those limits were reached, neither Congress nor the president could spend a dime unless they either cut something else or raised new money. How the caps would be put into effect and who would monitor them was a complex question: just the sort of complexity that Byrd, among few members of Congress, understood. His colleagues viewed him as a master of the Senate process and deferred to his judgment in working out a deal. It would be weeks before a budget was finally passed by Congress and signed by the president, weeks featuring all manner of political grandstanding and brinkmanship by both sides, including a shutdown of the government for a few days. But the essence of the budget was the deal reached between the monied son of a New England industrialist and the adopted son of a West Virginia coal miner. Darman got his caps. Byrd got his pork.

"Darman is a realist," another former White House official said. "He knows that if you want something, you've got to pay for it. Pork is currency."

The ultimate question became, Did Darman get what he paid for? He insisted that the caps would result in a meaningful reduction in the deficit, but his success or failure wouldn't be clear until after the 1992 elections because one wrinkle in the deal was that it was designed, by Democrats and Republicans alike, to push the deficit problem beyond the election, not unlike what they had done with the savings-and-loan crisis in 1988.

Some things were soon clear, however. Under Gramm-Rudman, the deficit would have been gone by 1992. Under the Darman-Byrd deal, it was supposed to be about $250 billion, but as this book went to press, it was actually $399.6 billion and growing, making the total debt of the U.S. government something around $4 trillion.

What was also clear was that the caps were anchored about as securely as a bad hairpiece. There were many ways to get around them. Just after the deal took shape, Scott Hodge, a budget analyst at the Heritage Foundation, had a particularly concise assessment. "Darman paid a very high price to get those spending caps because he thinks he's trapping the Democrats. Since they can't increase spending, they have to choose one program over another. They have to make trade-offs, which is what everybody keeps saying is the only way to make government spending rational. Another way to look at this is, if they want to expand programs, they're forced to eat their young, to gut something already in existence. Darman thinks he's got them in a box.

"But the deal is more clever than substantive. You're not forcing trade-offs because you're not reordering government. You're not resolving the question of what is the role of a national congress, a national government. You're just throwing a bunch of competing congressmen into a room and forcing them to make decisions based on who's the most powerful. They'll do it to a point, but as soon as it gets too tough, they'll change the rules. If it comes down to the Democrats blowing the caps off or eating their young, they'll blow the caps."

There was also this. When you looked at the budget deal, stripped of its intricacies and slyness, it did three things: it increased taxes, it increased spending and it increased the deficit.

New taxes, which came from a variety of places including gasoline, liquor and cigarettes, amounted to $164 billion dollars, by some estimates the largest onetime boost ever.

The so-called cuts weren't really that. They were "a reduction in projected federal spending," meaning the government was simply going to spend less than it had originally planned and that amount would be called savings—even though it was still spending more each year than the year before. This is something you can do only when you're using someone else's money. It would be like your husband coming home and saying that he decided not to buy a $500 television set and instead bought a $300 suit. So you "saved" $200. Try telling that to the guy at the bank when your check bounces.

But there was also the reassurance that one group in America would not be bouncing checks as a result of the deal: federal employees. At a time when businesses across America were laying off thousands of people to cut costs and when the federal government's income statement made Chrysler look like a hugely successful company, not one federal worker lost his job. All 3 million were apparently absolutely essential to the functioning of the country, as were all of the programs they ran. Every single one.

Anyone who could understand how all this made the budget deal of 1990 a truly great deficit-reduction package, could surely begin to understand how Washington really works.

## 3

# HOG HEAVEN

**W**HEN THE PALE, SQUINTY-EYED MEN EMERGED INTO THE sunlight from their mess hall at Andrews Air Force Base with a proposed budget deal in hand, Capitol Hill erupted in a roar of wounded outrage that echoed through every television market in America.

Congressmen fumed with what, to the untrained ear, sounded like genuine shock and amazement that taxes were being raised and spending programs cut without their knowledge. "I'll die in my seat before I let a gasoline tax go through!" some as much as said. "Medicare cannot be cut as long as I breathe!" others postured (meaning, in the wonderland language of Washington, that the rate of spending increases for Medicare couldn't be slowed; actual Medicare spending was going to blast through the roof no matter what happened, the only question being how big a hole it would leave as it blew the shingles off).

The reality was that the average congressman knew pretty much exactly what the proposed budget deal was going to be *before* it arrived on the Hill—and he knew that in the end, he wouldn't have much to say about it. But he had to have the chance to stamp his feet and show the voters that he was conscious, alert and fully aware of the sound of the Republic crumbling around him. "Have we become a house of political eunuchs?" Congressman Arthur Ravenel of South Carolina asked, no doubt fearing the answer.

So the bottom line that autumn was that the deal as it emerged from Andrews was unacceptable. It would have to be redone, with a lot more people putting their fingerprints onto it—because the average congressman resented the fact that the proposal had been forged by a handful of insiders with little consultation of the many second-level fiefdoms on the Hill. All the dukes and barons and earls of Congress were going to have their say in this matter, as well as some of the vassals and groundlings.

As the deal disintegrated, President Bush, who once served in Congress and should have known better, began racing around the country like a chicken on speed, bashing Washington in general and Congress in particular. "Oh, how nice it is to be out where the real people are, outside of Washington," said this consummate creation of the permanent government, his voice rising an octave or two into a whine of insincerity. The public sensed his phoniness and rewarded him with a precipitous decline in the opinion polls. After all, it was *his* lackeys who had called for the summit in the first place and then concocted an incredibly complicated deal that was bound to make Congress revolt, but still made their boss look bad by making him break his signature campaign promise: "No new taxes."

How stupid did Bush think the voters were? Could they have forgotten Candidate Bush in speech after speech? "No new taxes. . . . I am not going to raise taxes. Period. . . . There are those who say we must balance the budget on the backs of the workers—and raise taxes. But they are wrong. . . . The Congress will push me to raise taxes, and I'll say no, and they'll push and I'll say no and they'll push again and I'll say to them, 'Read my lips: no new taxes.' "

But at least the man who ran for president wasn't as deluded as the man who took the office. Candidate Bush knew that giving money to Congress was like giving Old Crow to an alcoholic. In 1988 he said, "Unless you can control Congress's spending, increased revenues will go to increased spending." And of course it did. Because once Bush permitted a deal to go through that involved new money coming into the federal treasury, there were some masterful old hands waiting in breathless anticipation to spend it. Not surprisingly, the first in line was Bob Byrd.

That fall, the senator from West Virginia was oblivious to the chaos around him. He carried himself with the confidence of a man heading for the bank with a paycheck in his pocket. Byrd in action provided as choice an example as you could hope to find of the two worlds of Congress. While Democratic and Republican leaders wrung their hands and resumed the imprecations needed to get enough votes to pass a budget, Byrd set about with his usual humorless discipline to carve up the pork pie. In the C-Span Congress, earnest men with circles under their eyes—led by those twins of dourness, Senate Majority Leader George Mitchell and House Speaker Tom Foley, looking like beleaguered small-town bankers—floated new wrinkles and waited in trepidation to see if anyone was buying. "The American people have begun to lose faith in our ability to do our business," Democrat Richard Gephardt moaned, only to be topped by Republican leader Bob Michel's memorably simpy attempt at pun making: "We can pick apart the agreement with a thousand points of spite. If we do, we'll not only lose the agreement but our ability to govern."

Byrd said nothing. He and the key members of the Senate and House appropriations committees met in secret to hear the pleadings of their supplicants and quietly hand out new projects as they saw fit. That the president decided to shut down the federal government for two days because the fiscal year had ended with no new budget was not a matter for the appropriators. These veterans of many seasons knew that in a few weeks somebody would work out a new deal and that after all the gas was expended—millions of words worth of gas in speeches, press releases and interviews—all the blame spread and the partisan advantages gained, it would be a lot like the deal that had emerged from Andrews.

And so it was. As often happens on the Hill, the sound and fury signified not much. The outlines, as worked out by Byrd and Darman, remained. What the leadership of the Congress spent three weeks doing was arguing over which crayons to use to color inside the lines. When the benumbed representatives finally voted on the Omnibus Budget Reconciliation Act of 1990, OBRA in Congresspeak, in the wee hours of the morning, it was a mere formality. Hardly anyone knew what was in it, except for a handful of insiders. "We didn't vote on a budget," Congressman Chris Cox said, "we voted on a two-foot-high stack of paper tied up with string. It wasn't even the same paper. It came from different copy machines all over the Hill and got slapped together just before we got it. I don't think anyone—and I mean no one—ever looked at the whole thing from start to finish."

But passing a slapdash budget with little thought or discussion by anyone other than the key members of the key subcommittees was business as usual in the fantasyland of Capitol Hill. The *serious* business that year had been elsewhere. If you knew where to look in the few weeks before the final budget vote, you could see that the halls of Congress had come to resemble a frantic Middle Eastern souk. They might as well have draped the bronze statues of Washington, Jefferson and Jackson with Persian carpets and started smoking hookah pipes in the hearing rooms. For a few tense days, people scurried and dialed, begged and cajoled to make deals. Not the least of these were the fourth branch of government, the lobbyists who represent every imaginable interest in America hoping to grab a slice of the vast budget pie. These were men, mostly, whose unnaturally shiny shoes matched their briefcases, men who lingered outside mahogany doors and spoke from behind their hands, men who had traded in the charcoal gray Brooksgate suits they had worn as congressional aides for custom-tailored models in the same shade of gray but with about a thousand dollars more luster in the fabric. Influence in Washington is always more subtle than one would imagine.

The mood recalled the words of the late Paul Powell, an Illinois politician of earthy tastes who used to say, when it came to deal-making time in the state legislature, "Mmmm, mmmm. I can smell the meat a-cookin'."

Because of Byrd's culinary skills—he is, after all, a former butcher—the aroma of meat was stronger than ever that year. Whatever anyone could say about the strange spending habits of the Reagan years, his budget hounds, notably Jim Miller, the last director of the Office of Management and Budget and a man known around the Hill as "Dr. No," had eliminated a lot of pork from the budget. Darman was not nearly so vigilant, or concerned. "The word," said one lobbyist, "is that the cash register is open."

The result was a spectacular season of porking that marbled the budget with probably thousands of projects—worth, depending on your definition, $50 to $100 billion—that were at best postponable in the midst of such fiscal hard times and at worst truly wasteful in the most prosperous of times. They ranged from the ridiculous to the obscene.

For some reason commemoration was a favored theme that year. Tenderly, Congress slipped in spending to memorialize a host of second-tier patriots and causes. The monument to Lawrence Welk was merely one in a series. Ralph Regula, an Ohio congressman, got $320,000 to buy the home of President William McKinley's *in-laws* in Canton, reasoning that since McKinley's own birthplace was no longer standing and certainly he needed to be remembered, why not buy his wife's parents' home, where he had lived for a few years, and donate it to the state of Ohio? And while they were at it, Al Gore, Jr., the senator from Tennessee, wanted $500,000 to create a park and museum at the birthplace of Cordell Hull, FDR's secretary of state, which happens to be just across the river from his own hometown of Carthage. This to go along with the money he had gotten earlier to reconstruct the Cordell Hull Bridge, which carries a state road across the Cumberland River. Then there was the restoration of the home of pulp Western writer Zane Grey in Lackawanna, Pennsylvania, and Gifford Pinchot, the father of the National Forest Service, also in Pennsylvania.

Red ink did not dissuade legislators from demanding—and getting—all kinds of museums, including $4 million for a new Japanese-American museum in Ontario, Oregon, and another $39,000 for an existing Japanese-American museum in Los Angeles that the government had already been subsidizing. Joseph McDade, the congressman from Scranton, Pennsylvania, secured $11 million to continue his personal obsession of Steamtown USA, a new national railroad museum (there are at least four national rail museums already) in downtown Scranton. Not far to the west, John Murtha, the congressman from Johnstown, got $13 million to start turning a string of abandoned factories into "America's Industrial Heritage," a sort of Rust Belt theme park that would cost a great deal more before it was through. Senator Barbara Mikulski sought to immortalize Christopher Columbus with a Marine Research Center in her hometown of Baltimore, notwithstanding that the same research was already being done in Michigan.

Culture, too, found that hard times were no impediment to subsidized good taste. North Miami Beach, not exactly a depressed area, got a $1 million Housing and Urban Development grant to build an arts center; Fort Meyers, Florida, into which many of the Social Security checks of America flow, got another $500,000 for the same thing. Senator Byrd bestowed $4.5 million on the citizens of Huntington, West Virginia, to restore what is no doubt the jewel of Huntington, the Keith-Albee Theater, into a four-screen multiplex worthy of any shopping mall in America. He tossed another half million to the sherry-pouring citizens of Fairmont for a "center for culture and the humanities," and signed off on the pet project of one of his protégés, Congressman Nick Joe Rahall II: a grant to "interpret the Hatfield-McCoy feud" in Matewan.

Among the stranger random items that found their way into the budget was $2.7 million to build a freshwater catfish farm in Stuttgart, Arkansas, taken at the insistence of Senator Dale Bumpers from the coffers of the National Oceanic and Atmospheric Administration, which is supposed to study the oceans. Bumpers also managed to wedge in $3.75 million for a Poultry Center of Excellence at the University of Arkansas, apparently to study how to make even more excellent poultry than was already being made by the several other federal poultry centers in existence.

Senator Daniel Akaka, a Hawaiian senator who was facing a tough reelection bid, got $2 million, allegedly to promote the sale of native Hawaiian handicrafts but actually to build someone a native canoe to sail around the islands, as well as a half-million dollars to study how to better sell mahimahi. He got further help when he teamed up with Hawaii's senior senator and a true spending power, Daniel Inouye, to get $1.2 million for something called "Hawaiian homeland infrastructure development" and another $1.3 million to save the jobs of Hawaiian sugar workers because they are "suffering continued economic hardship," which should not make the other 8 million unemployed American workers also suffering economic hardship any happier.

Cardinal Inouye, who headed the Senate's Subcommittee on Defense Appropriations, was a man who sometimes seemed to view the U.S. Treasury as his personal checking account, bestowing funds almost at will on Hawaii or whichever of the many defense industries he favored. He was responsible for a pork watershed of sorts when, in 1987, he inserted at the request of one of his major campaign contributors an item for $8 million of foreign aid funds to build religious schools for North African Jews living in France. The item, which generated Welk-like ridicule, was eventually withdrawn and may have ushered in the modern era of pork opposition. Not that it stopped Inouye; in the fall of 1990 he was also laying plans to score $50 million in federal funds to rehabilitate the private George Washington University Hospital in Washington for no apparent reason other than the fact that he is a graduate and trustee of the university.

Foreign aid funds are often thought of as funny money that satisfies the ego of congressmen more than their constituents. Stephen Solarz, the New York congressman who spends more time abroad than anyone else in the House and fancies himself a shadow secretary of state, generously sent $5 million to the citizens of the Solomon Islands, an independent nation in the South Pacific, so they could construct a new parliament building. He said when he visited there he was appalled that the parliament met in a quonset hut and that, since America had fought the battle of Guadalcanal on its soil fifty years before, we owed it something.

Other projects had a similarly whimsical quality, the sort of impulse buys a shopper makes when he's strolling through a well-stocked mall with an untapped credit card in his wallet. Senator Pete Domenici got it into his head one day that his constituents in New Mexico were in danger of being hit by the debris of disintegrating spacecraft, so he got a $100,000 grant to study the problem—in New Mexico only. One assumes that those in other states who might be at risk from falling space shards can get their own grants. Senator Tom Harkin, who cannot do enough for the people of Iowa, got $2.5 million to remove asbestos from the Rath meatpacking plant in Waterloo, a private business that traditionally would be expected to remove its own asbestos.

Harkin's House colleague, Neal Smith, who as a rule is inclined to do even more for the citizens of Iowa, came up with a curious plan that, while wasteful, is not apparently helpful to Iowans. He set aside $15 million (the first installment of a four-year, $105 million project) to give to states so they can hire small businesses to plant trees on state lands. Officials of the Small Business Administration, which Smith raided for the funds, didn't want to do the project, nor did the Small Business Committee in the House. But since Smith chairs his own appropriations subcommittee, he simply wrote the language into the budget bill just before it went to a vote. When asked by a reporter for *Time* why he had done it, the aging congressman replied testily, "Are you for tree planting or not?"

And there was so much more!

For instance, the Department of Transportation budget is always a favorite pot to raid for projects that have nothing to do with the national transportation system. Congressmen view new bridges, viaducts, railroad crossings, cloverleafs and road expansion as among the choicest pelts they can bring home from Washington. The fiscal 1991 budget was a banner year for this sort of thing and particularly rich in so-called "demonstration projects"—supposedly pilot programs to test new techniques of road building but usually just demonstrations of one congressman's clout.

The result are things like the Bud Shuster Highway, a wide, beautiful thirty-mile strip of road that carries virtually no traffic from the Bedford exit of the Pennsylvania Turnpike to Altoona —home of Congressman E. G. "Bud" Shuster, a self-made millionaire and a senior Republican member of the Public Works Committee who has devoted his life to getting what he can for the folks in central Pennsylvania. He often boasts that the road was completed at a cost of zero dollars to the people of his state. Its demonstration value must be in proving that if you build a nice road to a place where people don't want to go, they still won't go there.

Nonetheless, dozens of Bud Shuster Highways were getting their start that fall. Typical was $3.4 million to begin widening the road from Prestonburg to Paintsville in the hills of eastern Kentucky. The stated purpose: "to show the safety and economic benefits of widening and improving highways in mountainous areas." The real purpose: a little gift from aging William Natcher, the Lou Gehrig of Congress who hasn't missed a vote on the House floor in almost forty years, to his fellow Kentuckian, Chris Perkins, son of a onetime old-boy powerhouse, the late Congressman Carl Perkins. Being wily country boys, Natcher and Perkins knew all along that wider highways are better than narrow ones, especially if you don't have to pay for them. No need to demonstrate that. But Natcher, the number two Democrat on the Appropriations Committee and a man who's considered one of the most scrupulous members of the House—he accepts no campaign contributions and has virtually no staff—is nonetheless always willing to steer some federal money Kentucky's way, something he and Carl Perkins often did together. Young Perkins, who narrowly won reelection in 1990, was worried about squandering Daddy's franchise. Maybe something called the Chris Perkins Highway (perhaps with a Bill Natcher Overpass or two) just might save him.

There were other individual memorials that served as testament to the leverage, persuasiveness or butt-kissing abilities of various congressmen, things like $10 million secured by Senator Robert Kasten to build a ramp to the Milwaukee Brewers stadium parking lot and a $1.7 million first installment on a $19 million project to turn Miami's plush Biscayne Boulevard into an even more plush "exotic garden for people to enjoy the richness of city life," featuring new plants and sidewalks and a ninety-foot-wide median strip. This last was courtesy of Florida's William Lehman, the semicomatose chairman of the Appropriations Subcommittee on Transportation, who has showered Miami with such goodies as an unwanted subway that costs more to move passengers than door-to-door taxi fare would and a multi-million-dollar people mover to shuttle around all the folks who aren't taking the subway.

The farm appropriations bill was its usual county fair of delights and oddities. Three million dollars was allocated to study the dreaded pecan weevil in Oklahoma and many millions more to study all forms of pests and plants, everything from aflatoxin to zebra mussels, that had somehow missed scrutiny in the previous two hundred years of American agriculture. Some of the projects were probably even useful, although $37,000 to study how to handle manure seemed a bit much, and don't we know all we need to about wheat smut? Most precious was a $19 million study of cow flatulence which, on its face, sounded like the worst example of pork-barrel spending in the history of politics. But some environmentalists pointed out that cows emit a tremendous amount of methane gas, which may contribute to global warming, so the hecklers held their tongues until more information was in.

One amazing category of spending was projects dedicated to the memory of Thomas P. "Tip" O'Neill, the former Speaker of the House and now motel room pitchman, who has many friends for whom he's done many favors over the years. O'Neill comes from the unabashed school of spenders, whose battle cry is "All spending is good spending!" In his autobiography, he talks at length of all the money he was able to steer to causes he deemed worthy. And somehow, years after his retirement, he just kept on giving. It was as if someone had opened an attaché case at one of the Appropriations Committee meetings and out popped the bulbous Boston pol, flushed from nineteen holes of golf. He stuck out his hand and asked, "Where's mine, boys?" So Tip got $20 million for the International Fund for Ireland, which includes a project to study Irish ancestry, production of a video touting Irish golf courses and a program to promote the sale of Irish goods in Boston. His pals also shepherded through *$184 million* for a new federal office building in downtown Boston, the Thomas P. O'Neill Federal Office Building, to go along with all the other federal buildings O'Neill put into that city's massive Government Center. And finally, there was more money for Tip's legacy, the Central Artery project, in which the state highway system of downtown Boston will be rebuilt with about $3 billion of federal funds in one of the largest government construction projects ever.

Equally amazing, though involving a lot more money, was the defense budget. The most remarkable fact was what *didn't* happen: *the budget wasn't cut.*

Despite a radical change in the shape of the world and a virtual consensus that the Pentagon was spending much more than it needed to, *no major weapons were eliminated.* The Pentagon budget actually *grew*—it just didn't grow as fast as the Pentagon had originally said it would, so the move was portrayed as a cut. For all the talk of a peace dividend, when the time came for actual cuts, there was no swelling sentiment in Congress to take big pieces out of defense. This was in large part because almost every congressman had a substantial military presence in his backyard—whether it was a base for training web-belt repairmen or a factory that made overpriced toilet seats. Here was pork of a higher sort.

But there was plenty of low-down pork as well. Depending on whom you believed, somewhere between 10 and 20 percent of the Pentagon budget was attributable to bloat from pork-induced spending—a total of $30 to $60 billion added on as a sort of tax for keeping Congress happy. Some of the biggest unnecessary dollars in fiscal 1991 were spent on the National Guard and the reserves, often for new armories and training facilities, which are very visible manifestations to a voter about what his man in Washington is doing for him. All told, about $8 billion was split up among facilities the Pentagon didn't even want, with almost every state getting something to show.

As part of the generosity lavished on the National Guard, John Murtha, the Pennsylvania congressman who oversees defense spending, continued his plan to buy a fleet of Gulfstream IV jets for Guard commanders to use. *The Washington Post* discovered that with the backing of the Georgia delegation—Gulfstream employs four thousand people in Savannah—Murtha pushed through language requiring the Pentagon to buy two more of the $25 million planes to go along with three purchased the year before, and sources suggested that he didn't intend to rest until he had given a personal plane to each of the fifty state Guard commanders. Called the C-20 by the military, the Gulfstream is like a super corporate jet, the kind of toy coveted by chief executives the world over.

There were many more specific projects as well, some of them unfathomable to the naked eye. As it had in the past, the military was producing obsolete ammunition, acquiring vast stockpiles of unneeded spare parts, funding useless bases and paying to have its weapons built at the highest possible cost in order to keep one congressman or another voting the Pentagon's way. But some items leaped out because of their bizarreness. Coal, for instance, seemed to be a preoccupation of the Defense Department. One provision in the defense bill said that U.S. bases in Europe couldn't buy foreign coal or burn natural gas to heat their facilities, but instead had to ship in anthracite coal—no substitutes would do—from the United States. Overall, the Pentagon annually buys 300,000 tons, or 10 percent of the nation's output, of high-sulfur anthracite coal, a less desirable fuel than bituminous coal, that nevertheless costs the federal government several hundred million dollars extra to acquire and use. Currently, the Pentagon has a ten-year supply. There was even a $3 million project to see if jet fuels could be made from coal. Curious—*until* you realize that John Murtha and Joe McDade, both from Pennsylvania anthracite coal country, are the ranking Democrat and Republican on the Defense Appropriations Subcommittee and that coal is still close to the economic heart of Bob Byrd's state of West Virginia.

The Pentagon was also forced to buy a similar stockpile of unneeded depleted uranium, the residue of nuclear reactors that's used to make tank armor and armor-piercing shells. But *The Wall Street Journal* discovered that the government has enough depleted uranium to last for a hundred years—of war. If we were shooting at people every day, we'd still have enough on hand today to keep the ammo coming until late next century. But the Pentagon will spend $200 million to buy another 36 million pounds of the stuff from a company called Nuclear Metals Inc., which happens to produce it in South Carolina. Who put the item into the budget? South Carolina Senators Strom Thurmond and Ernest Hollings.

No congressman was more creative with defense spending than Pennsylvanian John Murtha, who had an all-star year. He forced the Pentagon to pay $10 million to establish a new intelligence center for the Drug Enforcement Administration and required that it be built in that hotbed of narcotrafficking, Johnstown, Pennsylvania. This despite the fact that there was already such a center in El Paso, Texas, and that the CIA, Coast Guard and Treasury Department each had its own drug intelligence center. The Justice Department, which oversees the DEA, had just had funds for the project knocked out of *its* appropriations bill. But since Murtha was the main man when it came to writing the defense bill, he simply inserted funds for the new center into *his* bill.

There was also a pot of $140 million for educational grants that went to all sorts of universities with only tenuous connections to defense research for projects the Pentagon didn't want. The grants were so outrageous that an angry and bewildered Senator Sam Nunn, chairman of the Armed Services Committee, whose job it is to oversee how the Pentagon spends its money, stood on the Senate floor and demanded that his colleagues put the money back.

"I am anxious to learn the military merit for using $15 million to build a children's museum in New Jersey," he said in his nasal Georgia drawl. "And to learn about the military contributions that require $4 million for a Japanese-American museum in Oregon. . . . I am anxious to learn why the navy's existing laboratories and design bureaus are so limited that we must add $24 million for a nonprofit consortium formed by Lehigh University to study shipbuilding design and manufacturing methods . . . and $10 million to build a building at the College of Pharmacy at Drake University."

But despite his pique, one needn't worry that Nunn was excluded from the spending party. As always, he had a variety of Georgia projects in the bill—the military builds lots of things in Georgia—including Tacit Rainbow, a badly flawed radar intercepting missile that would have been canceled years ago, were it not built near Nunn's hometown of Perry.

Nunn shouldn't have been too upset. Education spending was being used and abused all over the Hill. A total of about $500 million in unrequested education grants was forced down the throats of places like the Department of Energy and the General Services Administration, the agency responsible for building and leasing federal office space, which found itself putting up $20 million worth of private university facilities. Like planting trees, it's hard to argue with money spent for education, until you realize that it's often of questionable merit. The grants aren't bid out or reviewed; thus there's no determination of whether the work serves any purpose other than to give some third-rate university a shiny new building. Places such as Somerset Community College in Kentucky, Wheeling Jesuit College in West Virginia and St. Norbert's in Wisconsin were suddenly being treated as preeminent centers of learning not because they competed and won but because some congressman said so.

Another often-overlooked corner of the budget was the National Park Service, which has, in recent years, become a favorite of legislators looking for a quick buck to please the folks back home. The service used to take its role of designating national parks and historic sites quite seriously by assigning the task to a commission of noted scholars. But in the Reagan years, the budget cutters eliminated the commission, reasoning that they'd put an end to the proliferation of historic sites. Remember, these are the same folks who thought they could stop sex by stopping sex education. The gland in congressmen that creates the urge to spend money is likewise not so easily foiled. Congress just took on the job itself, and individual members began to tell the Park Service what constituted a monument. Thus, at a time when budgets were being slashed and rangers laid off at places such as Yellowstone National Park, one found the appearance of such items as many millions of dollars for the town of Harpers Ferry, which is commended by two factors, in ascending order: its significance as the site of abolitionist John Brown's attack on federal troops in 1859 and its location in the home state of Robert Byrd.

But West Virginia was by no means the only state that found itself with a disproportionate share of federal money. When the bill that funds energy and water projects emerged, some members were surprised to see that of all the money being spent on waterway improvements—for the entire country—approximately half of it, or some $300 million, was going to Louisiana, which certainly doesn't have half the country's water. What it does have, however, is Senator J. Bennett Johnston, the dapper, light-footed boss of the Subcommittee on Energy and Water Appropriations. With a smile and a shuffle of his spectator shoes, Johnston can be counted on to cook up a bill that takes care of his home state's many, many tributaries and bayous by dredging them, reversing them, straightening them or swaddling their shifting banks with concrete mattresses that the Army Corps of Engineers says only cost about as much per square foot as "carpeting your home with good-quality carpet." No doubt about it, stopping nature in its tracks is an expensive, never-ending proposition, but Johnston is an energetic man. And since he doles out a fair amount of smaller projects to take care of the rest of the water in the country, who's to challenge him? Johnston is a backslapping testament to the lesson that's never lost in the world of the Money Congress: The big dogs eat first.

Of course, there are dogs farther up the food chain than Johnston. And they all displayed some rather revolting table manners as the 1991 budget was thrashed out. While publicly preaching fiscal restraint, most of the leading figures of Congress were intently trying to wangle their own deals in private.

David Bonior, a Michigan Democrat and then the fourth-ranking member of the majority, got the Transportation Department to start building a forty-mile, ten-foot-wide bike path through his well-to-do suburban county of Macomb, northeast of Detroit. This was another "demonstration project," which would surely demonstrate the fact that wide, new bike paths were pretty darn nice things to have. The initial appropriation was for $1 million, but as one transportation official said, "It's going to cost a lot more by the time it's finished." A second $1 million bike study also emerged in the transportation bill, this one pushed by Martin Olav Sabo of Minnesota and intended to discover why people don't ride bikes more often. The answer may be because they don't have enough nice, free bike paths.

Dick Gephardt, the majority leader, cajoled and wheedled until the new tax on beer was cut from thirty-two cents a six-pack to sixteen cents. As the congressman from Budweiser, it was his duty. The high-minded George Mitchell paused from his duties as Senate president to make sure the new tax on luxury yachts applied only to boats costing more than $100,000, dismissing those $50,000 and $75,000 boats that the average guy buys. Would it be a surprise to learn that a lot of boats are built in his home state of Maine? He also tried to slip through a tax break that would have saved a Portland insurance company about a billion dollars—and cost the taxpayers an equal amount—but his colleagues found it too outrageous even for their standards.

Across the aisle, the Senate minority leader, Bob Dole, was working all the angles when he wasn't working on the budget deal. Dole is a man who inhabits both the Money and Gas congresses. In one maneuver, he used a ploy similar to Mitchell's to bump up the luxury tax limit on private airplanes from $100,000 to $250,000; coincidentally, Beechcraft and Cessna both make many airplanes costing more than $100,000 and less than $250,000 in his state of

Kansas. Corn is also grown in Kansas, so Dole renewed a hefty tax credit—worth $200 to $500 million over five years—for the continued experimental production of ethanol automobile fuel. As a Dole staffer told the *Los Angeles Times*, "Ethanol is a fuel made from grain and, since we represent a state that is grain producing, we have an interest in creating markets for grain." What he didn't mention was that the main beneficiary of the tax break is Dwayne Andreas, the head of Archer Daniels Midland Corporation and a longtime pal and contributor of Dole's.

Equally thoughtful was Bob Packwood, the Oregon senator who's the top Republican on the Senate Finance Committee, which writes tax legislation. Part of the tax package intended to help bring down the deficit was a boost from three to twenty-one cents on a bottle of wine. Packwood conned through a change that would exempt what he called small wineries, or those making less than 150,000 gallons a year. He said the extra eighteen cents a bottle would kill them, so his colleagues were sympathetic. What he didn't say was that all eighty-five of Oregon's wineries fall into that category. In news releases sent back home to his state, Packwood saw it as "a victory for Oregon's wineries." Others might see it as a loss of about $500 million for the taxpayer at large.

Oregon, then, was getting a double bonus, first by shirking the wine tax and second by being on Santa Mark Hatfield's shopping list. One wouldn't ordinarily think of Oregon as a politically rapacious state, what with its self-image as a whole-grain, track-shoe, respect-your-fellow-man sort of place, but the combination of Packwood and Hatfield, the senior Republican on the Appropriations Committee, make it a pork paradise. Among the projects snared by Hatfield was further funding for a subway to nowhere in Portland and an $8 million grant to build a space-age pedestrian bridge from the Portland Veterans Administration hospital to an adjacent private hospital. The VA had long contended it had better things to do with its money than build footbridges so doctors wouldn't have to take the shuttle bus, but Hatfield insisted they get the bridge. The steel-haired, stately senator has a reputation as a deeply religious man with a skewed ethical compass. Over the years he and his wife and children have taken gifts from all sorts of people who may ask a favor now and then. But then, what can you expect of a West Coast senator whose top staffer once wrote a guide to New York restaurants while on the senator's staff and while traveling to New York at taxpayer expense?

The leaders took care of their own comforts, as well. In a series of items that bore no fingerprints, they found enough funds to spend $8 million for new Senate elevators; $6 million to upgrade the Senate's private subway; $250,000 to study the best placement for television lights in the Senate; $2 million to refurbish a House restaurant; $375,000 to renovate the money-losing House beauty parlor; $25,000 to study the best location for a new House gym; and $40,000 for new wastebaskets.

Then there was Byrd. After all the work he had done in cadging the money out of Darman, it would have been naive to think he'd sit back and watch other people spend it. He didn't disappoint.

What Byrd got for West Virginia in the 1991 budget was an awesome display of pork power hitting that would surely rank as one of the best seasons in history, if records were kept on such things. It totaled about $700 million worth of special projects above and beyond the normal federal spending for the state.

Admittedly he got an early start, so purists might argue that he deserves an asterisk qualifying his accomplishment—similar to when Roger Maris topped Babe Ruth's home run record, but in a longer season. In the spring, Byrd pounced on a so-called "emergency supplemental" budget bill that the White House needed to funnel some promised foreign aid to Nicaragua and Panama, which we'd just devastated while nabbing Manuel Noriega in the world's largest manhunt. The bill had started out seeking a modest $800 million to preserve democracy in Central America, but by the time it went to the floor of Congress it was packed with so many special projects it had become a $3.4 billion sow belly with the mission of preserving Democrats (and a few Republicans) throughout America. Byrd's piece was the biggest. This time, Darman had bought his cooperation with a $185 million down payment on a plan to move the FBI's fingerprint lab from downtown Washington to Clarksburg in the heart of West Virginia.

When fall rolled around, Byrd had already lined up the choicest morsels in every spending bill moving through Congress. His biggest score was in the area of roads as he managed to bleed off $140 million in special grants—fully one third of all the money spent in the country for that purpose. These were more of the infamous demonstration projects and included a bewildering array of improvements to roads in desolate parts of the state. For instance, $33 million was set aside "for the purpose of carrying out a demonstration of methods of eliminating traffic congestion" in Mingo

County, a coal-mining area on the southwestern edge of the state that has been losing population since World War II and would no doubt be delighted to experience the slightest bit of traffic congestion. Another $50 million went to Buckhannon, a metropolis of 6,820 people in the desolate corner of the state.

Byrd got even more road money from the Appalachian Regional Commission, an obscure relic from Lyndon Johnson's war on poverty that's become the private preserve of a handful of congressmen, notably Byrd, Jamie Whitten of Mississippi and Tom Bevill of Alabama. No coincidence, then, that the supposed antipoverty agency—which every president since Richard Nixon has tried to eliminate—spent most of its $170 million budget on building roads in West Virginia, Mississippi and Alabama. Water money was a close second for Byrd, with $155 million in projects for some of these same desolate areas, including a vast network of locks and dams and funds for the Stonewall Jackson dam, which even the local congressman, Bob Wise, said was a bad idea.

There was much more, notably Harpers Ferry, which seemed particularly blessed as Byrd continued his campaign to turn plans for a small Fish and Wildlife Service training center into a sort of Disney World with aquariums (although the National Aquarium is only ninety minutes away in Baltimore), wildlife habitats (although the National Zoo is only ninety minutes away in Washington) and a gym and indoor pool for the trainees—all at a cost of about $100 million. Officials of the service were said to have initially opposed the grandiose plans as being much more than they needed. But when Byrd explained that he could get them the money without the usual red tape, they soon were reported to be "extremely enthusiastic" about the project. Harpers Ferry also got one of the more unusual expenditures, an $85,000 grant to its local police department for no apparent purpose. One staffer described it as "sort of a tip at the end of a big meal," though perhaps the extra police were needed to protect all the new federal money coming in.

Byrd himself had little to say about his accomplishments. With the terseness seen in many of the greats from Ruth to Aaron to Mays, he said modestly, if absurdly, "What helps West Virginia helps the nation."

After such a spending spree, it was no wonder that when Congress adjourned in early December, 1990, the members all looked so exhausted.

# 4

# PORKBUSTERS

NOT LONG AFTER THE BUDGET PASSED AND THE CULPRITS HAD skulked home to their districts, a small man who appeared to be a cross between Truman Capote and Howard Beale took the podium at the National Press Club before a packed room of Washington reporters and the all-seeing cameras of C-Span. His vintage dark suit set off the strands of white hair floating dementedly up from his balding, freckled head. He seemed distracted, shuffling papers and clearing his throat, until he looked up from beneath droopy lids and flashed hard little beads of blue eyes.

"Washington," he said in a gravelly lisp, "is not just a city without *guh*-tssss, it's a city without in-*teg*-ri-ty. And a city without *mo*-rals! Because . . . *elected* . . . *thieves* stole your *tax* dollars in the *tax* bill last month. And they've *lied* to you about it ever since!"

J. Peter Grace, a seventy-four-year-old rich man who saw no reason to be polite, had come to pay a courtesy call on his favorite city. The man who once said, "I can't believe what shits congressmen are," had returned to offer his thoughts on the budget deal. He wasn't pleased.

What some saw as mischief, he saw as a crime. The budget deal was robbery of a sophisticated order, and he was here to blow the whistle.

"When I first came to Washington, I was a virgin. Oh, I was a dumb cluck. I thought people came here to serve the *public*.

"Hah!"

He left the word hanging in the air like a belch in church.

Grace is a cult figure among Washington's porkologists, the small but persistent band of folks who make it their business to rail against wasteful government spending. The chief executive of family-controlled W. R. Grace Company since 1945 ("My first words were 'Thanks, Dad,' ") and a Democrat, he'd first come to Washington in 1982 at the request of Ronald Reagan to conduct a blue-ribbon study of government waste. But unlike in many blue-ribbon studies, Grace took to his job with gusto and assembled a team of first-rate professionals who volunteered thousands of hours to comb through the rat's nest of government programs.

The Grace commission had 2,478 recommendations that would have saved, by their accounting, $425 billion. They found three-cent screws costing $91; light bulbs at $511; 332 different accounting systems that meant the government never knew how many people were on the payroll or how much money was being spent. The commission was prescient in picking up on the potential for abuse at HUD, in the Pentagon's purchasing process and in the loosened regulation of the savings-and-loan industry. All three blossomed into fat, ugly, expensive scandals.

When the report was first released, some of the recommendations were actually followed—saving, by Grace's count, $200 billion. But most have sat on a shelf, fueling his frustration with Washington in general and Congress in particular. Three quarters of the reforms required congressional action, and Congress, it became apparent to Grace, was not about to reform the government when it came to cutting spending, wasteful or not. But Grace, a man who has his name on a forty-story office building in New York also has no need to indulge Washington's rituals of deference. Instead he made government waste his personal cause and has delivered as many as a hundred nettling speeches a year on the subject before any group who'll listen.

"In this town, if you spend more than you did last year but not as much as you would have if no one were looking over your shoulder, that's considered a saving," he lisped, throwing his arms up in a gesture of amazement that, after all these performances, still seemed genuine. He was playing not to the jaded reporters—who were amused by the antics of this sincere boor in a town of suave hypocrites, though unmoved by the rhetoric—but to the legions of news junkies tuned to C-Span, the all-day cable channel that mainlines the unedited juice of Washington straight to the cortex of the heartland. For that, he was willing to bulge a few neck veins.

"Listen to this quote: 'The budget should be balanced, the treasury should be refilled, public debt should be reduced, the arrogance of officialdom should be tempered.' Sound good? Sound like what we're facing today? That was Cicero in 63 B.C."

Rome paid the price for its self-indulgence, he said, and so would we.

"I mean, if this keeps up, by the year 2000 we'll be a banana republic."

He began to snap his fingers and twirl in front of the podium, " 'I'm Chiquita Banana and I'm here to say . . .' "

The audience tittered. He stopped in midtwirl.

"Oh?" he fixed the front row with that hard glare. "You don't think so? Well, believe me, we'll all be singing it, baby."

There was still hope, he said, but the opportunity was fast slipping away. And the folks who ran Washington just didn't get it. He reserved particular scorn for Budget Director Richard Darman, whom he saw as the evil architect of the deal.

"The future of Mr. Darman ought to be reevaluated," Grace sneered. "The Office of Management and Budget has adopted an elitist view that if you employ enough smoke and mirrors, the working stiffs who pick up the tab will never catch on.

"Well, the taxpayers are starting to wage war. They simply have to get madder and increase the volume like I'm doing today! We have a hotline. It's 1-800-BE-ANGRY. That's it! *Be angry!*"

His face grew flushed and bubbles of saliva collected at the corners of his mouth. He began to slap the podium with his palm.

"Let's tell them we're not going to *take* (slap) it anymore! Let's get *mad* (slap), *mad* (slap), *mad* (slap)!!"

He finished to polite applause. How he went over in the land of C-Span was anybody's guess.

"You know, I used to do this a hundred times a year," he said in the hall after his talk. "I'm still so damn mad at the bastards. But I've had to slow down. I'm getting a little tired."

Then he climbed into the back of a black stretch Cadillac and headed off to the airport.

Grace is one of only a handful of people who, for reasons of genuine concern, ideological pique or commercial gain, have tried to make it their business to stop the government from wasting money. These are people who, when asked the question "What's wrong with a little pork now and then?" answer, "Plenty." They know that pork isn't the whole problem of government waste, but it is one of the most visible symptoms of a sick system. They take as their maxim Senator Everett Dirksen's saying "A billion here and a billion there and pretty soon you're talking about real money."

Estimates of how much pork is produced each year vary from $10 or $20 billion to as high as $100 billion, depending on your definition. Those are big numbers, but not overpowering when you consider that the total federal budget was $1.4 trillion in 1991. An argument often made by those who endorse pork—or by cynical newshounds and Hill rats who dismiss it—is that even if you cut all the pork out of the budget, you wouldn't make a dent in the deficit, then running at about $300 billion a year. Which is a lot like saying, "I'm already overdrawn on my checking account, so I may as well buy those season tickets to the opera and the vacation in Bermuda." But never mind. That logic works in Washington.

There is, in fact, a good case to be made that by eliminating pork spending you could do a lot to reduce the deficit. But putting aside the dollars for a moment, the best argument the reformers make against pork is how it corrupts the system.

"The mentality that gives you Lawrence Welk gives you a $300 billion deficit," said Bill Frenzel, a former congressman from Minnesota who had long opposed soaring budgets. "It's that simple. The process is all about people spending someone else's money. Nothing has a real price tag because as a congressman, you're not paying for it. So why not help your state out with a museum? I'm sure you can come up with lots of good reasons to have it. Or a highway or a dam or whatever. You'll find that very few of these projects are outright silly. They all have people who support them and can make a good case for them."

A new congressman learns early on that there are no rewards for those who resist the pressure to spend. "Somebody, somewhere will praise you for spending money," said Frenzel. "People say nice things about you, they give you campaign money and they even reelect you. But nobody's going to say, 'He did great this year, he saved a lot of money.' "

Amazingly, the more wasteful the spending, the better. "The system makes no distinction between money well spent and money ill spent," said James Dale Davidson, head of the National Taxpayer's Union. "All money spent by congressmen is well spent in that it's good for them, even if it does nothing for you. And sometimes the more wasteful the spending, the more valuable it is to a given congressman. It's no favor to buy a hammer for five dollars from a company that sells hammers for five dollars. But to buy one for five hundred and thirty-five, now that's a favor. That's something people are grateful for, and more than likely they're willing to demonstrate their gratitude."

The pursuit of pork in all its various forms has created a kind of institutional corruption, in the view of Scott Hodge, the Heritage Foundation budget analyst. "We have a Congress so caught up in parochial interests that it can't deal with the big issues. I see pork as anything that's beyond the scope of a federally elected Congress. It's federal officials superseding the role of state, local or private interests, going well beyond their role as representatives in a national body. There's something undemocratic about a family in Santa Fe having to pay for John Murtha's drug intelligence center in Johnstown, Pennsylvania, because he wants to create jobs in his district. We need a major debate to redefine what the role of a national Congress is."

One thing it's not is an efficient organization primed to make quick, hard decisions affecting the largest business in the world, the U.S. government. What it's turned into is 535 individuals, "every one of whom thinks he's Sam Rayburn," as one congressman put it, referring to the legendary, autocratic Speaker of the House. They all develop their own areas of expertise, whether it's the merchant marine, space or highways, and proceed to tell those parts of the government how to conduct themselves. But what anyone who's ever run a business can tell you is that decisions to cut spending are the hardest kind. They need to be made by a handful of hard-nosed executives willing to take the heat, not by committees of individuals who aren't held responsible for the outcome of their decisions.

This leads to all kinds of mismanagement. "We call it micromanaging," said Jim Miller, a budget director under Ronald Reagan and the only one in the last fifteen years who can take credit for actually reducing the deficit on his watch. "It's Congress trying to get its hands on the way government departments do business. There is a clear correlation between micromanaging and growth in spending. You can't run a business with 535 chief executive officers. A lot of waste comes when the committees on the Hill tell the government agencies how to spend their money. A guy gets appointed by the president to run some agency and he thinks he's in charge, but he quickly finds that he has little control over one of his most important tools—the budget. I remember a subcommittee chairman telling me once, 'We don't want the agencies to do what the president wants. We want them to do what we want.'"

And what Congress wants usually has nothing to do with efficiency and everything to do with spending money in a highly visible way. No sight is more pathetic than some hapless agency administrator, say the head of the Federal Highway Administration, testifying in front of an array of members who each wants to know whether a certain new highway will be coming home to him.

"The instinct to get pork is a powerful one," marveled Miller. "When I tried to limit pork projects, I got an amazing amount of protest. I had some success, but eventually I had to give up because I wasn't getting the support I needed from the West Wing," he said, referring to the warren of offices occupied by the president's top staff. Other officials from the Reagan administration confirmed that Miller was eventually judged to be an out-of-touch zealot who was antagonizing Congress for no good reason.

But without such zealotry, the porkologists argue, there's no way to reverse the pressure to spend.

"The machine can't be turned off," said Frenzel. "Congress is set up to fund causes it favors and is then rewarded for funding them. The system has helped create a spending machine. Once something gets in the budget, it stays. The attitude is that if one program falls, all are in danger. So you get this institutional logrolling. And I'm not talking about just 'I'll trade you my vote for your support on this bill.' It's the whole place saying each member must defend every other member's spending or he runs the risk of losing his."

Such pervasive self-interest, according to Frenzel, creates unending support for the web of megapork programs that affect whole blocks of congressmen such as subsidies for farm products, milk and timber, cheap power in the West, mass transit money for the cities, textile quotas and maritime grants. And then there's what some say is the hugest pork of all, the so-called entitlement programs such as Social Security, Medicare and student loans, which largely benefit the middle class and are considered so sacred that in recent years they have not even been touched. Yet these are the fastest-growing parts of the budget. They've been taken out of the budget process and made automatic, so each year they're given increases for inflation and growth of population without Congress even having to vote.

"Washington isn't a place where the fundamental questions ever get asked," said Davidson. "I mean the hard ones, such as 'Why the hell are we spending all this money on this project in the first place?' Or how about asking people, 'What would you be willing to do without if you knew you had to pay for it out of your own pocket?' Because, of course, all spending in Washington comes out of the same pocket. Taxpayers just don't see it that way. They think they're getting something for nothing. That's the big inside joke in Washington. The people who really know this town are in on the gag. Everybody else is a dope, as far as they're concerned."

The best congressmen are the ones who can give you back some of your own money and make you grateful for it. Hilarious.

Of course the gag is an old one, as old as politics. The challenge for Davidson and the rest is to make people see that it isn't funny.

"The old rules can't apply anymore," he said. "Since 1960, federal spending has increased by three hundred percent in inflation-adjusted dollars. But average earnings, which peaked in 1973, have now slipped back to 1961 levels. That means the average guy is making what his father did, but he's paying for three times as much government."

Actually, given that the government borrows about 20 percent of what it spends, the real gag is that your congressman is giving you back your own money *and* your children's money and making you grateful for it. Most of the porkologists are driven by the notion that if people realized that this was the way the system works, they'd revolt and demand that it be changed. So far, they've been wrong.

"The paradox of the deficit," said Miller, "is that you find poll after poll showing that people think Congress is overwhelmingly wasteful. But their own congressman is fine. In the abstract they worry about waste, but they expect their guy to bring home the bacon."

Frenzel, the former congressman, thinks this paradox explains why his former colleagues act the way they do. "Congress is a representative outfit. They spend because people want them to. Congress will begin to restrain its spending the day its constituents say, 'Stop spending or we're going to take away your favorite toy, your seat in Congress.' Until then, members of Congress will spend because it profits them."

Of course, Frenzel's solution depends on how you define constituents, and for many congressmen it has nothing to do with the traditional notion of those who could cast a vote on election day. About half of eligible voters don't bother to vote, so the hell with them. The other half who show up at the polls may or may not be influenced by pork. But the folks who really care are the special interests—everyone from dairy farmers to roadbuilders. They turn out votes and contribute money in amounts well beyond their numbers.

A big part of the pork problem, then, is that more than Congress thrives on the notion of perpetually increased spending. All of Washington does. The culture of spending extends well beyond Capitol Hill to the vast empire of special-interest lobbyists who make up a fourth branch of government. Forget what the civics books say about the press being the fourth estate. In Washington today the relative handful of reporters who write for a general-interest audience takes its place in line well behind the legislative directors of the American Association of Retired Persons and the American Petroleum Institute, to name two of thousands.

Peter Grace, for instance, may be a rare bird for a number of reasons, but the most unusual is that he is a fat-cat patrician who has chosen to work in a field populated mostly by those at the lower end of the Washington food chain. Lobbying *against* spending is not exactly a growth industry. People who lobby in Washington lobby *for* money. When any given piece of legislation moves through Congress, there might be a couple dozen different perspectives tugging at members' sleeves begging to be heard. Everyone from, say, the Auto Seat Cover Manufacturers Association to the Committee to Promote the Use of White Sidewall Tires sends its high-priced advocates up the Hill with the same determination as the Marines on Mount Surabachi. But on no one's agenda will you find the words "Don't spend money." And this goes from chops-licking groups like defense contractors and auto manufacturers to supposedly noble causes such as the Children's Defense Fund or the Paralyzed Veterans of America. The dozens

of gleaming office buildings that sit like a great siege army northwest of the Capitol and the White House are filled with elegantly
polished men and women for the single reason that someone is
paying them to find a way to funnel money out of Washington.
They are paid to watch the actions of Congress and the White
House like chicken hawks and to pounce at the first sign of
wounded game. Sometimes the quarry is an outright grant, other
times the shading of a regulation, a delay in enforcement, maybe a
little twist of the tax code. Often the lobbying is legitimate; just as
often it is about blatant favoritism. But never is it about saving
money. Lobbyists in Washington aren't buying top-of-the-line
BMWs because the insurance agents in Omaha or the sludge haul-
ers in St. Louis have suddenly become concerned with good government. They're concerned with government that is good *for*
*them.*

One astonishing statistic was revealed recently in a study by
economist James Payne for his book *The Culture of Spending.* He
added up witnesses who testified for and against increased spending at an assortment of congressional hearings over the last several
years and found that among 1,060 witnesses on subjects as diverse
as farm credits, housing and job training, *only seven people* spoke
against spending more money.

Still, people like Miller and Davidson and the others seem to be
carving a tenuous beachhead in Washington as they slowly manage
to transmit their arguments to the rest of the country. They have
begun to have some success playing to that loose but growing
constituency of Middle American couch potatoes who leap up from
tartan plaid settees and yell at the latest government-sponsored
atrocity on their television sets. And the budget deal seemed to be
a tailor-made atrocity.

"This is like Charlie Brown and the football," said Davidson.
"Everybody in Washington knows what a crazy deal this is. They
know it won't work. They knew it before they started. I mean, my
God, the whole deal was premised on the fact that we weren't
going to have a recession in 1991, but we were already *in* one when
the deal was made.

"We have to find a way to convince taxpayers that the people
who run this government are just like Lucy. No matter what they
say, no matter what assurances they give us, they're going to pull
the football away every time we try to kick it. Will we ever learn
that?"

. . .

The spirit of J. Peter Grace, if not his eccentric self, was in the room in the winter of 1990, when representatives from several of those groups held a first-ever war council with the idea of trying to capitalize on the discontent they were sensing. They had decided to join forces and see if they could take the issue of waste right to the floor of Congress. The agenda was to figure out how to draft a bill to slice out the worst pork-barrel projects and bring it to a vote.

They and the people they represent were an odd stew of self-described budget geeks and policy dweebs, earnest government reformers, porkologists, libertarians, right-wing ideologues and for all anyone knew secret covens dedicated to eliminating the income tax and returning to the silver standard.

The most prominent members of the group were J. Marc Wheat, the budget expert from Citizens for a Sound Economy; Tom Schatz and Margaret Hill of Citizens Against Government Waste, an off-spring of the Grace Commission; Scott Hodge, the Heritage Foundation budget analyst; Terry Cooper from Americans for a Balanced Budget; and Jill Lancelot of the National Taxpayer's Union.

Several members of Congress had dared to send staff members to the meeting as well, including Senators Bob Smith of New Hampshire, John McCain of Arizona, and Dan Coats of Indiana and Congressmen Harris Fawell of Illinois and Tim Penny of Minnesota.

In the first order of business, they decided to call themselves "Porkbusters."

"Pork is something everyone can understand," explained Wheat. "The average person cannot comprehend the idea of a $3.6 trillion national debt or a $300 billion annual deficit. It's just too abstract. But spending a half million for Lawrence Welk's home, now that gets people's blood boiling.

"I think this year we've got a real chance to get some attention, to get some people mad," added Wheat, a former aide to an Illinois congressman. "They've gone too far, and a lot of people realize it. There's a bad taste from the budget deal that's going to linger for a long time. And if we can show that the result of all that battling, of shutting down the government and then pushing through all kinds of tax increases is just these huge amounts of pork, we've got a chance to make some gains."

Most of the Porkbusters were seasoned Washington hands who knew that victories inside the Beltway are usually measured in tiny increments. Contests aren't won or lost like a football game where the clock runs out and everyone shakes hands. They knew that although sports analogies abound in Washington's macho, competitive culture—the halls of Congress resonate with boasts like "We kicked their asses," "We stroked that baby into the cheap seats" or, ruefully, "We may have to drop back ten and punt on that one"— success often comes to those with Zen-like patience who are willing to wash in and out like the tide and wear boulders down into grains of sand.

The idea for the "Porkbusters Bill" was to find a billion dollars worth of the most egregious projects in the 1991 budget and ask that Congress cut them out. They would be projects that met a strict series of tests. They had to have been secretly put into the budget, never considered by the rest of Congress, never considered in competition with similar projects and have no national value; in short, the essence of pork.

This was not a simple task. Hodge pointed out that much pork was deliberately obscured, dropped into various committee reports, drafts and bills in cryptic language that had to be deciphered by retracing a paper trail. Coming up with a pork list was going to take hundreds of hours of work.

They agreed that the Porkbusters Bill didn't have to become law to be a success. It was a first step. Merely getting it into the system, and perhaps getting some kind of vote on it, would be a victory.

"Let's be realistic," Wheat cautioned. "I'm not sure we can get a vote in the House. We can use the bill as a way to attract cosponsors and see how enthusiastic people are. But I'm sure they're going to bottle it up in committee."

"They" were the various forces of darkness who represent the power structure in the House. Any number of key members can find ways to ensure that a piece of legislation never sees the light of day. The Rules Committee, which is controlled by the Speaker of the House, is supposed to act as the traffic cop of Congress, moving bills along on a rational schedule. But just as often it is used to send those bills—both the sound and the stupid—into a never-never land from which they won't return. Often they're steered to hostile committees that never quite get around to considering them. "Further study" is the euphemism for "Killed in action."

"I'll bet they send it to the Appropriations Committee," Wheat predicted with a grimace. That would be like appointing John

Mitchell as the special prosecutor to investigate Watergate. On Capitol Hill, it happens all the time.

The Senate was another story. The courtly men's club usually allows its members to bring whatever is on their minds to the floor and, if they insist, to have their colleagues vote on it. But the Senate has evolved its own means of moderating unpleasant issues. The unwritten rule is that each senator has a certain amount of political capital and goodwill that can be expended in the delicate trading of votes that goes on throughout the session. It is considered impolite—and therefore dangerous—for a senator to force contentious issues on his colleagues and make them cast a vote. Your capital account can quickly be depleted if you make yourself a pain in the ass.

Pork is that most unpleasant of topics, best kept private. To trot a bunch of pork projects out on the floor and force the members of the Senate to vote up or down on them is a risky venture indeed.

"My boss says he'll do it," said Tom Hodson, an aide to Senator Robert Smith, who had just begun his first term from New Hampshire.

For a moment, it seemed a little too good to be true. Oh, sure, *Mr. Smith Goes to Washington.* All the political junkies in the room had probably seen the 1939 Frank Capra movie a half-dozen times. Jimmy Stewart plays Jefferson Smith, head of the Boy Rangers, who finds himself appointed to the Senate as the unwitting dupe of the political machine that controls his state. When he arrives in town, Stewart goes slackjawed at the majesty of Washington, touring the monuments and taking to heart all the bronze-inlaid slogans about liberty, justice, equality and government by the people, for the people. "Gosh!" he says over and over, as only he can. Meanwhile the wisecracking newshounds and Hill rats chuckle in their cocktails at the quaint naiveté of this bumpkin. But Stewart proves to be nobody's fool when he stumbles upon—this gets eerie—a colossal pork-barrel project, specifically a dam that the greedy machine bosses are trying to hide within an appropriations bill. In a memorable twenty-four-hour filibuster, truth, justice and the American way prevail and the porkers are sent packing. "You think I'm licked," Stewart gasps just before collapsing onto the Senate floor from righteous exhaustion. "You all think I'm licked. Well, I'm not licked. . . . There's no place out there for graft or greed or lies. And if that's what the grown-ups have done with this world that was given to them, then we better get those boys' camps started right away and see what they can do. It's not too late."

The real Mr. Smith was a little more worldly, but not much. A former teacher and the owner of the Yankee Peddler real estate agency, he'd served on the Wolfeboro school board before being elected to three terms in Congress. He had been elected to the Senate on a pledge of flinty fiscal conservatism—New Hampshire being a state where people turn the thermostat way down to save oil, pay minuscule taxes and say they expect little from the government. Pork seemed a natural enemy, even though he knew it would be an angry one.

"We know we're going to catch a lot of shit for this," Hodson told the Porkbusters, "but he says he's willing to take it on."

There was, everyone agreed, an important role in Congress to be played by an economic reformer. There had been no dominant voice raised against excess spending since William Proxmire retired in 1988. There was a legacy waiting to be assumed, and Smith was the man to lead the troops in the Pork War of 1991. If only he knew the condition of the boots he was stepping into.

Some weeks later, the bony, spotted hand of William Proxmire slowly moved up and down his cheek as his eyes focused on the carpet and his brain tried to resurrect a memory. His great dome of a head rested on a thin, ropy neck that rose from the center of his shirt collar, untouched by its fraying edges. An obsessive jogger before that obsession became widespread, he had kept the gaunt frame and starved features that once had given him an unassailable image of moral rigor. The hand continued to move over the indented cheek. Finally, after enough time that it seemed like another question was long overdue, he looked up with a limpid smile.

"I can't remember," he said pleasantly.

Proxmire had been the Great Porkbuster, the Oracle of Excess. As the righteous senator from Wisconsin, he could be counted on to take to the Senate floor and pop the veins in his neck at the prospect of some boondoggle about to be made into law. He even got a few of them stopped, including a $50 million dam in his own state. He was best known for the Golden Fleece, his monthly tribute to the most shameless abuse of the taxpayer. He once pointed out that the White House was spending $10,000 a year to buy playing cards for the vice president's guests on Air Force Two, that the National Science Foundation was funding research to see if giving tequila to sunfish would make them more aggressive and had another study going to determine why people fall in love. His biggest score was stopping the government from spending money to develop the supersonic transport plane. He was equally penurious about his own money, refusing Political Action Committee contributions and, the last two times he ran, spending only a few hundred dollars on his campaign—"Most of it on envelopes and stamps to send back contributions we didn't want," he said.

Since his retirement thirty-one years after he replaced Joe Mc-Carthy in the Senate, he'd been working out of an office in the Library of Congress's Madison Building. Proxmire, who was seventy-five, had a small cubicle in a hall of old congressmen, a refuge where former members who haven't prepared for a lucrative career after retirement come to write their memoirs or just read the paper about what is going on across the street. Many of his other colleagues had done very well. For instance, Russell Long, Huey's boy and the former head of the Senate Finance Committee, was lobbying on tax matters from an opulent suite next to the Willard Hotel. Howard Baker, the former Senate majority leader, was making more than a million dollars a year as a partner in a prominent law firm housed on Pennsylvania Avenue, and representing hostile governments such as Jordan. Even former senators such as Walter Mondale and Ed Muskie were living comfortably on the fees they received for representing various people interested in influencing the ways of Washington.

But though Proxmire had long headed the Banking, Housing, and Urban Affairs Committee, he was not lobbying for any banks. He had his Senate pension and an office that wasn't big enough to seat a guest in. At first he seemed old, tired and distracted even though the subject of pork was one of his favorites.

"I never took the attitude that pork was innocent," he said, staring at a point on the carpet about ten feet in front of him. "It's a fallacy to say it makes the system function. A senator has to sell his voters on the notion that they're taxpayers and nothing's for free. Whatever it is that government does, the people pay for it. Just because it's pork going to your district or your state doesn't mean it's free. If you get some project, well then, Washington State or West Virginia or whoever's in power will get at least as much."

But beyond the dollars, he was repulsed by the implicit message. "When you have congressmen grabbing for pork, you pervert the process," he said, warming to his subject and looking up. "You create a system that says it's all right for everybody to grab for as much as they can get.

"It's an attitude that's gotten us into a colossal mess. You know, when I came to Washington in 1957, the federal debt was $5 billion. This year it's going to be around $300 billion. It's the fastest-growing part of the budget, and it's totally useless. It doesn't house a single person or save a life or educate someone."

Didn't it frustrate him that despite all his efforts, the deficit had soared and pork was as popular as ever? He seemed annoyed at the question.

"You can only do so much," he said with a frown. "You're one person. You can't expect miracles. If I try to evaluate my contribution, I don't look at where the debt is but where it might have been. The point of the Golden Fleece was deterrence by humiliation. Who knows how many people backed off projects because they were afraid of seeing a press release coming out of my office?"

But who knew what the pork connoisseurs were up to now with Proxmire gone and no one to take his place?

"Well, you would like to see some of the guys over there taking a more aggressive attitude about waste," he admitted.

The point, he said, is that someone has to try to stop it.

"I sound like some sort of old curmudgeon, but this can't go on. This spending is just plain crazy. It's got to come home to roost. The best thing for the Democrats in 1992 might be if they lose. The economy could just fall all over George Bush and you won't elect another Republican for thirty or forty years."

He smiled for a moment. Then he glanced up sharply from that spot on the carpet as if what he'd said was just too distasteful a way to prove his point.

"Anything else?" he said in a tone that indicated that there shouldn't be.

Then Proxmire walked back down the hall and stopped in front of a beige metal door. He rattled his key in the stainless-steel knob for a few moments. He looked back.

"Wrong office," he said, shaking his head.

A lifetime of fighting the forces of nature on Capitol Hill had taken its toll.

*5*

# BAFFLEGAB IN
DARMANLAND

RICHARD DARMAN MUST HAVE BEEN A HAPPY MAN THAT MORN-
ing in early February 1991. As he shaved and dressed in his spectacular home on a five-acre lot overlooking the Potomac River in
Virginia, he knew he'd be holding center stage in a few hours,
doing what he liked best. Perhaps he took a little more time to craft
his appearance of carelessness. He dressed the way you learn in
Boston prep schools: baggy charcoal gray suit, blue button-down
shirt, shiny black cap-toed brogues and, for a hint of wildness, a tie
with a slightly loud stripe to it. His hair was slicked back in the
style of a Wall Street investment banker—but cut, awkwardly, by
his own hand instead of a $30-a-session stylist. A man who had
inherited substantial wealth, Darman could have afforded a far
better suit and the haircut of his choice, but he knew that in
Washington, a flashy appearance attracts the wrong kind of notice.
Not that he minded attention. His ego was enormous. He just
wanted to control that attention at every possible opportunity.

This was the day he would unveil the government's proposed
$1.446 trillion budget for 1992. They called it the president's bud-

get, but it was really Darman's. George Bush had neither the patience nor the interest to deal with the minutiae in the 2,029-page document that set out, line by line, how much money each department in the federal government could spend. Admittedly, in the winter of 1991 Bush was preoccupied with his own passion of foreign policy, specifically the war in the Persian Gulf, which was turning into a remarkable success. But then Bush had never concerned himself with the budget or, for that matter, with much having to do with domestic policy. He'd left those details to Darman, the director of the Office of Management and Budget, who had achieved the status of an unofficial vice president for domestic affairs. Darman knew that a budget is the most powerful political document imaginable, and he'd spent months shaping it to suit his needs. Now he'd show the world and wait for the reaction.

As he drove down the George Washington Parkway to his office next to the White House that frosty morning, the sun rose behind the Capitol dome and cast a soft pink light on the ranks of pale limestone buildings. The scene could have flowed from the brush of Monet, though its romance was thwarted by the reality that these were factories filled with bureaucrats instead of gardens filled with flowers. Still, for someone like Darman there were few more beautiful sights. More than almost anyone in government, he could claim that Washington was his town. He was the ultimate Washington creature and one of the great survivors in the town's history. He'd been here for most of his professional life, twenty years working his way through a succession of increasingly important jobs at the departments of Health, Education and Welfare; Defense; Justice; State; Commerce; Treasury; and then the White House. He knew the intimate workings of the machine coming to life that morning, and he understood the nuances, the language and, most important, the gamesmanship that is required to get something done in the huge, sticky mess that is the federal government.

But even the great gamesman had to be a bit apprehensive. This budget for the fiscal year of 1992, which would start in October, was phase two of Darman's greatest deal. He'd soon see if the stitches on the crazy-quilt compromise would actually hold together. Could Congress be trusted? And more important, were the numbers realistic?

Darman had to know that morning that the numbers were very wrong. Since he had taken over OMB, *all* his estimates had been wrong. The deficit had soared, and he was being fingered as the biggest-spending budget director in history. While trying to sell the budget agreement, he'd said the deficit could go as high as $230 billion without it. Now, with a straight face, he was about to present a budget that called for a $318 billion deficit, the largest in history. But even that figure was being launched on a sea of optimism.

The budget deal had been a compromise over what Darman thought was politically possible, and that meant playing into the hands of Congress. Pork and entitlements had been preserved. Perhaps when he had made the deal, Darman had thought again of the encounter with David Stockman a decade earlier, when they had just tacked $2 trillion to the budget over ten years and they wondered if they shouldn't try to modify the plan. In the immortal words of the pathologically confident Darman, "We win it now. We fix it later." But on this February morning, later was now, and Darman was about to present a budget that would only make things worse.

The budget itself had made its debut earlier that morning, when the Government Printing Office on North Capitol Street had offered it for sale. As always, the volume had become an instant Washington best-seller, with emissaries of the permanent government—law firm clerks, lobbyists' lackeys, think-tank interns, junior reporters—lining up in the cold an hour before the doors opened, then carting out boxes full of the seven-pound red-and-blue book that looked like the Manhattan phone directory and read, if you knew how to read it, like a sprawling Russian novel. The eye-glazing pages of numbers told the story of the government for the next year. Who was being cut? Who was being boosted? Where would the lobbyists have to go to work restoring funds, and where would they have to circle the wagons and protect their gains? Cries of triumph and anguish echoed from the ungainly document, if only you knew how to listen.

Congress also got the budget that morning, a not insignificant step since it was charged with turning what was really only the president's suggested budget into law. As one White House official put it, "The amazing thing is how little power the president really has when it comes to spending. We can recommend and lobby and pound the table, but Congress will spend what it wants." A president can get his way sometimes, but it is damn hard work. The circumstance had caused a sense of brow-throbbing frustration in most presidents for the past hundred years or so, though Bush seemed to be taking it to a new level of inaction.

The public unveiling came at a press briefing in the chateau-style edifice next to the White House known as the Old Executive Office Building. A standing-room-only crowd of 150 reporters and eleven television cameras packed the modern, blue-upholstered auditorium. They were mostly the serious gray-suited types of the economic fraternity, a subculture of Washington reporters who for the most part carried themselves with a disdain bred of their superior knowledge of money matters. Over the years, Darman had courted many of them, alternately feeding them exclusive tidbits of news and cutting them off if they wrote something that bruised his notoriously thin skin. Darman was viewed by the press as both useful and vindictive, but—most important by the rules of Washington—as someone to be handled very cautiously. As a consequence, he had enjoyed many years of kind stories.

Not surprisingly, the press conference was a polite affair. The conventional wisdom in Washington at that moment was that the budget deal was a masterstroke that had laid the deficit demon to rest once and for all. A *New York Times* editorial summed it up: The deal "met Congress's duty to control borrowing." In a flourish of Washingtonspeak, the *Times* added, "Even as the actual deficit continues to rise, the structural deficit continues to fall"—the structural deficit supposedly being the money borrowed just to maintain business as usual, as opposed to specific things like wars, recessions and bank crises. In the wake of this good cheer it seemed somehow churlish to point out that however you rationalized it, the budget Darman was then presenting contained, well, um, the largest deficit in history. Darman was asking everyone to trust him. And they did.

But you didn't have to take it solely on faith. He had charts. True, he said, the deficit may look a little high, but only because of the budget's honesty. He said, for example, that he was retiring "Rosy Scenario," a cynically disingenuous term that referred to the phony revenue estimates the White House and Congress had been pumping out for years. And if you don't believe me, here's Mike Boskin.

"The revenue figures in the budget are our best estimate," said the deadly serious former Stanford economics professor who heads the president's Council of Economic Advisers. "They could be off. We expect the economy to rebound by midyear."

Of course, even if it didn't rebound, the government wouldn't change the amount it was spending—only what was coming in. The shortfall simply would be tossed on top of that old deficit.

At that point, after the barrage of numbers and qualifiers and assumptions, a gaunt man in a green tie came to the microphone and cleared his throat. It was Nicholas Brady, the brusque, sour Wall Street banker who was Bush's closest confidant on economic matters. He had lurked in the background like a head coach while Darman ran the offense, but let no one mistake who was in charge here. As is his manner, he had little to say to the press, which he views with the sort of disdainful sidelong glare reserved for unruly servants. He just wanted to emphasize to everyone how tight this budget really was.

"It puts a box around the government's business," Brady said, "just like every family in this country has to do with its spending." Every family, that is, except the one that brought us Nicholas Brady, who is part of a Wall Street dynasty; Bush, whose grandfather was a wealthy investment banker; Darman, heir to a textile fortune; Secretary of State James Baker, grandson of the founder of one of the biggest law firms in the country; Vice President Dan Quayle, whose family owns a chain of newspapers; C. Boyden Grey, Bush's lawyer and an heir to the Reynolds tobacco fortune; and Robert Mosbacher, the Commerce Secretary who is the son of a wealthy investor and has made many millions on his own. The Bush administration is led by so many patricians it might be the closest thing in American history to a plutocracy. Somehow it just didn't ring true that anyone there knew anything about tight budgets.

Darman went back to his charts. He seemed charmingly disheveled, not at all the arrogant technocrat his résumé would suggest but an earnest, almost breathless graduate student defending his thesis. He dropped a few charts onto the floor, had to be reminded to speak into the microphone and kept up a patter of explanations that involved terms like "placeholders," "negative outlays," "baselines," "consolidated policy budget," "off budget" and "structural deficit." The main point seemed to be that "in the out years" the deficit was really declining as a percentage of the country's gross national product, the total of goods and services produced each year. Never mind that in the "in" years it was continuing to grow. With a wink and a nod, Darman was telling the assembled economic scribes the same thing he'd been saying in private: "I know I gave away a lot last year, but you fellows are smart enough to read all these charts and see that I've got this thing licked."

An observer not accustomed to this kind of theater might be

forgiven if he were left with the unsettling feeling that he'd just been goaded into purchasing more insurance than he needed.

Even when Darman got to the part of every budget where he says he's going to attack waste, the words rang false. His pork list was accurate but halfhearted. He defined the problem very narrowly and came up with about $2 billion he said should come out.

This was a departure from his predecessor, Jim Miller, a big, loud country boy with a doctorate in economics who had railed at the top of his lungs on the subject of pork and spending in general. Miller's relish for warring with Congress had left him with a reputation among insiders as an uncouth asshole. Each year he had provided President Reagan with a list of pork projects—almost $6 billion in 1987 and a whopping 150-page tally of $11 billion in 1988—that the president had sent to the Hill and demanded that Congress cut. They never had, but it might have kept them honest. Miller's watch was the only time in more than a decade when the deficit actually declined.

"You've got to show that you care about the small spending, or the whole thing goes out of control," Miller once said. "You've got to fight every day if you expect to make any difference at all."

Darman wasn't a fighter. He was a deal maker and a pragmatist. Some people said that, like Bush, he had no grand strategy. Did he really care about reform, or was he just consumed by the game, enmeshed in a million little details and obsessed with winning by his own scorekeeping? Had he become so much the consummate Washington game player, a man so adept at understanding and manipulating the process, that beating the process had become its own end?

Pork was a case in point. How could Darman possibly attack pork in the budget when he was the guy who had put it there in the first place? He was the one who'd handed Bobby Byrd the keys to the larder three months earlier and said "Help yourself." Sure, Darman had put a few pages of pork projects into the budget and called for them to be cut, but nobody expected to hear a word about them after the press conference ended.

In fact, the budget showed that Darman was really kind of a softie. He was eager to talk about the *nice* things in the budget. Sure, he proposed to cancel 238 programs, but he had added 250 others. Many of them had to do with shifting a few dollars here and there to child welfare programs such as Head Start or, his passion, scientific research. This was the Dick Darman who was "the secret good guy," as Marjorie Williams wrote of him in *The Washington Post*. She quoted one congressman as saying, "There are people always in this town that let you know that they're the secret good guy. They're really fighting hard inside against these other people for the right things. . . . And I think Darman is a master at being a secret good guy."

On the other hand, his growing number of conservative detractors might have called him a closet commie. Clearly this was a man who believed in government, who believed in spending money to solve problems. Spending was growing faster under Bush than under Jimmy Carter. Darman's performance was "the most disastrous failure in the history of the job," according to Warren Brookes, the late syndicated columnist who was revered by the porkologists.

Darman even had his own pork in the budget, including vast sums going to NASA for space exploration. "Rocket Richard," as some called him, ultimately wanted to see a man on Mars (a $400 billion proposition), but would settle for insisting on $40 to $100 billion to build the controversial manned space station. Maybe there was merit in the project. Maybe not. But it sent a bad message when the budget director made it known that he was going to climb into the back room with Congress and deal for his own pets.

Surely it wasn't that Darman didn't understand the problems. At one point in his budget presentation, he was startlingly candid. Putting up a chart which showed that mandatory programs had grown from 20 percent of spending to 52 percent, he said, "You cannot be serious about reducing the deficit unless you deal with this fastest-growing part of the deficit." Which could be taken as an admission that the deal the previous fall hadn't been serious, because both sides had quickly taken these entitlements off the table.

And Darman said the right things. "We want a debate of ideas. We're trying to start this debate. Given a level of spending, what do you want to spend money on? You have to make hard choices, and we've made ours."

But it wasn't really a debate at all. The new budget adhered to the goals of the previous fall's budget deal—which were simply to box off spending into certain categories and prohibit, say, defense money from being used for domestic purposes. The new budget cut defense hardly at all, maintained the high level of domestic spending put into place by the budget deal and didn't touch entitlements.

Some could view it as a blown opportunity. You might buy the notion that in the fall of 1990 Bush had been hamstrung by the crisis in the Persian Gulf and that, to preserve tranquillity in Congress, he had given them the budget deal they wanted. But in 1991 he was riding high, soaring in the popularity polls with a bank account full of political capital. Besides, it wasn't even an election year. If he was ever going to go after the issue of government spending, this was the moment. But the budget the White House delivered was cautious, pragmatic, sneaky, and in some ways well intentioned—kind of like Darman himself.

Or, in the words of his Darmanesque introduction, "Though less grand than a New World Order, steps toward a new domestic order can continue to be advanced—at least at the margin of practicable change."

The press was underwhelmed. The enormous size of the government's budget wasn't news anymore. It met no editor's test of man-bites-dog to say that for the umpteenth year in a row federal spending had reached a new record. Even the huge deficits attracted scant attention, deficits also being something of a ho-hum story. It was a budget of "minor modifications," *The Washington Post* said. And minor interest.

The porkologists saw it a little differently.

"You could say that it keeps spending down because it only grows by 2.6 percent," said Scott Hodge. "But you could also say that it accepts as gospel all of the new spending that was put in a few months ago. If you look at the 1991 budget's increase of 8.3 percent and this one's increase, that's an average of 6.5 percent over two years. You have to see them as part of a package."

"The total national debt goes to at least $3.6 trillion, $14,500 for every man, woman and child in America, and that's not a story?" wondered Marc Wheat.

*The Wall Street Journal*'s conservative editorial page noted that the budget represented the first time since World War II that the federal government would spend more than 25 percent of the nation's annual wealth. One dollar of every four "will be handed over to Congress and its various Departments of Good Intentions." Calling it "a phenomenon of the Bush years," the *Journal*'s acerbic editorialists wrote, "With the country in recession, families are having to scrimp, while states and cities are slashing budgets. The only place where it's spending as usual is Fat City USA."

But at least Darman's boss was happy. Deluded, but happy.

Days before, he'd given to Congress a State of the Union address as chock full of platitudes as any in recent memory. In essence it said: "civil rights" (for), "hate" (against), "farmers" (for), "strong banks" (for), "crime" (against). But his most fervent banality referred to spending.

"We must begin with the control of federal spending," he said, a line which got—from Congress—an ovation second only to his praise for the troops who'd fought in the Persian Gulf but begged the question of why he was only now starting this campaign two years into his term.

"I'm submitting a budget that keeps spending to less than the level of inflation. . . . It's time to rise above the parochial and the pork barrel—to do what is necessary, what's right and what will enable this nation to play the leadership role required of us."

But rhetoric isn't action, and the point buried in the pages of the budget that Bush would have to take responsibility for was that he wasn't at all serious about taking on pork or any other kind of spending. The president was either too weak or too cynical. The lessons of his days in Congress had stayed with him. When it came to money, he would go along to get along. The message to his former colleagues was that the pork store was open for business.

## 6

# BEST OF SHOW

EVEN IN EARLY SPRING, SCRANTON, PENNSYLVANIA, THE HOME of the federal government's very expensive railroad museum known as Steamtown USA—the year's very best single example of pork—gave new meaning to the word "bleak." The oily gray clouds looming over the butt end of the Pocono Mountains continually coughed out stinging globs of sleet while along the highway bare trees did little to hide the brutal rock formations pushing their way through the soil. The scenery-chill factor made the air feel ten degrees colder than the allegation on the thermometer.

This is, after all, a town where people remember the good times as the days when plumes of smoke would rise from the hideous heaps of coal slag that guard Scranton's approaches like angry dogs. Ah, yes, that beautiful toxic haze and the prosperity that came with it, those days when the coal waste—they call them culm piles—was steaming and all was well with this aged industrial town in the northeast corner of Pennsylvania. But the piles hadn't steamed for many years.

Scranton is a five-hour drive north of Capitol Hill and about as far as you can get from that world of marbled formality and endless hors d'oeuvres trays. This is a city, like hundreds of others across the country, whose best days are long behind it. A hundred and fifty years ago the blast furnaces of Scranton were stoked by Scottish and Irish immigrants who turned much of the country's iron into the beams and rails that helped slake an insatiable appetite for expansion. Because the hills and valleys surrounding Scranton were blessed with a combination of water, iron ore, limestone and coal, prosperity seemed assured. But iron was soon replaced by steel pouring from the mills of Chicago at the turn of the century— just as the output of Chicago was later replaced by that of Japan, Korea and a dozen less-developed countries. At the end of the twentieth century, the golden age of Scranton is a very dim memory.

The road to ruin had been a smooth one, though, because it was paved by one of the most shameless, bragging, flamboyant, hall-of-fame-quality porkers ever to serve in Congress: Daniel J. Flood, congressman of Wilkes-Barre, an equally aging industrial town a few miles down the Wyoming Valley from Scranton. The highway that led from Washington was one of his many gifts.

Flood, a former Shakespearean actor and Harvard graduate, could have been a character who wandered out of a comic opera, with his waxed Snidely Whiplash mustache and black cape, onto the floor of Congress, where he indulged himself in the delusion that the business of the House was the greatest play ever written. "The curtain rises . . ." he would announce on the occasions when he took his turn presiding from the rostrum. But make no mistake: underneath the white suits, the velvet Edwardian coats with ruffled sleeves and the silk top hats was a man who knew how to bring home the bacon.

Like most of the legendary characters of Congress, Flood, who was first elected in 1944 and served thirty-six years, was singularly devoted to his job and its preservation. Politics consumed him; he had no other life. And thus the notion of private and public became blurred to the point that Flood believed the federal treasury, in all its many manifestations, was there to serve him in *his* mission of providing things for the 500,000-odd residents of his district, who would then gratefully keep him in office. The symbiosis was as logical and perfect to him as the relationship between, say, the giant Borneo pig and the wood partridges he allows to pick ticks off his hide.

Flood often worked until late at night, then swept down the steps of the Cannon Building and into his waiting car, where he would berate his driver to break all speed limits on the way to Wilkes-Barre. Naturally, he needed a first-class road, and when he noticed that plans for a new Canada-to-New Orleans superhighway were routed far to the west, he snarled, "This won't do *me* any good!" Thus Interstate 81 jogs to the east through Wilkes-Barre instead of through Pittsburgh.

As a feared vicar of the College of Cardinals—he was vice chairman of the Defense Appropriations Subcommittee—it was Flood who first forced the Defense Department to buy useless anthracite coal for its bases in Europe, at one point making it a crime to convert the furnaces there to oil or gas. He got counties in northern Pennsylvania declared part of Appalachia so they could hook up to the intravenous drip of federal War on Poverty funds, and he helped create the Economic Development Administration, a candy store for congressmen that gives low-interest loans to businesses in what are liberally determined to be depressed areas.

But not everything Flood did was so clearly wasteful. When Wilkes-Barre was devastated by a flood in 1972, its representative by the same name mobilized the entire Defense Department. According to a memorable story by George Crile in *Harper's,* Flood hauled Defense Secretary Melvin Laird out of bed at 3 A.M. to borrow his helicopter. "This is going to be one Flood against another," he growled to an aide as he approached the city in full melodramatic glory. Once on the scene, he browbeat the military to come up with another forty helicopters while calling in aid from practically every agency in the federal government. He was credited with saving many lives, just as his bare-knuckle campaign to push compensation for black lung disease through Congress has likely helped innumerable miners, though at enormous cost.

However any of this behavior played in Washington—and Flood's imperiousness earned him numerous enemies—his constituents reveled in his antics and showered him with fierce loyalty at the voting booth—a fact which was never more evident than when he was reelected while under indictment for thirteen counts of perjury, bribery and influence peddling for improperly obtaining government contracts. But all the loyalty in the Alleghenies couldn't keep the prosecution off his neck. After one mistrial and with his health shattered by cancer surgery and a longtime diet of painkillers and sleeping pills, he pled guilty to a minor charge and left Washington, a footnote in the roster of absurd congressmen.

What people in northeastern Pennsylvania remember, though, was the parochial politician who went to war on their behalf, the man whose wife, Catherine, according to George Crile, used to exhort him as he went off to battle each morning, "Cut 'em deep and let 'em bleed!"

Into those shoes stepped Joe McDade.

For all Flood's originality, McDade was commonplace: a pug-nosed little Irish back-room deal maker who could have sprung from the clubhouses of any urban ethnic ward in America. Yet McDade had what Flood had: a seat on the House Appropriations Committee. In fact, by 1991 McDade had become the most senior Republican on the entire committee. He also had federal prosecutors on his trail investigating assorted allegations of sleazy behavior. But in the grand tradition of Pennsylvania politics—and those of quite a few other states—he was reelected in a 1990 landslide in which he won *both* the Republican and Democratic primaries.

What McDade lacked was Flood's sense of the dramatic, as well as his bond with the folks at home. After almost thirty years in Congress, he had become a Washington creature, spending virtually all his time in a comfortable McLean, Virginia, home and rarely visiting the small apartment he maintained north of Scranton. The son of a minor coal baron who had grown up on the best street in Scranton, politics was not so much a calling for McDade as a job, but a good job nonetheless and one that he had no intention of risking. A Republican in a largely Democratic district, he knew that pork was his ticket to a safe seat.

In 1990, *The Scranton Times* practically held its nose when it endorsed him for reelection. Noting his ethical lapses—including a friendship with a man later convicted of smuggling seven and a half tons of cocaine into the country, a law school scholarship presented to his son by a defense lobbyist who had sought his support on numerous spending items, his acceptance of huge contributions and perks from coal companies, and his involvement in steering navy contracts to a man who later pleaded guilty to defrauding the government of $40 million—the *Times* still concluded, "He is acknowledged to be a great asset to this area, using his clout in our nation's capital to get a great deal of federal plums. . . . We endorse him on the basis of the federal help he can bring to our region."

Which explains why McDade could say, as he did in 1984, "The deficit demands that the defense budget be part of the reduction process," but could vote consistently to give the Pentagon whatever it wanted—as long as some defense contractors set up plants in his district. Or why he could call the deficit "the country's most serious problem" but back wild boondoggles such as the Synfuels program (hint: it uses coal); fat urban development grants (Scranton has gotten several major ones); and Small Business Administration loans (they fund all sorts of office parks in his district). It explains why he had achieved the porker's dream of a living memorial, in fact, *two* living memorials, in the form of the University of Scranton's spanking new Joseph M. McDade Center for Technology and Applied Research and the county's McDade Park with its Anthracite Coal Museum. This brand of politics also explains why the homes of Western pulp writer Zane Grey and the father of American forestry Gifford Pinchot were made into national monuments, soon to be followed by an assortment of abandoned factories in and around Scranton which together would make up the Heritage USA museum, supposedly memorializing the reasons that this part of industrial America had declined—as opposed to the reasons other parts of industrial America such as southwestern Pennsylvania, northeastern Massachusetts and eastern Connecticut had declined and which, because they share the common good fortune of being represented by influential congressmen, will soon have *their* empty factories turned into heritage museums *strictly on the basis of merit*. Or why, in one of the best examples of personal political service, McDade simply put a line into an appropriations bill to give a constituent $1.1 million from the Veterans Administration after an appeals court had thrown out the man's claim that because he had to wait too long for treatment he had developed a "nervous condition."

The need for pork also explains why McDade has fought so hard for what he must intend to be his greatest legacy, a project that would have made Dan Flood proud and that consequently has been derided as one of the most wasteful government endeavors in recent memory, a virtual pork poster child: Steamtown USA.

To find it, you drive past the coal mounds and around a bend in the river to what remains of downtown Scranton. As in many towns in America, there is little of what one could call private business there. Scranton has been a sponge for tens of millions of government dollars, yet it still looks a wreck. The showplace buildings —heavy stone structures restored to their nineteenth-century appearance—house the federal courthouse and other federal and state offices. Nearby are several commercial buildings such as the Scranton Electric Company headquarters, restored with the help of Housing and Urban Development funds and occupied, such as they are, by a variety of lawyers doing business with the federal and state governments. On the edge of downtown is the Erie-Lackawanna Station, also rehabbed with federal funds and turned into a hotel by Hilton, which has since abandoned it to another operator whose success has at best been minimal.

Perhaps guests stay away because they feel uncomfortable over-looking one of the nation's largest ammunition factories, just across the tracks from the hotel. The U.S. Army's Scranton Ammunition Plant sits like a brooding medieval castle festooned with red-and-yellow signs that warn "Danger!" Alongside it is a strip of vacant stores with once-interesting facades that the town is planning to tear down and replace with a shopping mall—once the grant from HUD comes through.

And back there behind all that is a gate that announces "Steam-town National Historic Site," accompanied by the arrowhead logo of the National Park Service, those fine folks in the tan ranger hats who brought you Yellowstone, Yosemite, the Grand Canyon and dozens of other awesome natural wonders, as well as an assortment of historic wonders such as Fort Sumter, Gettysburg and Valley Forge.

The wonder of Steamtown is why it looks like a shutdown factory yard waiting for the scrap dealers to arrive. The forty-acre expanse is lined with rails, among which an assortment of interesting weeds has grown. Dotted around in no particular order are locomotives and passenger cars, most of them battered and rusting as they stand unprotected from the raw Pennsylvania winter.

There is some evidence of construction—a trailer, a crane, piles of brick and lumber outside the huge repair shop called the round-house—but people are rarely, if ever, in evidence. Anyone could just wander in, though there appears to be little to steal. Several of the locomotives and passenger cars seem to have been restored, but they are unspectacular specimens and not particularly old, not unlike what someone growing up in the 1940s or '50s near a rail line would have seen every day. Oddly, for what is supposed to be America's national railroad museum, the only two restored engines in the immediate vicinity are labeled "Canadian Pacific" and were in fact made in Canada. Other Canadian locomotives have been painted to look like American-made engines.

There is, in short, little evidence of the $40 million that the federal government has pumped into the project and no indication where they are going to put the estimated $30 million to $40 million more—though surely someday there will be something to show. The original timetable called for the museum to open in the spring of 1991, and a sign does announce visiting hours, though if there *were* any visitors it's likely their disappointment would be profound.

But then, the surprisingly long life of Steamtown has always been disappointing. It began almost twenty years ago in Vermont, where a wealthy private collector named F. Nelson Blount assembled a motley assortment of retired coal-fired engines along with their passenger wagons and tried to promote them as a tourist attraction. Most of the equipment was Canadian, and only a few of the cars were considered historical, including a Union Pacific "Big Boy," supposedly the largest locomotive ever made. But the tourists didn't come, and Blount was forced to auction off some of the best cars, finally putting the rest of the collection up for sale.

In 1984 the city of Scranton bought it. The old trains were to be their salvation, they decided. There was something of a community consensus that Scranton needed a boost, and a world-class train exhibit right downtown seemed the ticket. Rail buffs and city boosters formed the Steamtown Foundation, and the city responded with an outpouring of enthusiasm and contributions.

The day the trains arrived from Vermont, steaming and whistling down the tracks, it was as though a medicine man from the East had come to a cowboy town. Folks flocked to the rail yard to cheer their good fortune. This idea was going to work.

"There was so much enthusiasm," Mike Wasko, the city's representative on the board, recalled some years later. "Steamtown added a dimension to the community, an imagination, a sense of excitement that Scranton really can be a destination."

Sister Adrian Barrett headed the fund-raising drive and astonished everyone when she announced that contributions were pouring in at the rate of $700 an hour. In short order she brought in $2 million. Over the next couple of years the city kicked in another $6.2 million of scarce funds.

Consultants were hired to come up with a plan. They said to start small: restore some of the cars, build a museum facility and see if people come. But the board sensed greatness. They decided to make Steamtown a working rail yard that would send passengers out into the Pocono mountains for scenic excursions on old trains. They bet a whole lot of people would pay $19.50 to take a four-hour train ride.

They were wrong.

"More energy went into the celebration side than into the nuts-and-bolts side," Wasko said ruefully.

Within two years, Steamtown was a flop. The money was gone, most of it apparently sucked into the vast pit that is an operating railroad, let alone one run by amateurs. The trains, some of which hadn't run in decades, were far more expensive to restore than anyone had imagined. Mechanics had to be found to work on equipment that had been obsolete for years. At one point a team of mechanics was imported from Poland because they were familiar with their own country's antiquated equipment.

But train cars are only part of a railroad. The excursion scheme meant that track, as well as bridges and crossings, had to be maintained. And no one ever bothered to make a survey to see if once the railroad was running there would be enough paying passengers. Steamtown was about to become history in more ways than one.

Then someone telephoned Joe McDade. Among his responsibilities in 1986 was a seat on the appropriations subcommittee that oversees the Department of the Interior and its ward, the National Park Service. He was one of the key people responsible for putting money into the NPS checkbook—so when he asked if they'd be interested in taking over Steamtown, even though it was a site of questionable value and to acquire it this way would totally circumvent the Park Service's elaborate historical review process and come at the expense of several more established museums, they said sure.

Now he had to get Congress to agree. Since his House colleagues weren't about to question the wishes of a senior appropriator, he knew his real problem would be with the Senate. John Heinz and Arlen Specter, Pennsylvania's two senators, did what they could—the prevailing attitude in the Senate being that any money spent in your state, no matter how wasteful or absurd, accrues to your benefit—but this was an expensive, strange proposal that their colleagues were not thrilled about approving. McDade's maneuver through the money maze was a classic.

In the fall of 1986, Congress was facing its usual end-of-session fiscal crisis, trying at the last minute to cobble together the giant reconciliation bill that would authorize spending for the 1987 fiscal year—which had already begun. This last-minute scramble is not thought to be an especially good way for the nation to conduct its business, but it *is* considered fertile ground for mischief making by those who know the system best. And McDade certainly knew the system.

Two principles of pork are: the bigger the bill or the later the hour, the better the chance to slide something by. McDade had both advantages. He chose a vastly complicated, $576 billion piece of legislation to camouflage his modest request that the Park Service take over Steamtown and spend $35 million on it. His leverage came from his seat on the conference committee where hand-picked members of both houses try to work out their differences and devise a passable bill. A conference committee is a pork mating ritual where a lot of side deals are consummated at the last minute.

This time McDade sat across the table from James McClure, the Idaho Republican who was a master in his own right at sidling up to the pork barrel. At that very moment, McClure was scheming to win Idaho everything from energy contracts to tourist facilities, including an authentic Bavarian resort. As so often happens in these cases, the gentlemen reached an accommodation. McClure drove a hard bargain: he cut McDade's request to $20 million but agreed to move it through the Senate on his behalf. The dollar figure didn't matter; McDade understood another of the enduring principles of pork, the secret of the camel's nose, which says, "If the camel gets his nose into the tent, it's only a matter of time before he gets the rest of himself in, too." Once a project is written into a bill, it's damned hard to pry it out.

Within a few days, the government owned Steamtown. Within a few years, it would be committed to spending a truly impressive amount of money on it.

Not that the Park Service would be tricked into going down the same foolish road as the private citizens of Scranton, mind you. "The federal government will not become a dumping ground for white elephants," said Park Service spokesman Duncan Morrow gamely. The service was willing to display some of the cars, but "If Steamtown officials just want our money so they can continue to operate the excursion, we are not interested," Morrow told *The Scranton Tribune*.

Two years later, the Park Service was operating the excursion. In fact, they had signed on whole hog to an even more ambitious plan to turn the place into one of the greatest theme parks anywhere. It would be a working rail yard, one Park Service official said, with eighteen or twenty coaled-up locomotives steaming away, machine shops humming and trains leaving for "a variety of excursions . . . varying in length, scenery, destination and price," according to the service's newsletter. There would be new bridges, walkways and amphitheater seating as well as a school to teach the skills of loco-motive restoration. The Park Service was in the railroad business.

It was, according to one of the government's preeminent experts on trains, "a prescription for financial collapse." William Withuhn, the Smithsonian's curator of transportation, said the project was so large it would cause "an eventual financial hemorrhage" for the Park Service. John White, a former Smithsonian transportation curator, called Steamtown "a third-rate collection in a place to which it had no relevance." *Locomotive and Railway Preservation* magazine published a piece in 1988 that claimed there were already better collections in St. Louis, Baltimore, Sacramento and Strasburg, Pennsylvania. The magazine noted the poor condition of the cars and said it would take $30 million to $50 million just to restore them.

And all this came at a time when the Park Service was already squeezed and cutting back at its most popular attractions. *News-week* reported that Yellowstone and Glacier parks, among others, were cutting hours and staff. Salaries at places such as Yosemite were so low that employees were applying for food stamps. *The Wall Street Journal* discovered that in Philadelphia, not far south of Scranton, Independence Park was a shambles. Almost half of the nineteen-building site, including the home where Thomas Jeffer-son had written the Declaration of Independence and Old City Hall, where the Supreme Court first had met, had had to be closed down for lack of maintenance funds. Despite its 5 million annual visitors, the hallowed park was ninetieth on the Park Service's priority list.

At the top of the list were places such as Steamtown; the Hun-tington, West Virginia, theater that Bob Byrd was turning into a cineplex; Newark, New Jersey's Symphony Hall, which Frank Lau-tenberg had the Park Service purchase for purposes unknown; the Connecticut home of Julian Alden Weir, an obscure painter who was given immortality by Sam Gejdenson, an obscure congress-man; John Murtha's heritage park scheme to restore factories—a scheme that had proved so ingenious that dozens of representatives were vying for similar parks.

And sure enough, Steamtown proved to be even more costly than had been projected. The amount to repair one crumbling bridge shot up from $2 million to $7.5 million. The rail yard was found to be densely contaminated with PCBs from transformers and had to be cleaned at a cost of several million dollars. There were few surviving buildings in the yard, so most would have to be built from scratch, making a mockery of the notion that anything was actually being restored or preserved there. The trains themselves proved tricky to run. During the second summer of Park Service excursions in 1990, all eight passenger cars on one train came uncoupled while traveling at speeds up to fifty miles an hour. "They have to learn that this is not some Christmas tree train," said Arnold Embleton, one of the first conductors and a man who had spent forty-two years on the Lehigh Valley Railroad. "They're going to have to start railroading by federal rules and regulations, or they're going to get somebody killed."

But the money kept coming. In fact, in the 1991 budget McDade expanded the project to include all the major bridges and overpasses as well as track along the excursion runs. The Park Service now owned a complete railroad. Agreeing that it was certainly an expensive project, the Park Service's local superintendent, John Latschar, confessed to *The Scranton Times* that McDade's mysterious ways were the secret to Steamtown's success. "He gets the money through a Congressional funding add-on," Latschar noted with disarming candor. "McDade is an expert with add-ons. That's how we've gotten all our funds here at Steamtown to date."

What he meant was that $40 million later, there was still no official authorization by Congress for the Steamtown project. It had been built with money shipped out the back door. Normally any project is supposed to be first approved by the authorizing committee in the House and Senate. In the case of parks, that meant the House Interior and Insular Affairs Committee and the Senate Energy and Natural Resources Committee. The textbook says those bodies are supposed to hold hearings to take testimony from all the various interest groups, weigh the competing proposals before them, then decide which projects have the most merit. Does the nation need another railroad museum, or would the funds be better spent on a new park? These can be tough decisions that go right to the heart of the democratic process. With a limited amount of resources for anything the government is asked to do, hard choices have to be made and the losers aren't often happy.

But at least the authorizing process is sometimes fair and logical. Everybody takes his or her best shot. A decision gets made. You live with it and move on. Only then are the appropriations committees supposed to get involved. Their role is supposedly to approve the spending portions of projects already decided on. At least, that's the theory.

What McDade and other appropriators routinely do is to short-circuit that process. Steamtown is as good a case as any of the way some legislators can make solo decisions and carry them out with few other members paying attention and even fewer having much to say in the matter. The outcome is based purely on power. McDade got it because he could. Not that it was always easy. Even among the appropriators there is fierce competition for available pork. And of course every member of the appropriations committees is besieged by other members of Congress with their own special pleading. But somehow, those with the power seem to get what they want.

"Funding for Steamtown is always a problem since it is one of the two or three most expensive projects funded by the Department of the Interior," McDade's aide Debbie Weatherly once admitted. For each of the first five years of the project, McDade had to start from scratch and put the Steamtown funds into the House Appropriations Bill. Since the Senate would not put the money into its bill, McDade would then have to battle it out in the annual conference committee, where both houses do horse trading based on a complex array of personal relationships and political favors. Each year he succeeded in getting the money he wanted. He revealed his ace in the hole when he crowed to *The Scranton Times* after getting more Steamtown money into the 1991 bill: "Fortunately, Senator Robert Byrd is a personal friend of mine. We've worked close to thirty years together." In addition to heading the full Senate Appropriations Committee, Byrd also chaired the subcommittee that handled interior appropriations. It's certain that he would accommodate McDade, as long as McDade would accommodate him in some area where the Pennsylvania congressman had particular influence—say the defense budget. The hidden cost of Steamtown had just gone up again.

By the fall of 1991, when McDade had cajoled and backscratched his way to another $12 million, he decided he was ready to go the legitimate route. Steamtown now had more than half the funds necessary to complete it, so he finally brought the project out into the open and went to the authorizing committee to ask for permanent funding: *another* $40 million to finish the project and $6.5 *million for every year thereafter* to run it. He was ready to test another principle of pork, the paradox of "halfway done is well begun." This says that the worst thing a congressman can do is to break a project up into stages and complete the stages one at a time. That may be the way a logical business spending its own money would do it, but, well . . . you get the point.

The idea is to have a lot of partially completed parts, each with a good deal of money invested. Then you can evoke the great cry of the porker: "We've got too much invested to kill this project now! Think of all the money we'd be wasting!" When John Stennis and Jamie Whitten teamed up to build the Tennessee-Tombigbee Waterway through Mississippi and Alabama, they started it at both ends *and* in the middle. When the pressure to kill it or scale it back built up, they argued that it would just be a useless billion-dollar ditch if they stopped now. The only solution that made sense, they argued, was to put in another billion-some dollars and finish it up. Otherwise people would say, "There goes Congress, wasting the taxpayer's money again." Never mind that new studies were showing the same thing the old studies had showed: that there was no point in building the thing in the first place. It was too late for that now, the smug old southerners argued. Best to just suck it up and do what's right. Naturally, Congress went along.

So there was the answer to the question of why, with all the evidence to the contrary, the Park Service didn't let Steamtown grow naturally. After all, the hapless citizens of Scranton had already learned the lesson the hard way. Why not restore a few cars and see who came? Maybe the admission fees would generate enough cash to expand, the way a business would. If enough people came, then maybe a case could be made that excursion trains were a risk worth taking. Maybe ten years from now there'd be a full-service railroad yard the way the Steamtown dreamers had envisioned. Or maybe there'd just be a handful of nicely restored train cars and a pile of money that could be used for more popular purposes elsewhere in the country. After all, just to operate Steamtown, which the most optimistic predictions say will attract 500,000 visitors a year, will cost more than twice what it takes to operate Acadia National Park in Maine, which sees five million visitors a year. But this argument flew in the face of the contorted logic of congressional spending. Decisions aren't made on such a rational basis.

The minor $20 million deal that McDade hammered out had mushroomed to a project that, over ten years, would cost more than $100 million. At the April 1990 groundbreaking, the prediction was that the facility would be open in fifteen months. Two years later, it is still two years from completion. But McDade is on the verge of scoring the long-term protection that makes such estimates meaningless. He's about to make Steamtown a permanent stop for that most welcome of all trains, the U.S. government gravy train.

Meanwhile, back in Scranton, there are few gripes, and any skeptics are quickly laughed out of town. "The complaint by detractors is that Steamtown is (gasp!) a pork barrel project," *The Scranton Tribune* smirked in February 1991. "Perhaps it is. But it is a small slice."

In Scranton and elsewhere, that's the prevailing mentality, the one that makes it possible for people to say, "Congress is filled with a bunch of free-spending bastards who deserve to get thrown out— all except for that free-spending bastard who brings federal money to *my* district."

Or, as one seasoned Scranton pol summed it up with admirable bluntness, "McDade could shoot a nun on the courthouse square and if you were an eyewitness, people would say you got it wrong. The attitude is, he may be a prick, but he's *our* prick."

Perhaps the best example of this approach to government is Bob Cordaro, a bright young lawyer who ran a tough campaign against McDade in 1988. Though he lost, the stocky Scranton native showed the easy charm of a veteran campaigner and put the champ to the ropes a few times with clever charges that McDade was an absentee representative who'd amassed an enormous campaign war chest thanks to PACs. He talked the fiscal conservative line that seems to be increasingly prevalent among politicians of his generation: "The government is spending too much, and it's got its nose in areas where it doesn't belong." He worries about the deficit and has an uneasy feeling that spending in Washington is out of control. But when it came to Steamtown, he had a soft spot in his heart.

"I can't be too critical of Steamtown," he said after reciting a litany of McDade's faults while sitting in his office overlooking Federal Square. "If it's good for the district, what can I say about it? You know what I mean, right? Bringing money to the district, that's what people want to hear.

"When I campaigned against McDade, I hit him for not delivering the funds fast enough. He announced that he had gotten the Steamtown grant nine different times. The same funds. I also found out the district to our south got more total federal dollars than we did. I said in a two-year term it was worth a billion dollars if we could do as well. I said that since I was a Democrat, I could work with the House leadership and get more. That's what people want to hear. For this district, Joe McDade defines a congressman in the modern era. Most people have never known another congressman. If he's good at pork, then that's what people will judge any challenger on. They want to know if a new guy can deliver as well. Personally, I think McDade is a walking advertisement for term limits. But if you're going to take him on under the current system, you're going to have to play by his rules."

Later Cordaro, who had served as a Hill aide, talked about broader economic issues. "Scranton's not as bad off as some people think. We're a microcosm of the country. We're no more hard hit than anywhere else. The problem is, the whole country's dragging. And I think a lot of it goes to that huge chunk of money the federal government takes. What is it, more than twenty-five percent of gross national product? Then there's the part they can't even pay for. That's the deficit. It's like this huge anchor pulling you down. Pulling everybody down."

He never made the connection.

## 7

# PORK IN ACTION

**A**BOUT THIRTY SECONDS AFTER SCORING ONE OF THE BIGGEST victories of his career, Senator Dan Coats knew he was in trouble. As the clerk's gavel came down and the 56-to-44 win was sealed, he and two of his staffers congratulated one another. Then they stopped and realized what they'd done.

For the moment, that late March afternoon, they'd taken away about $700 million from some of the most potent people on Capitol Hill. They'd brazenly challenged the power structure, trifled with the forces of nature and gotten away with it. For the moment.

Their accomplishment recalled the story a few years back of the small-time gang of break-and-entry artists who picked clean a well-apportioned house in a quiet Chicago suburb—only to discover that it was the residence of Tony "Big Tuna" Accardo, boss of the Chicago mob. Uh-oh. Over the next several months, each of the "alleged perpetrators," as they say in Chicago precinct houses—or at least substantial parts of them—was discovered in the trunks of cars parked in various locations throughout the Chicagoland area. Fortunately for Coats, Congress is often more polite. But as he retreated to his Dirksen Building office to await the inevitable, he also knew there were several very angry political bosses—we are talking here mostly about the Allegheny twins of John Murtha and Joe McDade, and to a lesser extent their Senate colleague Arlen Specter—gritting their teeth and plotting revenge because an obscure senator had won a major victory in what looked to be the first battle in the Great Pork War of 1991.

Coats, a lean, hard-eyed, forty-eight-year-old corporate lawyer from Indianapolis, was a former staff aide to Senator Dan Quayle, who was later appointed to fill his boss's modest shoes before winning on his own in 1990. He had convinced a majority of his fellow senators that the pet project of the delegation from Pennsylvania—a fat contract for the Philadelphia Naval Shipyard—was nothing but a wasteful piece of pork-barrel spending that deserved to be stripped from the "dire emergency" spending bill they were considering.

The mere fact that Coats had introduced such an amendment was something of a shocker to those on the Senate side of the Capitol, where dozens of lean, hard-eyed lawmakers—all white and, with two exceptions, all male—really do conduct themselves with the decorum, civility and remarkable unwillingness to intrude on anyone else's business that you would expect to find at some musty old men's club. This despite the fact that the Senate is actually a place where some of the most contentious issues of the land are supposed to be hashed out and where one might think it in the interest of the public, if not the members, if a few of them were less concerned with maintaining cordial relationships than with raising a little hell when they thought something was out of line. Such insurrection was more evident on the House side, where the rabble made up largely of former insurance agents and ex–car salesmen with bad suits and unflattering haircuts could sometimes produce someone who would raise his voice and redden his face in indignation at the prospect of wasteful spending. But in the Senate, this was considered bad manners. When it came to another member's pork, senators, with few exceptions, could be found resolutely staring at their shoes. Coats was thought to be too inexperienced to realize that challenging someone else's piece of pie just wasn't the way things were done. No one gave him a chance to win. But he did, and that evening the Hill was wondering what came next.

Amazingly, Lawrence Welk was at the heart of this matter, as well.

When Congress returned from Christmas break and began its

102nd session in late January, the humiliation of the Welk memorial was very much on the minds of several members and they vowed to do something about it. The Welk fiasco had come to symbolize a Congress out of control and had helped to energize an increasingly militant group of members, mainly Republicans but some Democrats, who'd been threatening to challenge the pork-barrel system. With federal red ink flowing at about $300 billion annually, there was a growing sense among many members that the old rules had to change.

"Pork has been part of the system since the first congress," said Congressman Harris Fawell, an Illinois Republican who had taken that fateful step and signed on with the "Porkbusters." "Whether you called it the old-boy network or just larceny, we let it go on because we could afford it—until now. Only since the advent of these tremendous debts has the damaging effects this pork mentality become so very, very apparent. We're spending close to three hundred billion dollars just to pay interest on the old debt as well as adding more than three hundred billion in new debt each year. That's outlandish. It's gone too far."

This loosely allied group included Dan Burton of Indiana; a Texas trio of Richard Armey, Tom DeLay and Charles Stenholm; Bob Walker of Pennsylvania; John Kasich of Ohio; and Tim Penny of Minnesota. They had volunteered to push the antipork bill and try to bring it to a vote on the floor of the House.

But Jim Slattery, an eight-year veteran from Topeka, decided not to wait. He broke from the group and went after the Champagne Music Maker on his own.

"I was burning about this Welk thing from the time the session ended last fall," he said. "Members had just cast some very tough votes to restrain spending and cut some programs, and they resented the fact that right before these cuts there were some people who did business as usual."

He got his chance in March, when Congress began to consider a "supplement" to the 1991 budget, intended mostly to cover the costs of the Persian Gulf War. It would be the first major money action of the year, and Slattery and Kasich had teamed up to toss in an amendment that would prohibit the government from spending any of its money to rehab Welk's home.

It made a great press release. But that was about as far as Slattery figured it would go. Amendments such as his usually end their lives in the House Rules Committee, perhaps the most cultlike group on the Hill, which, for all anyone knows, makes decisions by slaughtering goats and reading the entrails. They often meet in secret, rarely explain their actions and issue terse rulings that can cripple initiatives that members have spent months preparing. Their role is said to be that of the House traffic cop, scheduling time for debate on bills and deciding which are proper amendments to introduce and which aren't. In reality, the committee, run by the boyo South Boston pol Joe Moakley, acts at the whim of the Speaker of the House and takes wide latitude in reshaping legislation to his liking. Pork hunters, in particular, are usually foiled by the Rules Committee, which refuses to allow most amendments offered on money bills.

But mysterious things were afoot that winter. With no comment, Welk was allowed to proceed to the floor.

"I have been here for nine years now, and I have never seen a vote on an individual pork project like this," Kasich marveled.

At 7 P.M. on March 7, a Thursday evening during which many members of the House were hoping to head back to their districts for the weekend and many had already left, Slattery introduced his amendment to bar any funds for the restoration of Welk's birthplace. It was, he said, a simple measure to recoup some of the embarrassment the House had suffered in recent months. He asked for its approval.

A few rows from the front of the chamber, from behind an oversized desk, a lumpy, big-headed man with steel-frame glasses and slicked hair rose from his seat.

"Mr. Chairman," he said in a voice that sounded like his tongue was otherwise occupied trying to pick the remains of a Moon Pie from his back molars. "I am opposed to the amendment."

Here was a problem. The man was Jamie Whitten, the greatest living relic in the House, then serving his fiftieth year as the tribune for the people of the great state of Mississippi. At eighty-one years old, he was older than all but a few members, but there were none with more seniority—and, due to his chairmanship of the Appropriations Committee, few with more power. He was one of the most fervent defenders of pork in recent memory. Whitten called it "federal spending for local interests," and he claimed it had made America great. "The wealth of this country has increased forty-one times since we started using federal money to take care of local interests," he would say at every opportunity, though no one knew exactly where he got his figures.

Whitten, everyone left on the floor quickly realized, was going to make a stand on Welk.

"May I say that we have here a national program in which we have tried to help communities throughout the country. I have some mighty good friends from North Dakota"—including Senator Quentin Burdick, his partner in crime on all the country's farm spending—"and they are the best ones to decide how they wish to do those things."

Then he squinted across the empty desks at Slattery through eyes so deep inside the folds of skin that the whites were invisible. He looked as menacing as a small-town southern judge just before he sentences a Yankee speeder.

"I know that my *friend*, the gentleman from Kansas, *means* well," he began again in a tone oiled with the exaggeration that told everyone he believed just the opposite. "But now this committee"—by which he meant the Appropriations Committee, many of whose members were then on the floor—"received this letter on March 5, from the gentleman."

As Whitten held up a sheet of paper, Slattery shifted in his chair, knowing what was coming.

"He wants us to add five million dollars for a project in Kansas. For—what is it?" Whitten squinted. "What is the word here?"

Whitten drew it out, peering intently down at the letter and getting stifled grins from other members. They'd seen it before. He was toying with his prey.

"Oh, yeah." He smiled at his apparent discovery. "The Hall of Fame in *Kan*-sas!"

He meant the National Agricultural Hall of Fame in Bonner Springs, Kansas, a project that on its face was as much of a boondoggle as Welk's home, and considerably more expensive. Slattery had indeed asked the mighty appropriator if they would put it into a bill for him. Whitten knew well the dirty secret that in the eyes of the appropriators, few men ever have clean hands. Now he was letting everyone else know.

"But he is against this rural development project in North Dakota," Whitten continued, shaking his head in seemingly genuine puzzlement. "I just cannot understand that. I will not list the many things we have put in our bill for *Kan*-sas, but I could. It is quite a large number. I would point out that five million dollars for a Hall of Fame in *Kan*-sas is a whole lot more than five hundred thousand dollars for North Dakota. And I think the senators from North

Dakota are the best judges of what they want in North Dakota."

And so came the classic veiled threat of the appropriators: Leave well enough alone, or else. We know where you live. We know what you're used to getting, and we know how to take it away from you. In the world of Congress, it was a chilling ultimatum.

After Whitten sat down, North Dakota's only congressman, Byron Dorgan, launched his own assault. Visibly agitated, he agreed that a half-million dollars for Welk was too much money. He proposed $75,000. But he considered the attack on his state to be an insult that he wouldn't stand for.

"This notion that what is in your district is waste and what is in my district is fine is a notion that we ought to explore in some depth," he fumed before proposing an amendment to slash such ventures as a Pony Express Visitor Center and a new park in Kansas, the restoration of the home of William McKinley's in-laws in Ohio, and a $4 million plant research center at Kansas State University that the Department of Agriculture had concluded was "the responsibility of the state of Kansas" and not of the federal government. And surely Dorgan was right; this was all pork. The only problem was that the two projects didn't belong to Slattery or Kasich but to two powerful Hill insiders: Senator Bob Dole, the minority leader, and Congressman Ralph Regula, an Appropriations Committee member. Whoa! Things were getting out of hand.

"This may start a little civil war," a peevish Dole had told the Associated Press before the session. "We've got a number of [Kansas] projects I understand are going to be threatened." And Dole had plenty more at stake in the bill: he was backing a huge increase in the government's export subsidy for wheat farmers, which many people who aren't farmers think of as farm pork. A lot of people had a lot to lose; everybody's quiet deals were vulnerable if this went on.

Whitten quickly stepped in to oppose Dorgan's amendment. Even though he agreed with Dorgan, there were bigger stakes here, and Whitten was not about to have someone declare open season on his appropriations bills.

Then another amazing thing happened. With a relatively large number of members milling around the House floor, someone called for a standing vote on Slattery's amendment. The chairman called for the ayes to stand, then the noes. He declared the amendment passed, 71 to 11. Just like that. Normally a member from the winning or losing side will press the issue and demand a recorded vote as a way of putting everyone on record—and sometimes changing people's minds. A standing vote is rarely used for important issues because it's almost like a secret ballot with no fingerprints and no accountability. But for some reason, no one wanted to go any further. The winners were happy to take their gains and go home; the losers were nowhere to be seen.

Only later did it become clear that the deal had been rigged. It had been too easy. The leadership, which meant Speaker Thomas Foley, wanted Welk to go away because most members of the House did. Despite the usual practice of protecting pork, this one was too hot to handle. From the curious decision by the Rules Committee to the evening vote when most members were gone to the nonrecorded ayes and noes, the skids were greased for this unpleasant matter to slip from sight the way a mob family would take care of an out-of-control hit man. In both Congress and a well-run Mafia family, displays of excess are considered bad for business.

But rigged or not, the Welk victory let the demons loose. Revolution scented the air, prompting mere mortal backbenchers to start talking tough. "This is the beginning of the end of business as usual with the way Congress spends taxpayers' money," Harris Fawell said with intoxicated optimism. Emboldened by Slattery's success, a handful of brave souls started combing the rest of the supplemental spending bill for other porky items they might try to chop off. All sorts of unusual things were showing up in the various drafts of the bill, which was only supposed to provide funds for the "dire emergency" of the Gulf War. There was so much proposed pork, in fact, that it became known around the Hill as "the dirty sup."

It was a hog trough. There were things like new furniture for the Library of Congress, a new building for Chicago's Loyola University, a dam in Wyoming, all kinds of farm subsidy increases, $100 million for the District of Columbia government and $5.8 million for flood control on the Passaic River in New Jersey. Even most of the items that had to do with defense weren't exactly emergencies, let alone dire, which means desperately urgent. The attitude of many congressmen was that in the wake of the Gulf victory, no one could beef about money going to the Pentagon. The only problem was that the Pentagon didn't want a lot of this stuff, yet to remedy this desperately urgent emergency it was being told to spend, for instance, hundreds of millions on the military health care program, including $5 million for something called the Fort Bragg Mental Health Demonstration Project. Another provision, inserted by Senators Al D'Amato and Barbara Mikulski, demanded that $1 billion be spent on refitting F-14 fighters, not because the navy needed them—even at the height of the war, the navy was using less than half its planes—but because they're made in New York and Maryland. Another $200 million was allocated to the development of the V-22 Osprey tilt-rotor aircraft, which the Pentagon didn't want, but which had the strategic advantage of being made in Pennsylvania and several other key states.

Then there was this cryptic paragraph inserted into the bill:

(52) Sec. 203. None of the funds available to the Department of Defense may be used for advance procurement of material and other efforts associated with the industrial availability of the USS *Kennedy* other than the service life extension program for the USS *Kennedy* at the Philadelphia Naval Shipyard.

Don't worry. This is not meant to be understood by a layman. It is, in fact, written to be obscure. But an experienced porkologist could smell a rat. And staffers for two gentlemen from Indiana did just that.

Independent of each other, Senator Coats and Congressman Burton discovered that the navy wanted to spend about a half-billion dollars to overhaul the aging aircraft carrier *Kennedy* and get another five years of service out of it before mothballing. But several members of the Pennsylvania delegation had other ideas. They were insisting that the ship essentially be rebuilt, or given something called a service life extension program (SLEP), which would extend its life by fifteen years and cost about $1.2 billion. The difference in cost: $700 million.

The Pennsylvanians were intent on this because a SLEP could be done only at the aging Philadelphia Naval Shipyard, which employed nine thousand people and was itself a facility the navy no longer wanted. So as Coats and Burton saw it, taxpayers were being asked to shell out a huge amount of money to maintain not one but two dinosaurs, the ship and the shipyard. The whole deal was, in essence, a $700 million toilet seat.

One afternoon, Burton made a gallant charge up Pork Chop Hill and moved to throw out the shipyard item.

"Mr. Chairman, the amendment I propose will save seven hundred million dollars, and I think it is something everybody in this body ought to embrace."

He was instantly challenged by John Murtha, the Pennsylvania Democrat who heads the Appropriations Subcommittee on Defense. A towering marine veteran who, at the age of thirty-four, reenlisted so he could go to Vietnam, Murtha is physically and professionally an intimidating presence. In terse remarks, he explained that despite the fact that the navy said it didn't want this repair of the *Kennedy*, his subcommittee had decided that they should have it. "We have had a lot of experience in dealing with the navy," he said patronizingly. And whether the navy knew it or not, "this is better for them in the long run. They'll get more use out of the ship this way and not have to come back in a few years and ask for more money."

But of course the proposal had little to do with the USS *Kennedy* or the U.S. Navy and everything to do with Pennsylvania politics. The real reason was that the Philadelphia shipyard was in imminent danger of being shut down and this would keep it open. The government was getting ready to come up with a new list of obsolete military bases to close in a world where the threat of war with the Soviet Union had diminished considerably. There were hundreds of unnecessary facilities, maybe thousands: everything from training depots with no recruits to air bases with no targets, and high on the list was the Philadelphia yard, which was outdated and expensive.

But there was one thing the Philadelphia yard could do. It was the only yard set up to conduct a complete overhaul on an old carrier like the *Kennedy*. Forcing the navy to rehab the *Kennedy* would at least keep the yard open for a few years while the job was going on, and maybe justify its continued existence.

So unlike Welk, this was not a deal the appropriators were about to give up. This wasn't small change, and it wasn't the sort of comic subject matter that would cause a storm of embarrassing headlines. This was the real business as usual in the Money Congress. The word was passed that the appropriators considered this an important project. To reinforce the point, most of the members of the committee wandered onto the floor when the vote was taken. Members could challenge them at their own risk.

"I would urge the members to vote this amendment down," Murtha boomed. It lost by a resounding 315 to 105. The forces of nature were back in balance for the time being.

About a week later, it was Coats's turn. He returned to Washington on the dreary, cold morning of Tuesday, March 19, after a fact-finding trip to still-smoldering Kuwait. At a staff meeting, three of the aides, Gray Rather, Genie MacKay and David Hoppe, told him that the budget bill was moving fast and if he wanted to take a stand on wasteful spending, he had to do it now. Congress planned to recess for Easter at the end of the week, and everybody wanted this bill done. Coats and his staff went over the pork list once more, ruling out several items that might have a shred of justification, and settling on the shipyard because it had been shoved into the bill—with no debate—as a pure power play. The money was there because the delegation from Pennsylvania wanted it there, and who would dare to take it out?

Pennsylvania had a particularly powerful delegation when it came to fights like this one. The House Appropriations Committee boasts four members from the state, including Murtha and McDade. Senator Arlen Specter, a Philadelphian running for re-election in 1992 who had the most to lose if the shipyard closed, is on Senate Appropriations.

"Challenging the appropriators is always dangerous," Coats reminded his staff. The year before, after he had clashed with New Jersey's Frank Lautenberg over a bill to ban the export of garbage from one state to another (New Jersey was shipping its excess trash to, among other states, Indiana), Lautenberg had joked ominously, "There's no bitterness. Amtrak just doesn't go through Indiana anymore." During another encounter, Lautenberg, chairman of the Transportation Appropriations Subcommittee, read into the record each of $180 million worth of highway projects scheduled for Indiana and suggested they could be in jeopardy if Coats pursued his amendment.

Coats said he was again hearing subtle threats from Appropriations Committee staffers who told him, "You don't know what you're getting in to."

At the same time, his own aides told Coats they were having a hard time gathering many allies. Among those who had let it be known that they didn't want a public fight with Appropriations members was the secretary of the navy and his boss, Secretary of Defense Richard Cheney.

"It's the classic Washington story," observed one Hill staffer. "Everyone wants the dirty work done, but no one wants their name on it."

Wednesday was a warm and spectacularly beautiful day. "This is not only the first day of spring, it is also the first spring day," Senator Robert Byrd commented benignly at the start of the session. Appearances, like senators, can be deceiving. The clock was ticking on the emergency money bill, and Byrd, who was supposed to manage its passage, wanted it done before the recess. As the day wore on, he coaxed and berated senators to get to the floor with their amendments or comments and get the bill moving. This is the untidy part of democracy that someone with Byrd's dedication to the process is forced to tolerate. Members are rarely on the floor, instead spending their time in a numbing array of committee hearings, staff meetings, closed-door chats with lobbyists and campaign contributors and grip-and-grin photo sessions with constituents on the steps of the Capitol. Why couldn't they all be as devoted and disciplined as himself? Byrd as much as said as he strutted up and down the center aisle in annoyance.

At times like this Byrd would entertain his fellow legislators—or at least amaze them—with his photographic memory of history. For example, that afternoon he told the story of the Battle of Metaurus, where Hannibal's brother, Hasdrubal, was defeated by the Roman consuls Marcus Livius and Caius Claudius Nero—not the Emperor Nero, he reminded anyone silly enough to confuse the two, but another Nero. The victory, he suggested, had been a lot like General H. Norman Schwarzkopf's battle plan in Operation Desert Storm—and, in fact, not dissimilar to the maneuverings by the Black Prince, son of Edward III, at the Battle of Poitiers in 1356, or at the Battle of Crécy in 1346.

"It is well, I think, to reflect upon history as we deal with the events of our own time," Byrd mused while waiting for business to begin.

Coats's amendment to slash the *Kennedy* funds was introduced late in the afternoon. His real intention, he said as he stood up to plead his case, was to illustrate the need for the line-item veto, a powerful antipork tool that would give the president the ability to reject specific projects such as this and force Congress to debate and try to override his action. If a two-thirds majority of both houses wanted the project and was willing to vote on it in the open, fine, they could have it. As it was, the president's only choice was to sign or veto an entire spending bill, so he almost always signed.

The shipyard, Coats said, was merely one of "dozens" of examples of "items attached to this bill that have nothing to do with

Desert Storm and arguably have nothing to do with an urgent dire need for funds. . . . They are items that were not requested by the administration and in many cases are items that even the department receiving the funds does not want."

While Coats talked on the Senate floor, his opponents from Pennsylvania and New Jersey were strangely absent. They were all next door in the ornate ceremonial office of the vice president, working over Defense Secretary Cheney in what one participant described as "a rubber hosing." Cheney had been hauled to the Hill, where Murtha, Specter and the others were verbally trying to beat him into submission on the shipyard issue, at times almost shouting their arguments into his face. If Cheney agreed that he wanted the *Kennedy* rebuilt, the debate would be over. But the former Wyoming congressman, who seemed genuinely to want to reform the Pentagon, wouldn't budge.

Specter and several other senators such as John Heinz, Joe Biden and Frank Lautenberg, returned to the floor, unsatisfied and testy. There was much talk by these amateur military strategists of how the navy really needed more carriers, how Cheney really wanted a re-habbed *Kennedy*—he just wouldn't say so—and how spending more money now would really be cheaper in the long run. Then Bill Bradley of New Jersey, a big-issues, good-government type who wanted to be president some day and seemed to have little stomach for this sort of parochial horse trading, cut through all the windage to hit on the real issue: jobs for Philadelphia, New Jersey and Delaware. After a few desultory comments about the need for saving money by spending more, he said for all to hear that the navy's real motive was that it wanted to close the Philly yard and "if you knock out the SLEP program then you can slip in and justify closing it."

Finally, an honest man! Waste and pork-barrel jobs were the real issue here, dammit, and somebody had to point that out. But then it became apparent that Bradley, who had suffered a big election scare in 1990 in part because he had spent all his time on Major Issues of the Day and none of it on tending to the folks at home, was arguing in *favor* of all this. Sure it was a boondoggle—but it was *his* boondoggle.

Finally, Specter, too, came clean. His first concern was for national security, he wanted his distinguished fellow senators to understand, but there was this other matter that he, well, he hated even to bring up. "This will probably kill the Philadelphia Naval Yard," Specter said forlornly. "My basic concern is for national defense"—of course, Arlen, we believe you—"but there is a consideration for my state."

It was a last-ditch appeal and the kind that ultimately prevails in the sympathetic Senate. The logic unfolds simply: "If he doesn't get his pork, the poor guy could lose jobs in his state and, worse, he could lose *his own* job. Worse still, if it can happen to him *it could happen to me* when I need something." And then the deal closer: "Besides, it's not my money." It doesn't take a Rhodes scholar to figure how to vote on that one.

But this time it didn't work.

When the clerk called the roll, the vote came in 56 to 44 in favor of Coats. The majority was a broad cross section including liberals and conservatives. As with many Hill votes, there is often no precise explanation of why things happen the way they do. Unlike issues with hardened positions, say abortion or gun control, these kinds of votes represent a confluence of forces that join for a moment, then move on. For instance, one key block of votes came from all the members of Sam Nunn's Armed Services Committee, who were miffed at what they saw as the appropriators usurping their role of overseeing defense policy.

"There was some turf war here," agreed an Armed Services staff member. "The Armed Services guys were furious at having this shipyard shoved down their throats."

"I think this is one of those rare cases of an issue that won on its merits," another staffer said with a touch of wonderment. "The carrier is such an obviously bad idea. Coats made the case, and people voted the way they felt. I think they surprised each other."

But it wasn't over, as few things are ever over on the Hill. There's always another shot, if not this year, then next year. In the case of the shipyard, it was the next day.

Thursday was to be the day of the conference committee. This is where selected members of the House and Senate appropriations committees get together to reconcile the two versions of the bill that each chamber has just passed; only when there is a final compromise that both houses approve is it sent to the president. Conferences are also where wheeling and dealing can be most acute. Often an item that was taken out by one chamber will be put back in by the members of the other. Many of the critical decisions of Congress are debated in these conferences, and rarely are they public.

"The first thing to know about a conference committee," a

veteran Capitol Hill reporter explained, "is that they don't want you there. They don't want the press, and they don't want most of the members of Congress. The second thing to know is that if it's an open session, they won't talk about anything you want to hear anyway. The deals will have been cut before they sit down."

Just finding a conference committee on a fast-moving bill can be a little like investigating a murder in Little Italy. Nobody knows nothing. At some point, members from both houses and their key staffers have to sit down in the same room. But when and where are not the easiest things for an outsider to discover. Staffers refer the curious to the committee clerk's office.

"We haven't picked the conferees yet," said the cheery-voiced woman on the House side.

"And when will you pick them?"

"Whenever Chairman Whitten decides it's time."

Oh.

"And how will anyone else know when that time is?"

"Well, the people in the conference will know. We'll tell them."

To anyone trying to make sense of all this, the pull of the rabbit hole seemed stronger now.

"We don't have a clue what's going on," Coats told his staff in early afternoon. "I'm getting a queasy feeling. The problem is always that the people who want something are going to be in the conference. The people who want to keep it out are going to be kept outside."

That's because the people in appropriations conference are always members of the appropriations committees. They are the people whose business is spending money and whose method is to get along with all the other members of the appropriations committees.

Coats's only hope was to get to some sympathetic members of the committee and try to stiffen their spines and get them to stand up for the Senate's position. Only he didn't know whose spines to stiffen.

Late in the afternoon, the secretaries of the House Appropriations Committee began telephoning various members to invite them to the conference. Anyone lucky enough to be hanging around the high-ceilinged lobby of the committee suite would have overheard that the conference was to be in Room H-140 at four o'clock—tea-party time.

Set among the maze of frescoed corridors on the floor beneath the House chamber is the George Mahon Room, named after the Texas powerhouse who chaired House Appropriations from 1964 to

1979. Through a pair of immense mahogany doors walked an odd procession: Byrd, chin up, white hair flowing; the shambling, eighty-year-old Whitten; barrel-chested, crew-cut Murtha; grinning Joe McDade, looking like an Irish ward boss in a new suit; and a line of very senior citizens who were all members of the House and Senate Appropriations Committees.

Inside is a thirty-by-thirty-foot room with a vaulted ceiling from which hang two brass chandeliers. Four long tables were squared corner to corner as at a peace treaty negotiation. The room was filled with middle-aged white men in gray suits—staff—thumbing through fat brown accordian folders.

A stranger, even one dressed in the uniform of the Hill, attracted immediate attention. No sooner had a visitor walked through the doors than conversation was suspended in midsentence and heads swiveled with the same suddenness as if Charles Manson had wandered in for a visit.

"This conference is closed," said an unsmiling woman in a very long skirt and brown pumps.

"You mean it's closed to the public? I've got a press pass."

"To the press, the public, everyone," she answered curtly as she pushed the visitor into the hall. Then she slammed the doors. First one set. Then the next. Double doors. You couldn't peek through the keyhole if you wanted to. It was 4:15, and business had begun.

"A conference committee is just absolute Let's Make A Deal," one Senate staffer observed. "Policy and philosophy go down the tubes just to settle what's on the table. Some of these issues have been debated for weeks, but these guys have to work it out once and for all in a few hours."

As the hours wore on, various members and staff left the room. They were usually tight lipped—but morsels emerged. There were several substantive issues to be worked out—a proposed hike in milk price subsidies, a plan to slash foreign aid to Jordan—and a couple of dozen quibbles between the House's version and the Senate's. Some were haggled out before all the members of the conference committee, but most were relegated to the various subcommittees that specialize in the issue. Most problems were worked out among eight people: the chairman and senior Republican on each subcommittee from the House side and the Senate side and, of course, their staff members.

The shipyard issue was tossed to the Defense Subcommittee, headed on the Senate side by Dan Inouye, the Hawaii Democrat, and Ted Stevens, Republican from Alaska, and, on the House side, Murtha and McDade. The discussion was simple. Murtha wanted it back in. McDade agreed. Inouye and Stevens, two gentlemen who have secured vast military projects for their own states, had nothing to say.

"I wasn't in on that discussion, but that's the sort of deal where Inouye and Stevens would say, 'We got no dog in that fight. Just let it go,' " an Appropriations Committee staffer explained. "Maybe they wanted something else."

"Nobody in the conference wanted to fall on their sword over this one," said another staffer who was in the room. "As far as I know, the Defense Sub staffers huddled somewhere and when they came back into the room that provision was in. I don't know what other deals were cut."

Contacted later, spokesmen for Inouye and McDade would not comment on the meeting. Stevens's press secretary said, "It was a decision made in conference, and there is really nothing we could add to that." Murtha's press spokesman, Brad Clemenson, said, "The congressman felt strongly about this issue, first because he believes we need a large carrier force and also because it could mean the loss of jobs to Philadelphia. He advocated the House position, and it was worked out congenially."

Democracy in action. The defense portion was finished by 10 P.M., and the whole conference report was signed at midnight. Dan Coats was home asleep.

By Friday morning the gray skies were thick with rain again and Coats came to work with that sinking feeling. The conference report was finally available at 10 A.M. Sure enough, the shipyard language was back exactly as before.

He decided to take one more shot by trying to amend the bill on the floor. He would have to urge his colleagues to vote the measure down because it contained this one provision that they had already voted against.

He didn't have much time. There were just a few more bits of business to be taken care of before the Easter recess, and he knew members weren't in a mood to hang around, even for $700 million. They had vacation plans, fund-raising plans and junket plans. Some had left already.

"There's a headlong rush for National Airport," he told his staff. "Let's see who we can round up."

Meanwhile, on the other side of the Hill, Dan Burton had the same idea. He hustled to the floor and offered a motion to reconsider the conference report.

"When we talk about waste and pork, this is it," he told the handful of members milling about the floor. "Not little things like a half-million-dollar Lawrence Welk memorial or library or whatever it was. We're talking about seven hundred million dollars, and they want it because they want to provide more jobs for the Philadelphia shipyard, not because they care about defense."

Burton, a former insurance salesman from Indianapolis, was selling himself into righteous lather.

"This is really a travesty at a time when we're facing monumental deficits, the largest possibly in American history—three hundred fifty billion in one year! And they're going to stick seven hundred million dollars that the Department of Defense doesn't want back in the bill? You should be ashamed of that!"

As the voting began, Burton discovered who was really angry: John Murtha. The Pennsylvania congressman said he took Burton's remarks as a personal insult—he might want to save the shipyard's jobs, but he was also a big backer of the U.S. military. He loomed over his colleague, stabbing the distance between them with his finger and telling him loudly enough to be overheard, "That was B.S.! You better think twice if you want to come before the Appropriations Committee for something!"

Back on the Senate floor, John Warner of Virginia, the top Republican on the Armed Services Committee, was also coming unglued when he discovered that the shipyard item was still in the bill.

"Given the rather decisive vote by the Senate yesterday," he asked Byrd irritably, "would the managers kindly tell me what was the evolution by which this now reappears in the conference report?"

Byrd was impassive. It was his committee, his report, but he wasn't about to take the heat for this one.

"That was negotiated by Senator Stevens and Senator Inouye," he said mildly. "What was said, I am not privy to."

Stevens and Inouye were nowhere to be found. Warner suddenly looked like a man spoiling for a fight in an empty bar. The clock ticked.

Finally, the results of the House vote came in. Burton's motion was thrashed by 291 to 95. Watching this on the television in his office, Coats decided to throw in the towel. He couldn't find many of the people who'd voted with him two days earlier. His only hope would be to introduce a motion and demand a roll-call vote, meaning that every senator would have to be found and brought back and that Dan Coats would be a very unpopular senator.

"We made our point," he told his staff. But of course the money was still in.

At 2 P.M. the $4.7 billion "Dire Emergency Supplemental Appropriations Bill" passed the Senate by voice vote. Even Arlen Specter, who had more to lose than anyone, had already gone home to Pennsylvania.

What had also survived was the amendment to bar the government from funding the Lawrence Welk Museum. Contrary to what the Porkbusters had anticipated, the Senate had not stripped the item out in conference. They were pleasantly surprised.

But in those final intense hours before the Senate cleared out for the holidays, there was a brief statement made on the floor that few people noticed. Senator Burdick wanted to have the last word on his friend Lawrence Welk.

"Mr. President," he began, "I address the provision in the bill stating that certain funds may not be used for the restoration of the birthplace of Lawrence Welk. None of the funds will be used for restoration. That has been accomplished using private resources. Rather, the funds provided are for additional rural development work connected with the project."

He said the money would go to promoting tourism and to a *second* museum, a "German-Russian interpretive center."

No wonder everyone thought Burdick was such a crafty old beaver. He knew that in the arcane maze of the Money Congress, battles were not fought head on unless you knew, without doubt, that you'd win. The guidebook here was Sun Tzu's *The Art of War*, which advocated deception and stealth. While the Welk-busters were just waiting for someone to try to beat them head on, Burdick had slipped out the back door. The Slattery amendment had been written so narrowly that it referred only to Welk's home, so the rest of the town was fair game.

It now seemed as though the 650 people of Strasburg, North Dakota, might have ah-one and ah-two museums.

## 8

# THE CARDINALS
# CONVENE

Otto von Bismark once said, "If you like laws and sausages, you should never watch either one being made."

He was certainly right about the sausages. Those sizzling links next to your eggs-over-easy start with a pig squealing for dear life in the killing room of a meat-packing plant. The poor beady-eyed beast knows his number's up—pigs are surprisingly intelligent animals—so he scrapes his hooves frantically against the white tile floor until the moment when the man with the pneumatic hammer slams it into the center of his skull and the lights go out. Unless he's only been stunned. Then he really goes crazy as the hammer man tries to land another shot. Once you've heard it, the sound of his last high-pitched cry will never leave your ears.

The limp pig has a hind leg hooked to a chain hanging from a moving conveyor belt on the ceiling. His first stop is in front of a man with a huge, well-honed knife who slits the carcass from belly to throat. The steaming guts, all slimy and purple, spill out with a plop. They'll be saved for sausage. While the blood drains to the floor, the hairy hide is skinned off, the head severed and the car-

cass hosed down. Then it's sawed into pieces—the belly for bacon, the ribs for chops, the haunches for smoked ham, the feet for the pickling jar. The odds and ends—scraps of meat, gristle, a little bone, ropey sinews, slabs of fat—are tossed into a big pan that's also carried into the sausage room. There, in the small, cold chamber, men who look like battlefield surgeons in bloodstained white coats feed all manner of particles—the quality of the viscera depends on who's making the sausage—into a stainless-steel shredder from which emerges a pinkish-gray paste speckled with globs of milky fat. This is forced into a long, thin tube that's twisted at intervals of a few inches, then coiled like the intestine it once was. Breakfast, anyone?

The curious procession of mostly old men who trooped through the glass doors of the House Appropriations Committee on May 14, 1991, wore somber suits instead of white coats. They shambled, some of them, but their eyes were as bright with anticipation as their minds were sharp with details of the day's work. They had come to make their kind of sausage.

There were thirteen of them, one for each of the subcommittees that oversees a portion of the government's budget. The oldest by a month was Sid Yates, born August 27, 1909, in Chicago—when Teddy Roosevelt was still president and the Cubs had won their last World Series. Next in line, born in the gentle hills of central Kentucky, was Bill Natcher, white-haired and bowed like a hickory branch. Jamie Whitten, the chairman, was eighty-one. He was followed by William Lehman, who, at seventy-eight, had watched Miami grow from a swamp to the capital of Latin America; Ed Roybal, seventy-five, who'd seen much the same thing in Los Angeles; former Iowa farmer Neal Smith, seventy-one; and Tom Bevill, seventy, who'd come from the clay hills of northwestern Alabama. There was something of a second generation as well, led by John Murtha, 60, and ending up with Vic Fazio, 48, a onetime reformer from Sacramento, California who was, for the appropriators, suspiciously articulate and outspoken.

This was the College of Cardinals, men who shun the klieg lights of public Washington but dominate the business of Congress. While wars raged in foreign countries and debates on all manner of social issues had swirled about the Capitol for the past few months, they'd gone about their methodical work of getting ready to spend the government's money. Now they were coming together for their first formal discussion on how to divide up the $500 billion that they would have to turn into appropriations bills by the fall.

"Appropriations" is one of those terms like "cloture," "quorum" or "ways and means" that seems designed to make the government about as easy to understand as a medical textbook. For instance, "ways and means" is an awfully confusing pronunciation for "tax," a term we all understand. The average person probably doesn't think about "appropriating funds" for, say, beer—but he understands the concept of reaching into his pocket for cash, which is more or less what the members of the appropriations committees do. They just do it by reaching their hands into someone else's pocket. But that's their job. Because no matter what goes on between the president and all the other committees of Congress that vote on budgets and approve programs and stamp their feet about money for this or that, nothing gets spent until the appropriators come up with a piece of legislation detailing exactly how it's to be spent and the rest of Congress passes that legislation. The Constitution says so. "No money shall be drawn from the Treasury but in consequence of appropriations made by law."

Not surprisingly, this would seem to give a great deal of power to the people who write those laws. They are, after all, making thousands of very specific decisions on how money is spent, then controlling the timing and the method by which those decisions get reviewed. It's like being the grillman at a barbecue. People can complain, but you're pretty much going to cook the meat however you want. And if you want to snack on a little here and there, who's going to stop you?

It's no wonder any member of Congress with a shred of ambition in his belly wants to have a seat on the appropriations committees or, barring that, to be very good friends with someone who does. They've been known to trample each other for an Appropriations assignment for the exact same reason Willie Sutton supposedly said he robbed banks: "Because that's where the money is."

"The key to status in Congress is how close you live to the Money River," is how one former staffer explains it.

There used to be a time, a century ago, when the appropriators were thought of as guardians of the public purse. They were supposed to be flinty-eyed curmudgeons who remained mighty suspicious of government officials spending the people's money. That discipline eroded for many years, then turned into a rout with the arrival of the New Deal, whose catechism that lots of government spending was good found many willing disciples on Capitol Hill. Such thinking's been rethought in recent years, but word hasn't really reached the appropriators, whose elders are all children of the Great Depression and unwavering apostles of the New Deal. They've seen government keep people from starving and return men their dignity by putting them to work. That's proof enough for these powerful men with narrow horizons. Their job is to spend.

Not that they have all the money, or all the power. The appropriators face limits. Under the budget law that was rewritten in 1974, mainly to keep Richard Nixon from trying to steal Congress's goodies, the budget committees of both houses are supposed to give the appropriators an overall spending limit. The budgeteers, who are meant to be serious members with the good of the nation at heart and can only serve a three-year term, study the president's budget, revise it to their own liking by shifting funds from one category to another and come up with broad guidelines that, more often than not, are close to what the president asks for in the first place. The reality of government spending in the 1990s is that all but a few percent of it is considered to be carved in stone. If you're not going to touch things like Social Security and Medicare, if the defense budget stays about the same, if you assume you've got to pay interest on all the money you're borrowing and if you believe that every department and agency in the government is truly necessary, then you don't have a lot left to argue about. In a $1.4 trillion budget, perhaps $100 billion is at odds.

Technically, the appropriators have to legislate about $500 billion in spending, the so-called discretionary funds. But in reality, they have the ability to play with only that truly discretionary $100 billion—still a lot of money. And play they do, running their own minigovernment, establishing policy, rewarding friends and punishing enemies. By the time they were through with the 1992 budget, for instance, at least half of the $100 billion would be magically transformed into what a reasonable person could define as pork.

It was that $100 billion that the College of Cardinals was eyeing when they began meeting in the spring of 1991. They had come to make the first cuts on the hog. And like the animal in the slaughterhouse, it would have to go through many steps before it was ready for the table.

Both the House and Senate would proceed along their own tracks.

Meeting in secret in their palatial conference rooms, the cardinals would decide how much money each subcommittee could spend. Then the subcommittees would hold hearings, taking testimony from all sorts of agencies, bureaucrats and cabinet secretaries—all of whom wanted more money. The House would draft its bill first and mark it up, or amend it, before sending it to the full House for preliminary passage. Once passed, it would go to the Senate subcommittee, which would make its changes and submit those of the full Senate. Then both versions of the bill would go to a conference committee, where any differences would be hashed out until there was agreement on a final version. If both houses passed that, it would be sent to the president for his signature. Only at that point, as the civics textbook says, does a bill become a law.

The appropriators do this every year. Unlike other members of Congress, who might manage a major bill two or three times in a career, most cardinals have managed a dozen or more. When it comes to putting together a piece of legislation, they and their staffs are the real pros on the Hill. And only those who pay close attention can ever hope to follow what they are doing. This distinction, coupled with a paranoia about publicity and a fondness for sticking together, make the appropriators less a committee than a secret society.

To a large extent, the process in recent years has been shaped by the personalities of the chairmen, Jamie Whitten in the House and Bob Byrd in the Senate. Each could not have been better bred for the role if they'd come off an Agriculture Department experimental farm.

Whitten, the longest-serving member of the House—ever—is the spiritual elder of spending. A former schoolteacher and small-town prosecutor, he is a furtive man made all the more cryptic by having an unintelligible southern drawl. His diction makes Strom Thurmond sound like a Shakespearean actor. But for those who can understand what he says—or who read the translation in the next day's *Congressional Record*—his message is usually simple: all money spent by the government is good money, and any funds spent anywhere help the nation as a whole.

"Since 1940," he says in an oft-repeated statement, "in those areas where the federal government has come in with programs to help meet the needs of the people, our national wealth has increased thirty-four times." Sometimes the figure varies—during the heat of the Lawrence Welk debate, he said wealth had increased forty-one times—and no one knows where the figure comes from anyway. But then no one questions Whitten. Ever. His own definition of wealth is "highways, bridges, schools, harbors, health facilities, national parks, research programs"—all, coincidentally, things his committee spends money on.

And he is an unabashed home-boy porker. As he puts it, "If you're in a key place and don't include your district in a spending bill, you wouldn't want to go home." In the latest budget, Mississippi was strewn with Whitten-engineered projects—from roads and waterways to NASA installations and every farm program imaginable. Whether he knows it or not, he's also engineering a little old-fashioned socialist redistribution of the wealth, once telling constituents, "These federal programs help to equalize opportunities in our state with those in the larger and richer states."

Not that his life's work has been motivated by any populist beliefs or even any humane instincts. Whitten's ideology has been the practical kind that starts and ends with his own reelection. A thick-headed southern conservative on most issues, he once had the FBI investigate people from Mississippi who'd appeared on a *CBS News* documentary to complain about hunger in the South. He has also, from his early years in public service, been happy to do all he can to support pesticide companies, including blocking the Environmental Protection Agency at every turn and even writing a book favoring the use of pesticides that several chemical companies purchased in bulk—the same sort of ethical lapse that helped send House Speaker Jim Wright packing more than two decades later.

His main interest in pesticides came from farmers who didn't want to be told they couldn't use them. And for fifty years, Whitten has been the American farmer's best friend. He stands as one of the best examples in history of how one man can dominate an entire function of government. They call him "the permanent secretary of agriculture"; as head of the Appropriations Subcommittee on Agriculture since 1949, he's been at the heart of a farm policy that many consider to be colossally wasteful and irrational.

He sees his work as supremely rational, at least in his public statements. America has a moral responsibility to protect its farmers, he argues. They are the cornerstone of the economy, and their lives are harder and more unpredictable than those of factory workers. None of them should be allowed to fail. Ever. So he has helped set up and enforced a crazy quilt of programs that to this day pump billions of dollars of grants and loans into rural America, buy surplus crops, pay farmers to grow things, pay farmers not to grow things, keep foreigners out of our markets, research every known aspects of agriculture and teach people how to hold a sewing bee. The original intent of these programs, when they were conceived during the Depression years, was to stabilize the prices of farm products on a temporary basis. However, thanks to Whitten, the programs have become permanent and often straight giveaways—farm welfare.

"When we put the federal government in is when our rural areas quickly became wealthy," Whitten once told author David Rapp.

Never mind that the nature of farming has changed from family farms to corporate factory farms and that almost half of the people getting subsidies are earning more than $100,000 a year. As James Bovard wrote in his 1989 book *The Farm Fiasco*, "Farm subsidies are the equivalent of giving every full-time subsidized farmer two new Mercedes-Benz automobiles each year. With the $260 billion the government and consumers have spent on farm subsidies since 1980, Uncle Sam could have bought every farm, barn and tractor in 33 states." Some of these programs are the ones that provide lavish incentives to grow a given crop and, when naturally too much of the crop is grown, provide lavish incentives not to grow the crop.

Whitten has masterfully maintained the programs through some of the wiliest, most brazen maneuvering the Hill has ever seen—including bullying cabinet secretaries, blackmailing presidents by holding up spending bills, handing out generous favors to his supporters, sneaking projects into obscure corners of bills and rewriting the rules with such complexity that virtually no one else knows where the money's going.

Over the years, even Whitten has seen his power diluted. But he's made a remarkable comeback. He was forced to adapt in order to protect his domain, so adapt he did. As the nation shifted from mostly rural to mostly urban, Whitten, an old bull segregationist who had fought as hard as he could against civil rights and any program that would help urban or rural blacks, worked to put together an amazing political alliance: the linking of farm programs to food programs, including food stamps, for the urban poor. The effect was that farm spending bills suddenly had a whole new constituency. In fact, today Whitten finds himself with the tail wagging the hog; out of $52 billion earmarked for Whitten's "constituency," more than 40 percent is for food stamps alone. The permanent secretary of agriculture is then left with $15 billion to play with, which he spreads among an intricate array of programs and locations in a bill that he is said to write, line by line, himself.

It's still a tidy empire. You could say of Whitten what he's so fond of saying of his opponents: "He has more power than a good man should want or a bad man should have."

With a boss like that, it is no wonder the rest of the committee was uncontrollably eager to get to the table and start carving as soon as they could. If Whitten felt so strongly about farmers, others on his committee could be equally passionate about water projects, urban housing, roads, military spending or memorials to aging television bandleaders. Whitten is said to run the committee in an almost collegial style with the twelve other subcommittee chairmen participating in the discussion of how the dollars are split up among them. Once the limits are agreed to, they all go in their own directions, spreading the money around as they see fit.

Though he shared a similar philosophy on the need to spend, Bob Byrd runs a much tighter show at the Senate Appropriations Committee, just a few hundred steps to the north on the floor below the Senate chamber. If Whitten is the leader of a jazz band— happy as long as music comes out and he gets in his riffs—Byrd is the maestro of a well-practiced orchestra. He controls the score and the tempo. In a marathon session, he met individually with each of the thirteen subcommittee chairmen—agriculture; commerce, justice; state; defense; District of Columbia; energy and water; foreign operations; interior; labor and health and human services; legislative; transportation; military construction; treasury and postal service; veterans affairs/housing and urban development—and asked them their desires. Then he told them what they'd get.

That winter Congress was in a foul mood. It was hung over from the gluttonous spending spree before the holidays and mindful that things wouldn't be that good again for some time to come. Still there was hope. As House Speaker Tom Foley said reassuringly, despite a war and a growing deficit, "There's room for some expansion of domestic spending."

One word on everyone's lips as the session started was "infrastructure." A big word, that. But some folks would just spell it p-o-r-k. It means roads and bridges and train tracks, and there's no doubt the nation has lots that need fixing. The key would be which ones would get fixed. There would be thousands of other requests as well for every kind of project imaginable—from potato blight studies in Maine to immigrant health care clinics in Texas. All were thought to be useful in some way to the people who wanted them. The appropriators would decide who got what.

From the late winter to the late spring, hundreds of appropriations hearings droned on in the office buildings on both sides of the Capitol. An endless procession of bureaucrats came with binders full of numbers and aides full of charts to justify their existence. "Mr. Chairman, I know the cinch bug has been eradicated in the lower Mongo Valley, but we're very concerned about an influx of gradnabits and think it would be a dangerous policy to cut down on the four hundred inspectors . . ." And so on. The minutiae was numbing.

"Appropriators are the car mechanics of Congress," one Hill veteran explained. "They lie there on their backs looking into the engine of government with grease up to their elbows. It's boring, grubby work. But one reason they're so successful is that so few people take the time to know how the engine runs."

On the House side, the third floor of the Rayburn Building is a warren of Appropriations hearing rooms. Here and there along the coldly efficient marble-and-stainless-steel halls are small chambers that exist as the seat of the various subgovernments of the United States. For instance, Room 2358 is the domain of the Subcommittee on Transportation. One afternoon in March, chairman William Lehman, the former Florida car salesman, banged his gavel and began to hear the pleadings of eight men representing the Federal Highway Administration. Lehman, a man whose slurred speech makes him sound like an understudy to Jamie Whitten, was perched three feet above his supplicants at the apex of an imposing half circle of black leather chairs, microphones and nameplates. On the wall behind his head were the round seals of his various wards: Federal Aviation Administration, National Transportation Safety Board, Coast Guard, Interstate Commerce Commission, Department of Transportation, Saint Lawrence Seaway Authority. Each of these entities would have its day in court before the appropriators.

Actually, Lehman did little of the questioning and periodically left the room. Most of the queries came from Lawrence Coughlin, a lean, bowtied patrician from Philadelphia's Main Line suburbs, who was the highest-ranking Republican on the subcommittee. At age sixty-one and in good health, he had more stamina for the butt-numbing work of taking testimony. He was also proof of an appropriator's maxim: *Cardinals check their party politics at the door.* Rare among congressional committees, the appropriators avoided partisan squabbling in favor of getting the job done. It seemed reassuring, until you realized that of all the committees in Congress, this one might benefit most from the Republicans exercising their role as skeptical mugwumps. Instead, they were brothers in conspiracy.

But the appropriators have a strong pull on their members. There was, for instance, Robert Livingston, certainly a contender for Congressional Hypocrite of the Year. A conservative Republican from New Orleans, he was elected on a platform of attacking government waste—then found himself with a seat on House Appropriations. He quickly converted to the cult of the cardinals and zealously joined in their butchering rituals. "There are times when you just have to swallow and support a bill because you've worked hard to get something in it," he admitted uncomfortably to *Congressional Quarterly's* George Hager, who added, "Livingston insists that he feels as strongly as he ever did that federal spending is out of control, but the Appropriations seat has clearly forced him to compromise." True enough, if you consider a compromise to be the complete revocation of your core principles.

So Coughlin, a country-club Republican who graduated from Yale a few years behind George Bush and didn't even have to worry about past professions of fiscal restraint, could be trusted to run the hearing. Of course he had help from the committee's clerk, or full-time staffer, who sat in front of several fat binders of data and constantly whispered into Coughlin's ear as the highwaymen droned on. On all the subcommittees, the clerk's position is one of enormous power because, despite the fact that most Appropriations members are unusually well informed about the departments they fund, the nature of government has become so complex—with spending formulas, budget caps, legal interpretations—that only a full-time professional can truly understand what's going on. Appropriations staffers tend to be among the best on the Hill, with long backgrounds in government and long experience in Congress. Often they've served several chairmen and managed dozens of bills. For this they are paid approximately $100,000 a year.

The questions that day were about asphalt quality, truck safety and intermodal transportation connections. The answers were crisp, detailed and unintelligible to an outsider.

What wasn't discussed openly was pork. Maybe everyone was just being polite. The FHA is one of the pork-richest agencies in government, with hundreds of so-called demonstration projects for new roads, bridges, bike paths, "smart highways," research centers and the like that would magically appear in the subcommittee's report, which was attached to the actual bill as an explanation. In the end, in an awesome display of micromanagement, Lehman's subcommittee would tell the Federal Highway Administration how to spend almost all of its money, down to which intersection would get a new curb.

Down the hall was the home of Big Pork. To get to the hearing room of the Subcommittee on Energy and Water, also meeting that day, you had to go through a long anteroom and be examined by three separate secretaries, each of whom asked, "Can I help you?" in a tone that suggested the opposite. These were the offices of Tom Bevill, a country lawyer who looks like a leaner version of Jamie Whitten and comes from the southern end of the same Appalachian Mountains that produced Bob Byrd, John Murtha and Joe McDade. He reveres pork. He was overseeing a bill that funded everything from nuclear weapons research to dams in Oregon to the Tennessee Valley Authority and contained many big-dollar, high-profile projects. So many congressmen from across the country came to plead for one deal or another that the carpet seemed prematurely worn.

Way back in the corner was a closed door. You wouldn't go through it unless you were looking for something, which, apparently, lots of folks were. The large room was smoke filled and packed with men in properly fitted suits. The hearings were in recess, and the noise level sounded like a cocktail party. Everyone seemed to know everyone else. But there were only a few congressmen and the bureaucrats were still at the hearing table, so who were all these people? Ah, *these must be lobbyists:* the human lubricants who make the machine of Washington run.

At the same time as public hearings were going on all over the Hill, private conversations were beginning as well. Like the crocuses of early spring, lobbyists were starting to appear, representing all manner of interests, pitching all kinds of programs.

Appropriations is fertile ground for the most skilled among this seductive breed. There are two types of lobbying done in Washington: retail and wholesale. In recent years, wholesale has been what happens on major legislation (such as bills to regulate the cable television industry or the Clean Air Act); the job is to shift political opinion by organizing coalitions of interest groups, marshaling grass-roots reaction through calls and telegrams. It's rare anymore that someone can change a congressman's mind because of a personal relationship; lobbying a major bill is like laying siege to Capitol Hill.

But retail lobbying is still the domain of the schmooze, the world of who you know. And Appropriations is an area where retail counts. "If you don't have personal contacts on the appropriations committees, you can forget about doing this kind of work," said one lobbyist who specializes in the process. "Just let some community group in the Midwest or wherever try to get something from Congress without knowing anyone. It doesn't happen."

That goes for municipalities as well. Most pork has some connection to local government. Think your town deserves a new federal bridge over Pupkin Creek? Think again unless you've got a congressman who's very close to the Money River—or you're willing to pay for the services of lobbyists who are. Merit isn't the issue; connections are. There are good projects and bad. And sometimes bad people get good projects. But what seems so appalling is the concentration of power. The spending decisions get made here by the 26 subcommittee chairmen and their 60 members; the other 449 members of Congress and their constituents can stand in line.

And they may stand forever if they challenge the appropriators. Like any successful tribe, the appropriators are fiercely protective. They take care of their own and they punish their enemies. After Jimmy Carter's attempt to slash water projects failed in the late 1970s, Senator Floyd Haskell of Colorado summed up the frustration at the appropriators when he said bitterly, "Six of the eight water projects restored by the Senate Appropriations Committee are in states which have senators on the committee. The committee saw fit to preserve these worthy projects, weeding out only, of course, those which are truly lacking in merit. Certainly the committee members cannot be blamed if all the bad projects are in someone else's state."

William Dannemeyer, a cranky Republican from Orange County, California, accused the appropriators of "blackmail" when he was pushing an amendment in 1990 to trim the transportation bill by 5 percent. In a speech on the House floor, he said, "There is one million dollars for Orange County in there for some kind of a transportation study. Somebody called my office and advised my staff that if this member [Dannemeyer] had the audacity to offer a five percent reduction to the transportation bill, would you believe that that one million dollars would have come out in conference? Now, that is hardball politics. But what it shows is the addiction of the spenders in this institution to have their way. Any member who seeks to modestly reduce spending is told, 'If you do not go along, you are not going to get along.' "

Harris Fawell, the congressman from Chicago's western suburbs, got his education several years ago, when he challenged one of the classic boondoggles in history, Senator Daniel Inouye's plan to build a religious school for Jewish immigrants in Paris—the one in France, not Texas. Fawell says his fellow Illinois congressman Richard Durbin, an Appropriations member, was dispatched to talk some sense into him. "Don't you understand you're insulting a member of the Appropriations Committee?" Durbin told him. When Fawell said he didn't see it that way, he was told, "Don't expect to bring things up there. If you want to do things, you've got to do it our way." Later he got a call from Dan Rostenkowski, the most potent member of the Illinois delegation, who chairs Ways and Means but shows an abiding interest in the appropriations process, "to ask what was the matter with me." Fawell said Appropriations Committee staffers called Argonne National Laboratories, the big government-funded physics lab in his district, to complain about him. Finally, after Fawell won his fight to strip out Inouye's ploy—a victory that stands as a lonely milestone in pork history—funds for advanced nuclear reactor research were cut from Argonne's budget. "It was later put back in, I was told, because Rosty asked for it. That's typical of the way they operate. They want you to be grateful for getting what you ought to have gotten anyway. It's disgraceful."

Others have all-too-similar stories. As one senator said, "It's subtle pressure, but it's always there."

Subtle pressure was the business at hand for most of the spring as the appropriations bills began to take shape in the closed committee rooms of the cardinals. For weeks those who pay attention to money in Washington burned with curiosity as everyone from budget aides at the White House to lobbyists for okra growers wondered what the cardinals would come up with this time. Finally, one at a time, the carved and dressed hogs were carted from the kitchen and put onto the table.

## 9

# PRIME CUT

THE UNSHAVEN, BLEARY-EYED PUBLIC DEBUT OF ANY PIECE OF legislation comes at a rite called a "markup." Once the hearings end, the private conferences complete, the furtive phone calls made, a bill is drafted by the staff and the committee meets to amend it, or mark it up. For most bills, this is a critical session when members of the full committee will have their first chance to wrestle with the proposed law, arguing with other members, demanding changes and sometimes questioning the whole premise. The markup is often rough-and-tumble democracy at its best.

But not in the appropriations committees. For the cardinals, a markup is like a show trial at the Inquisition. The fix is in. The friar will be fried. With few exceptions, any serious disputes have been resolved behind closed doors. That became apparent a few minutes into the Senate markup of that year's energy and water bill, also known as "Big Pork."

A line began forming outside the carved doors of the main Appropriations Committee suite an hour before the session's scheduled 4 P.M. start. For the public—which means lobbyists and a few members of the press—a markup is coveted because it's the first chance they'll get to see what made it into this version of the bill. If the markup is open at all—some aren't—space for spectators is extremely limited.

As those in the hall shifted expectantly from foot to foot, the members began to arrive. The guard at the door greeted each of them with a nod and a deferential "Mr. Chairman . . . Mr. Chairman . . . Mr. Chairman . . . ," no doubt figuring they were all chairmen of something. He had a point. The real chairman, Robert C. Byrd, swept through the doors, white mane frozen in place, nose pointed sixty degrees toward the sky, followed by three stern aides. They in turn were followed by J. Bennett Johnston, chairman of the Big Pork subcommittee, who seemed to dance into the room wearing a smile, two-tone shoes and a seersucker suit that recalled the courtly, sly politicians of his native Louisiana, not the least of whom were Huey "Kingfish" Long and his son Russell. Then there was Mark Hatfield—the ruggedly handsome Senator from Central Casting—who used to be the chairman, and Daniel Inouye, who was the chairman of the Defense Subcommittee, and so on. As each went through, the doors closed with a rattle.

For those who cared about this game, the sealed doors hinted at unseen deal making as provocatively as moans through a motel wall. At the appointed hour, committee aides pushed them open and ushered a handful of voyeurs into a domain that most Americans would never see. If you accepted the sarcastic but respectful analogy that the appropriators were the College of Cardinals, then this was the Vatican. Otherwise, you might think of it as a set for a live sex show.

"Can you believe they let the press in before us?" said one anxious young man in a blue suit. An older gentleman by his side merely put his index finger in front of his lips.

Reporters were escorted quickly through the paneled, carpeted, chandeliered reception room where several assistants sat at immense mahogany desks. Off to the left was a series of high-ceilinged offices, one leading to the next and ultimately ending with the entrance to Byrd's private chamber. To the right were the doors to the conference room.

Inside was what looked like the boardroom of the world's most successful company. Based on appearances, it would have to be an old, traditional sort of firm; the gold-leaf trim, the vaulted, frescoed ceiling, the double chandeliers of crystal and polished brass told you that. And a rich company as well. Clearly, no expense had been spared in decorating this room. The centerpiece was a magnificent table polished to a gleam, upon which sat twenty-nine identical yellow pads, twenty-nine pencils and twenty-nine water glasses. Around the rim were twenty-nine black leather chairs with one, at the center of the table, taller than the rest.

The occupants of those chairs told you that this company, with all its wealth and tradition, must be having a good year. The confident, handsome men around the table engaged in relaxed banter as they waited for the meeting to start. Nothing in their manner even hinted that this was a company in deep trouble. Were it a private firm hemorrhaging red ink at a rate of, oh, say, 30 percent of operating revenues, the faces of the directors would have been pale and tense, reflecting the torment in their Gelusil-coated stomachs. But no, these men, sitting there in those big black chairs, had the easy elegance of born winners.

Byrd sat in the largest chair. To his left was Hatfield, the ranking Republican. Johnston sat to his right. Around the table were fifteen or so others, among them Quentin Burdick, Frank Lautenberg, Daniel Inouye, Phil Gramm, Pete Domenici, Al D'Amato and Ernest Hollings. Behind the senators, the walls were lined with side chairs, each occupied by a nervous staffer who would periodically lean over to whisper into the boss's ear. The Whisper was a strange spectacle to witness, like some animal custom captured by the cameras of *National Geographic*. The staffer would cup a hand to the side of his mouth tightly as he tucked his chin into the space between his patron's neck and shoulder, sitting that way for minutes at a time while his eyes darted about the room. At one point, there were Johnston, Burdick, Lautenberg and Hollings, all in a row and each with an aide fitted into the crook of his neck.

The press was shunted into a window well in the back corner of the room and told to be quiet. There were no seats, and the dozen reporters stood packed in a sweaty cluster. One reason reporters don't like to follow the affairs of the cardinals is because they make it so damned uncomfortable. The other reason is that if anything important is going to happen, the cardinals do their best to make sure it doesn't happen when the press is around. Typically, those who show up are the reporters for specialized publications such as *Congressional Quarterly* and various newsletters on narrow subjects. Sometimes a daily newspaper will make a special effort to focus on the appropriations process and discover some fascinating stories, as Dan Morgan of *The Washington Post* and David Rogers of *The Wall Street Journal* have done in recent years. But if the average person wants to read about the sausage being made, he can forget about it.

At 4:10 in the afternoon, His Holiness Robert C. Byrd whacked down a wooden gavel with a shot that startled everyone in the room.

"Senator Johnston?" he said with exaggerated courtesy.

J. Bennett Johnston, a professional politician from Shreveport, Louisiana, is known among those who know the Hill as a major league operator. After all, this is the man who, because he is passionate about tennis, got a senators-only court built in the deep, dark recesses of the Hart Senate Office Building. He's viewed as very smart, very suave and somehow just a little too slick. He's come close, but failed twice, in his attempt to be elected Senate Majority Leader. Still, on anything that has to do with water or energy, he's a power to reckon with, chairing both the Appropriations Subcommittee *and* the full Senate Energy and Natural Resources Committee.

He is in many ways the perfect student of the system to run the Big Pork bill. This was the grandpappy of pork, dating to the old Rivers and Harbors Bill of two hundred or so years ago, when all the money of consequence spent by Congress had to do with things that floated. More recently, the bill has also included new fiefdoms such as the Bureau of Reclamation, founded in 1902 to bring water to parts of the bone-dry West. The bureau's done a great job—too great, some would say—turning parts of the West into tropical resorts. And once it mastered irrigation, the bureau naturally got its fingers into all sorts of areas including hydropower, flood control and recreation. No doubt about it, the cities, ranches, farms and suburbs of the West have prospered largely on the basis of lots of cheap water and power, paid for by all the taxpayers of the country. And the best part is that those who benefited have hardly paid any of the money back. The idea of the bureau was that it is supposed to be self-supporting with fees paid by all those who have profited so handsomely from the true gold of the West. But somehow, in 1992, we were still spending $900 million on this endeavor and bleeding taxpayers to ensure the continued growth of places like Phoenix and Salt Lake City.

Big Pork is, well, big. The Bureau of Reclamation, along with the Army Corps of Engineers, are the folks who brought you projects like the Cross-Florida Barge Canal, a scheme to join the Atlantic Ocean with the Gulf of Mexico, which merely succeeded in contaminating much of the drinking water in Florida with salt. Or the Kerr-McClellan Waterway, a ship canal in Arkansas and Oklahoma named for two awesomely powerful legislators who were nonetheless impotent when it came to making ships use their creation. Practically any Big Pork project costs a billion dollars—or two. It's almost like a poker ante. Not surprisingly, moving enormous amounts of earth and spitting in the eye of Mother Nature have always been expensive propositions. Not as obvious is the outcome: rarely is all this effort worth the trouble.

The best example of all is the Tennessee-Tombigbee Waterway, an attempt by Congress to do nothing less than duplicate the mighty Mississippi River a few hundred miles to the east. Now, you might ask why anyone needed to clone the Mississippi, one of the most useful ship channels in the history of man, but you'd be missing the point. This venture had nothing to do with boats.

William Proxmire called the project, completed in 1986, "The pork barrel's greatest monument." And true, it was monumental. To build the 240-mile waterway linking the Tennessee River to the Gulf of Mexico, they had to cut through mountains, build intricate locks and dams, and take out two and a half times the amount of earth scooped from the Panama Canal. But the real challenge was the political engineering.

Tenn-Tom was big in every way, especially the lies that were told to get it built. Its cost soared ten times from an initial bogus estimate of $300 million, while, in a nice bit of symmetry the amount of traffic it carries is about a tenth of what its backers predicted. The flagrantly fabricated cost-benefit analysis used by the Corps of Engineers to justify the project relied on an interest rate of 3.25 percent at a time when the prime rate was approaching 20 percent. The Corps said it would produce $125 million a year in benefits; the General Accounting Office, before a key vote on the project, said $12 million.

To put across such a fraud required a cast of all-star porkers, and Tenn-Tom had it, from Howard Baker to John Stennis to Tom Bevill to Jamie Whitten. Whitten was the best. Speaking at a ceremony held a few years ago to honor Whitten, his fellow cardinal Bill Natcher inadvertently spilled a few trade secrets on how Whitten had gotten Tennessee-Tombigbee through.

"Jamie said, 'Well, I will tell you what let's do as we go along.

Let's kind of rearrange the authorization, just a little as we go. . . . If we want this project to succeed that means so much to the State of Mississippi and so much to the United States of America, we must see that we start at the upper end of the project, that we start in the middle, and we start at the tail end of it. That is the way to bring Tombigbee along. If we start in one place in the beginning at the upper end of it, we will never carry it through.' "

Still, there were several close votes in the early 1980s requiring all kinds of arm twisting and favor promising. The most persuasive argument, though, was the famous "too big to butcher." As James Abdnor, a Republican senator from South Dakota who reluctantly voted for the project, said in 1982, "Today, you couldn't get this thing off the ground for love or money. But it seems ridiculous to have poured vast sums of money into it and then spend more money to shut it down." And that, at least, was the final reassurance to Tennessee-Tombigbee's harshest critics. It could never happen again.

Even on a lesser scale than Tenn-Tom, the cost of Big Pork was hard to justify. So much of it was purely regional, hugely expensive and often destructive to the rest of the country. If you live in Cleveland, does it really make sense to send your tax money to irrigate Arizona so that jobs will go there?

But if anyone expected a change in philosophy, they weren't going to get it in the 1992 budget. That became apparent as Johnston summarized his $22 billion bill. The highlights were that the superconducting supercollider—the giant magnet-driven atom smasher being built on the Texas prairie at a cost of $8 to $10 billion that some critics thought would soon be another candidate for the pork-barrel hall of fame—would not only survive but get a boost in funding to $508 million, and that Johnston had managed to find money to start fourteen new multi-million-dollar water projects.

"The House had more," he pointed out quickly. "And we'd like to do more," he shook his head ruefully at his project-hungry colleagues, "but if anything, we've been too generous."

You see, there were some ongoing projects that just had to be funded before others could be added, he said innocently. "We're concerned with Tug Fork, Red River and Garrison River"—names which meant nothing to those uninitiated to the coven, but everything to those who knew. Tug Fork was Byrd's, Red River was Johnston's and Garrison River was Burdick's. Once again, the big dogs had eaten first.

But then there was money for others as well. For instance, the nuclear weapons labs in New Mexico—Los Alamos and Sandia— got big boosts for weapons research. Admittedly, such funds were hard to come by in these peaceful times, but then Pete Domenici was a member of the subcommittee and even though he was a Republican who talked tight spending, he was a guy you could deal with. Jake Garn got millions for his Central Utah Project to move water through the desert and over mountains to keep the Salt Lake City area growing; Dennis DeConcini got the same for a similar ongoing engineering marvel in Arizona.

Sprinkled throughout were $10 million here and $10 million there for favored universities such as Louisiana State, Louisiana Tech, Oregon Health Sciences University and the University of Alabama, Tom Bevill's alma mater. One growth area was nuclear medicine, with new programs and buildings popping up all over the bill. Normally you might think of nuclear medicine as belonging in a medical budget, where it might be weighed against other medical needs and breakthroughs. But since the word "nuclear" is in the title, the same folks who brought you the H-bomb are now building wings onto hospitals—in their own districts—across America.

And the supercollider itself was a committee-friendly project that supplied choice contracts to the states and districts of many of the key appropriators, not the least of whom was Bennett Johnston himself, who had once opposed the SSC but came on board about the same time General Dynamics announced plans to build a $150 million magnet factory in Hammond, Louisiana. In some ways, the SSC was the keystone of all the excesses in the energy and water bill because the man who really wanted it was George Bush. It was a pork beard. As one Appropriations Committee source explained, "Once they knew how intent Bush was on keeping the supercollider, they could load the bill up without fear of his veto."

Looked at one way, the supercollider is the scientific equivalent of deregulating the savings-and-loan industry. It's a gamble, sure. There's a risk of sinking a ton of dollars into a black hole. But it's the kind of chance you're willing to take with other people's money.

The SSC is wacky science, according to the vast majority of scientists in the country. The plan is this: build a precisely engineered fifty-four-mile concrete tunnel in the Texas plains near Dallas; line the tunnel with eight thousand powerful magnets; turn on the switch; and try to smash atoms into each other with incomprehensible force. The intent is to duplicate the Big Bang, the supposed moment the universe was born. What they're looking for is to isolate the smallest particles that make up matter, called quarks. Specifically, they want to find the Top Quark. The experiment may find something, it may not—its biggest supporters admit this. What it finds may or may not have any relevance or application to the world we live in. The tunnel may turn out to be just a very expensive exercise in theoretical physics that will win somebody a Nobel Prize. As one of its developers casually told *The Washington Post*, "Physics is not rational, and physicists are not rational."

But politicians are supremely rational, and what the SSC has come to represent in the appropriations committees is merely pork of another dimension. The original cost estimate of $4 billion has gone to, according to one Energy Department study, $12 billion. Construction companies are calling it "The Big Pour." Dozens of universities in friendly congressional districts are getting multi-million-dollar research grants—and expressing support for the project. True, there is a growing outcry from the general scientific community that the SSC is draining funds from many other more relevant projects. And with about a billion already spent, the deal isn't yet at the too-big-to-butcher point. But this year's money was important because it was going to be used to start digging the hole. The magnet technology wasn't nearly ready yet, but they wanted that tunnel built because once it was under way, the project would be very hard to stop. Just ask Jamie Whitten.

At the markup, Johnston merely noted that he had decided to give President Bush all the funding he wanted. There was no other discussion of the issue by the Appropriations Committee. And only later did a footnote become apparent. In order to give the supercollider all the funds it needed, the appropriators slashed a project at Fermilab that might do, at a fraction of the cost, what SSC is supposed to do. Fermilab is part of Argonne National Laboratories, located in DuPage County, Illinois, the heart of the congressional district of Harris "Porkbuster" Fawell.

The other giant project in the bill was even quieter, creeping about on cat's feet—or was it brown-and-white spectator shoes? Over there, under the table. That $124 million line item snoozing away. Could it be . . . Yes, indeed. Son of Tenn-Tom!

For all those naive souls who believed Hollywood would never make a *Halloween, Part II*, there was a shock in store as Bennett Johnston tucked in what was likely the too-big-to-butcher installment of the Red River Waterway, a long-standing attempt to duplicate the Mississippi heading west.

The Red is one of the all-time great cowboy rivers, flowing through New Mexico, Texas, Oklahoma and John Wayne movies before it's rudely rammed into the back end of Shreveport, at which point the glamour ends and the nasty business of being an industrial alleyway and sewer begins. For many years, the ruling citizens of that unglamorous oil city have dreamed of a deep, tidy link with the mighty Mississippi, despite the fact that highway and rail connections exist. Their hired hands, Johnston and the once-almighty Russell Long, have been inventive and relentless in their zeal to deliver.

In the famous 1977 attempt by Jimmy Carter to purge useless water projects, Red River was at the top of the list. As if Carter didn't have enough problems, he soon had the Cajun cousins leading the opposition with Johnston pushing through the crucial amendment that kept him from shutting down *any* water projects. A few years later, Ronald Reagan got a lesson in reality when he proposed to cut out some of the early Red River funding—and found Long and Johnston on his doorstep, surely reminding him of all the trouble they could cause on a host of initiatives, not the least of which was his tax cut plan, which had to go through Long's committee. Red River stayed in.

The plan is to cut a 236-mile channel nine feet deep and two hundred feet wide through the existing course of a river that hasn't been much good to anyone since 1885, when the railroads came to town. The Army Corps of Engineers, which found Red River to be so wasteful it took a rare stand against the project, estimated the annual benefits at $28 million and the cost at $3 billion—meaning in another hundred years, you might have something to show for it.

But the Corps is a can-do kind of organization, and the goal is Shreveport by 1994. "We may not agree," said one Corps official, "but if Congress tells us, we'll get it done on time."

They said there'd never be another, but Shreveport '94, here we come.

Amazingly, despite these projects and more, the theme of Johnston's talk to his fellow appropriators was how tight things were. In fact, penury was what all the cardinals were preaching at all their sessions that summer. "We're doing the best we can within limited means," you heard over and over. You almost felt sorry for them, until you realized that most of their budgets were going up from the previous year's huge boost. Johnston, for instance, was up almost 5 percent on top of about 10 percent the year before. Not many working people this side of Lee Iacocca were getting raises even near that level. But overall, domestic spending was more than 20 percent higher than what the cardinals had been dealing with just two years earlier. Maybe the machine really was insatiable.

"We're operating under very tight constraints," Byrd reaffirmed at one point that afternoon. Of course, not tight when it came to Byrd. When the chairman introduced a minor amendment, he turned with a flourish toward Johnston and said, "That is, if the chairman has no objection."

"Mr. Chairman," Johnston replied with a grin that could melt butter, "I have no objection to your amendment. In fact, we have no objection to *anything else* you want to put into this bill."

"Verrry . . . well . . . said," Byrd oozed with mock deliberation and a smile to let everyone know that he knew Johnston was just joking. But of course they all knew he wasn't.

Still, not everyone got what he wanted. Even before they entered the room, Johnston, Byrd and Hatfield had made most of their deals, leaving some folks unhappy. An unusual moment came when Ted Stevens, the wiry senator from Alaska who wore a very unsenatorial short-sleeved shirt and had actually been snoozing on his forearms for part of the meeting, popped up to ask for some emergency funds to help shore up a riverbank that was eroding near a regional health clinic in Bethel. Stevens is another of those conservatives who projects an image of fiscal rectitude to the outside world, in fact a sense of frontier frugality, but sups up pork with astonishing vigor. Oddly, this time he might have had a legitimate cause.

"Look, I first raised this issue five years ago. The riverbank is washing away. It would take a million to start the project. I'm willing to take it out of the Kodiak Harbor project. I'm not asking for an increase for Alaska. I'm willing to take it away from the Kodiak fishermen."

Johnston knew this game. "What's the total cost, Senator?"

"About eighteen million over four years."

"So you just want a million this year, but then it goes up?"

"About eighteen million over four years," he repeated with his expression of perpetual peevishness.

"You say this is an emergency," Johnston noted dryly. "You first raised the issue five years ago."

"The riverbank is washing away," he snapped. "This is a health care clinic for Indians."

"Senator Hatfield and I don't like to say no to any member of this committee, especially one who has been such a strong supporter. We can give you Bethel in lieu of another project, but we can't have two new big mortgages. We've done what we thought was fair."

Stevens huffed out, vowing to get the money somehow.

Then there was the matter of the Army Corps of Engineers. For a hundred years the Corps has been a barnyard of pork. Its job has been to carry out wild schemes to dam rivers, make them change direction, stop them from flooding, reinvent harbors and generally reverse the course of nature at great cost—in both dollars and damage to the environment. To accomplish this and justify its own existence, the Corps has become the lapdog of Congress, eagerly telling all manner of lies about the tiny costs and grandiose benefits that will accrue from whatever harebrained ploy a member is willing to propose. Admittedly, some of the projects have worked. And, yes, some helped make America great. But after 150 years of this frenetic activity, there just isn't that much left to dam, dredge or dig. The Corps knows this. In recent years it's even tried to act more responsibly. For instance, it produced a plan to start consolidating its many regional offices, saving more than $100 million a year. The cardinals, however, were not at all happy about this.

Just how unhappy was made clear by the man who introduced the amendment to stop this foolish money saving, Senator Don Nickles, a Republican and self-professed fiscal conservative from Oklahoma who had recently made a Mephistophelian bargain, the terms of which would surely emerge as his career progressed. In some ways it was like asking a new Mafia soldier to prove his loyalty by killing a friend. At one point, Byrd praised him with a chilly smile. "The senator has been very cooperative. Very accommodating. He has proved to be a very able ranking member."

"Mr. Chairman, I have an amendment here," Nickles said quietly as copies were passed around the table. It said, "None of the funds appropriated in this Act or any prior Act shall be used to close any Corps of Engineers Division or District headquarters office."

Simple. If you don't have the money, you can't move. This is how the cardinals legislate, how they make policy decisions that have nothing to do with appropriating money. If the Corps wants to close its offices, there are other committees in Congress that might want to study the matter, but it's not the appropriators' business. In theory.

The best example of this was the northern spotted owl controversy, widely viewed by Hill insiders as one of the seediest backdoor scams in the history of the appropriations committees. A few years before, the same Mark Hatfield who sat grimly studying the Corps amendment—everything Hatfield did was grimly senatorial—had pushed through similar amendments at this very table to ensure that timber could be cut in the Northwest *despite court orders prohibiting it.* Hatfield was, among other things, the Cardinal of Timber and was willing to flout the Constitution to protect logging interests. When environmentalists got the federal courts to temporarily stop the logging of old forests in Oregon and Washington because they were being destroyed too rapidly, Hatfield stepped in. Certain that he wouldn't fare well if the matter were given a full hearing in Congress, every year from 1985 on he tacked riders on to appropriations bills that required the U.S. Forest Service to sell a certain amount of timber to private companies—including timber that was under court injunction. His fellow cardinals, of course, didn't challenge him, and the hundred-year-old fir trees were cut and the owls slowly exterminated while the naturalists screamed that they were being robbed. They were. In this quiet room, anything is possible.

Finally, in 1990 a federal appeals court said that the Hatfield amendments were essentially telling the courts what to do—an outrageous violation of the separation of powers. The case is now before the Supreme Court.

But the real issue isn't right or wrong, or sanctimonious tree huggers versus greedy lumber companies. The issue is abuse of power. Maybe it's best to save the trees, and maybe it's best to cut them down. There's a political process for reaching those decisions, and, as the judge in the case wrote, "While the loss of old growth is permanent, the economic effects of an injunction are temporary." But the appropriators, and more specifically, Mark Hatfield, made the decision for the whole country on how much of the ancient forest of the Pacific Northwest we want to cut down. And they did it for the same reason they do so many things: *because they could.*

Nothing so precious was at stake in the Corps of Engineers controversy. Just money. But for a moment it seemed the issue might take on grander significance. As he read the amendment, Bennett Johnston looked like he was eating a bad oyster.

"It might not be the best way to do this," he said with a frown. "That's a hundred and twelve million down the drain."

Then he qualified himself—sort of. "That's money that could be used for new starts"—new projects, he meant. Not saved. That wasn't his job.

"At some point," he said, placing his palms on the shiny tabletop and eyeing the assembled cardinals and lesser clerics, "we're going to have to face up to the fact that we're wasting a whole lot of money here."

There was stillness. No one spoke. Hardly anyone breathed. Was good ole Bennett going to stop this amendment? Was he going to let them fool with the sacred Corps? The mother of all pork? Was he losing his mind? But before anyone could delicately raise these notions, Johnston broke the silence, the momentary seizure of conscience having lifted.

"All in favor? . . . The ayes have it. Next item . . ."

*At some point we're going to have to face up . . . but not today.*

Some weeks later Johnston and a few other senators would get together with Cardinal Bevill and his monsignors at a conference committee to reconcile their differences, slight though they were. The final product would sail through both houses and become the first Appropriations bill passed into law that year. As expected, Bush would sign it without a second glance. Even Ted Stevens later got what he wanted, netting $5 million to fix his riverbank when the vote came to the floor of the Senate.

The odd thing about the markup of Big Pork was what *wasn't* discussed. You could have sat through the entire ninety-minute session and not have had a clue of what a controversial, pork-heavy bill was on the table. Decisions to spend enormous amounts of money had been made in a series of private discussions by a handful of members, then quickly rubber-stamped by the committee that had once been the guardian of the public treasury. And unless you were obsessively trying to discern the hidden meaning of this curious ritual, you wouldn't have understood the summary offered by one staff member of the Appropriations Committee who marveled at the bill by saying, "That's the first time I ever heard the walls oink."

## 10

# THE POPE OF
# PORK

ANY TRULY SERIOUS PILGRIMAGE THROUGH PORKLAND MUST include a side trip from Capitol Hill to the ancestral home of the Pope of West Virginia, a long day's ride whose tedium is relieved by the discovery of the many gifts he has bestowed on his native state.

Cross the Potomac and head out past McLean, the ritzy suburb where Robert Byrd now lives (in what is always described as a modest home) with his wife and sweetheart of sixty-some years, Erma. Go on out past Leesburg, Virginia, on Route 7 to Harpers Ferry and Charles Town in Jefferson County, the tip of the West Virginia panhandle that's slowly becoming part of the Washington sprawl. Here, for a hundred million dollars or so, Byrd's creating a giant new facility for the U.S. Fish and Wildlife Service. It is also where he hopes one day to move a substantial portion of the Central Intelligence Agency, at a billion-plus dollars, the most expensive office move in government history. Then swing up through Martinsburg, a tiny landlocked town that's now the home of the Coast Guard's computer operations and will soon have an upgraded airport and a new base to house Air Force cargo planes.

Straight west, two hours along Route 40, is Morgantown and West Virginia University, which has suddenly found itself showered with federal grants for all manner of research—from coal technology to wood products, NASA computers to Alzheimer's disease, job safety to veterans' medical care.

Unless you were making a career out of this, you wouldn't have time to drive up to the odd appendage of West Virginia that juts to the far side of Pennsylvania and contains Wheeling, home of Wheeling Jesuit University, another surprisingly in-demand academic institution that finds itself with a substantial amount of NASA research projects as well as a grant to design the "classroom of the future." More likely, you'd turn south on Interstate 79 and head for Clarksburg. That road, an uncrowded four-lane that runs all the way to the state capital of Charleston, is pork of a sort, but not from Byrd's barrel. The road was a present from John F. Kennedy after the 1960 election, when West Virginia proved so crucial to his winning the Democratic primary. He asked the burghers of Charleston what they wanted, and they said, "A good road so we can get up to see the WVU football games." It seemed like a modest request, but no one in Washington ever dreamed how expensive it would be to build roads in the Mountain State. Traveling in West Virginia, it quickly becomes apparent that there is virtually no flat land. Millions of years ago the earth here twisted and writhed into an endless series of sharp ridges and narrow valleys. "If you could smooth out the surface of this state it would be as big as Texas," one state official remarked.

Those hills have been the promise and the agony of West Virginia for two hundred years, holding endless deposits of the highest-quality coal in the world, yet, at the same time, isolating the people into tiny hamlets that allow them few options to earn a decent living. The handful of natural transportation routes through the state was discovered many years ago by people like Daniel Boone; from then on, anything beyond what meager access the land offered had to be chopped and blasted from it at a frightening cost. State officials estimate that to build a mile of four-lane highway in West Virginia today costs as much as $25 million, more than four times the cost of the same road in, say, Iowa. Just one outcropping at the center of Interstate 64 south of Charleston cost nearly $75 million to move.

But federally funded road construction in West Virginia is booming. Why? Because Byrd has insisted on it. And what's under way is just part of the story. You only need to look at the variety of "studies" that have been inserted into various appropriations bills—a million to study upgrading this route, two million for that one—to appreciate that these seeds will soon be blossoming into unstoppable $500 million projects.

It was that same insistence that got the Stonewall Jackson dam near Clarksburg finished—at a cost of approximately $250 million, making it the most expensive monument to the man who, to date, has been West Virginia's most famous son and finds so many civic projects named for him. But not for long. After all, General Thomas Jackson merely won some battles in a losing war. Students of state politics think Jackson's legacy will one day be surpassed by a man who's brought the same strategic brilliance and religious fervor to another sort of civil war, this one over the government's money and this one a winning effort. Already, for instance, the new high school in Clarksburg carries the name "Robert C. Byrd" over the entrance portal. And no wonder. Byrd has particularly blessed the town of 18,000, first through a huge upgrade of its tiny airport (in an attempt to attract aircraft maintenance work from around the country), then by setting up an aviation training center and most recently by decreeing that the Federal Bureau of Investigation move its aging fingerprint center here from Washington. It's a prize pork chop that includes a $250 million building and a network of road improvements.

Back on the road, if you were to detour west of Clarksburg along Route 50, you'd come to Parkersburg along the Ohio River. Here the government has a new headquarters for the Bureau of Public Debt, the agency that keeps track of the soon-to-be $4 trillion that the government has borrowed.

There aren't many pork landmarks between Clarksburg and Charleston. The center of the state has few people and little to recommend it. A series of old dams in obscure places stands as the legacy of another of the state's senators, Jennings Randolph, who was elected the same day as Byrd and who headed the Public Works Committee until he retired in 1984. He was an unrepentant New Dealer who believed that pouring concrete was the key to prosperity, a thesis that the barren landscape of central West Virginia would tend to disprove. But they're still trying, around the town of Buckhannon, for instance, where one of the old Appalachian Highway plans is being resurrected with new money. And far to the east, in the magnificent, unspoiled Monongahela National

Forest, is the $75 million radio telescope that Dick Darman gave to
Byrd as an enticement to get money for the Nicaraguan contras in
a recent pork deal.

In Charleston, the state capital, which has new airport facilities
and a new National Guard armory—thanks to the federal taxpayers—folks wait in anticipation for the groundbreaking of the new
$80 million federal courthouse while they enjoy new federal parks
along the Kanawha River. Both projects will surely offer work to
those who arrive at the brand-new federal Job Corps center.
There's work, too, farther to the west in Huntington, the state's
second-largest city, where much federal money is restoring the
historic Keith-Albee Theater into a cineplex, finishing an addition
to the David Harris Riverfront Park and building a new Air National Guard center.

From Charleston, it takes about an hour to drive southeast to
Beckley on the engineering marvel known as Interstate 64, which
dips and soars and dodges its way among the increasingly tight
mountain folds. Just before you get to Beckley, a few miles to the
east, runs the New River Gorge, which the National Park Service
is spending tens of millions of dollars to transform into a
whitewater-rafting paradise and the heart of the state's booming
tourism industry. Thanks to yet more federal money that's being
pumped into upgrading Route 19 and other nearby roads, even the
mined-out areas around Fayetteville are slowly being reborn as
vacation destinations. The biggest problem is the shortage of motel
rooms for the thousands of visitors who come in the spring and fall,
when the water runs fast. Could it be that tax dollars are even now
being earmarked for velvet paintings, magic-finger beds and other
essential motel furnishings?

The city of Beckley and its surrounding area, with 40,000 people, is becoming its own kind of wonderland. Aside from roads,
Byrd has steered about $200 million in new federal money to the
city that has long been known as the capital of the state's coal
belt—and more recently as the home of Bob Byrd. Near the airport, there's an agricultural research station. Across the road lies
the lavish National Mine Safety Institute. Ground will soon be
broken on a new federal building downtown as well as for a new
federal prison. Despite the fact that the state's veteran population
is declining, Beckley has not only managed to keep its veterans
hospital but to *expand* it with a new clinic. The Internal Revenue
Service is shifting its research facility here. There's even a move

afoot to build a statue of Byrd in the town center. It would only be appropriate that this, too, be cast with federal funds.

Already the Robert C. Byrd Highway runs west through the town of Crab Orchard (where Byrd worked as a butcher and taught Sunday school while starting his career in politics) and ends in Sophia (where—could this just be a coincidence?—Byrd also lived earlier in his life). Cutting through the center of Sophia is Silk Creek, a typical mountain stream which, from time to time, used to overflow its banks. Not anymore. In a showy display of man conquering nature, the federal government has brought it to heel—stabilizing its banks with tons of rocks and bridging it with a series of concrete-and-steel overpasses. Residents can now get to their trailer parks whatever the weather.

There is, too, a world beyond Sophia. But you can forget about seeing it on a day-trip. From there on, the map looks like a nest of angry snakes writhing among the tiny dots that signify coal-mining hamlets: places called War, Bias, Bald Knob, Matewan, Sarah Ann and Cinderella. Byrd's presence is known here as well. The Coalfields Expressway is under way, as is a 150-mile loop along the entire western border of the state, a public works project that is unimaginably expensive.

Already well along are a series of flood-control ventures on the Tug Fork and Big Sandy rivers, which define the western border of the state. These have long been nasty, unpredictable rivers with a tendency to flood their banks and wreak havoc on anyone unlucky or foolish enough to live too close. But bad luck would no longer seem to explain the condition of the 4,000 citizens of Williamson, who've been inundated by the Tug Fork four times in the last twenty years. Now the town has a fifty-foot steel-and-concrete wall surrounding it, another engineering marvel that's part of a *billion dollars'* worth of dams and flood-control projects for the area. "It is absolutely one of a kind," a spokesman for the Army Corps of Engineers told *Congressional Quarterly* magazine. "It is the most remarkable structure of its kind in the country, maybe in the world." The magazine noted that Byrd had lifted the federal requirement that the local government share some of the cost of construction. The good senator also came to the rescue when the Corps said that the project wouldn't meet its own cost-benefit rules. (A project is supposed to bring economic benefits equal to its cost—but, like all the really great pork, this one didn't come close.) Byrd suspended the rule.

There is the promise of more to come. Here, too, one finds evidence of "studies" of various rivers and lakes, studies that one day will be "site purchases" and finally "project development funds." The dwindling population of southern West Virginia will certainly be dry, if nothing else.

So a day—and a couple billion dollars—later, there you are at the end of the rainbow, at the end of one of the great money trails in the history of politics. It's exhausting, exhilarating, amazing. But if you're Bob Byrd, you just go back to the beginning and start over again.

To understand why Byrd won't stop, you have to understand where he started. It wasn't really Beckley; it wasn't even Sophia. That town backs up to a mountain, and if you head up over a twisty narrow road that skirts along the edge of five-hundred-foot ravines until you start to plunge down the other side, thinking for a moment that you're going to drive straight into the creek that runs like a tiny crack at the base of two soaring mountains, you'll come to Stotesbury, a onetime coal-mining camp that is Byrd's hometown. This is the start of coal country. Beyond Stotesbury are a thousand *more* Stotesburys, tucked into the crevices of endless coal-filled hills. From here west is a singular part of America, a remote region of proud, stubborn people that was home to the bloody Hatfield-McCoy feud a hundred years ago and later the coalfield wars in which miners and management killed each other by the dozen. Coal country is a place of scattered settlements called hollows—hollers, if you live there—where the same families have lived for generations, where they speak their own dialect of English and where they practice some mighty strange customs, such as worshipping rattlesnakes in church.

Byrd grew up on the edge of that world, but very much a part of it. Not the story of Abraham Lincoln, exactly, but about as close as one gets in modern politics. He came out over that hill and by sheer force of will worked his way back from Sophia to Crab Orchard to Beckley to Charleston to Washington and finally to the imperial suite of offices he occupies in the northwest corner of the Capitol. But he never forgot the holler.

He was actually born Cornelius Calvin Sale, Jr., to a North Carolina couple in 1917. His mother died when he was ten months old, so Cornelius was sent to live with his father's sister, Vlurma, and her husband, Titus Byrd. They settled in Stotesbury, where

Titus worked the mines for two dollars a day, like just about everyone else Byrd knew. It was a classic company town. The arched opening of the mine loomed like a pagan temple high above rows of identical houses that lined the railroad track. Everyone prospered or went hungry with the price of coal. Byrd was too young to witness the bitter, bloody struggle to unionize the miners, a decades-long conflict that tore up West Virginia but finally ended in improved pay and benefits. The memory of that war with "the bosses"—defined as everyone from the mine supervisor to Wall Street investment bankers—still lurks in most West Virginians, as does the collective consciousness of the mines: In the best of times an unrelenting life lived on your belly in a dark, wet shaft with shale falling onto your head and coal dust sucking into your lungs.

The best idea for a slight young boy with a good brain was to stay out of those mines. Byrd told friends that as a boy, he slopped hogs on a small plot his stepfather owned. During the year, he'd go from house to house collecting garbage to feed the beasts. When they slaughtered one, he'd repay everyone with some sausage or a slab of bacon. He walked miles along the railroad tracks to Mark Twain High School, where he made valedictorian and earned a partial college scholarship he couldn't afford to accept. He worked in a gas station and later a grocery store for three years while he studied a butcher's handbook and learned to cut meat for a supermarket in Crab Orchard.

"He was one of the hardest-working people I've ever met," said Thomas Lee Gray, who first worked with him at the Carolina Market. "He came in at 4:30 every morning to prepare his meat cases. He never walked, he ran from counter to counter. He knew every customer's name and usually their children's names."

In fact, he had a photographic memory, which he's used to great advantage in dealing with legislative minutiae. Gray, who runs one of the most successful lumber businesses in the Beckley area, recalled Byrd once coming to his church and asking him the names of the twenty-five people in the choir. "Robert thought they had sung so well. After the ceremony he greeted each one by name. He only got one wrong—and that was because I made a mistake."

Byrd's affection for church was always strong—he's told friends that if he hadn't become a politician, he'd have been a preacher. Folks still talk about his famous Bible class at the Crab Orchard Baptist Church. A few months after he took over the small Sunday school gathering, he was lecturing to standing-room-only crowds of five hundred.

"He was a natural-born leader," said Gray with a grin.

For a man with those gifts, the best job was in politics. So Byrd picked up his fiddle and headed for the hollers with the somewhat cryptic slogan "Byrd by name, Byrd by nature, let's send Byrd to the legislature." Whatever it meant, the voters of Raleigh County bought it and Byrd has never looked back. He has never lost an election, from the state legislature in 1946 to Congress six years later to the Senate in 1958. In fact, his only rough time was when an opponent made an issue of Byrd's onetime membership in the Ku Klux Klan. Byrd said it was because of the Klan's opposition to communism, so West Virginia voters, who have usually been supporters of civil rights, let it pass. Byrd had too much going for him. In a state that had been run more like a colony by various generations of coal barons, steel barons and union barons, Byrd was his own man.

"Robert never fit into the establishment," said Hulett Smith, a former governor who campaigned with Byrd in the early days. "He never took a position against the little man. Never wanted personal gain. He's still that boy from the coal camp."

Judge K. K. Hall, another coal country politician of Byrd's era who now sits on the federal appeals court, told of the time Byrd was first running for the House of Delegates and met with George Tittler, head of the powerful United Mine Workers of America Local 29. "Tittler wanted to make clear to Robert how he needed to vote on certain issues of interest to the mine workers. It had always been that way. But Robert sat there and told him, 'Mr. Tittler, I wear no man's collar.'"

Anyone who's followed Byrd through his career could see that. His independence has been noteworthy in everything from his voting record to his demeanor. At a time of television-conscious politicians, Byrd still styles his hair into a soaring, blue-tinted pompadour and gives windy speeches—a recent one lasted eight hours—crafted in Victorian grammar. For many years he favored cardinal red vests under his suits, a period cloakroom wags called his "aging bellman phase." Byrd seemed unaffected.

Not that he didn't have some insecurities. Judge Hall recalled the young Byrd wincing when he was introduced at West Virginia political events. "They'd say, Let's welcome so-and-so who's a lawyer from here, and this one who's a lawyer from there and then they'd come to Robert. They'd say, 'that butcher and fiddle player from Raleigh County.' One night I remember he said, 'But one day I'll be a lawyer, too.' " And one day he was, taking night school courses while serving in the Senate and earning his J.D. in 1963 at the age of forty-six.

That same sort of drive has been apparent in everything Byrd has done on the Hill. He is obsessed with his work, putting in endless hours and rarely taking a vacation. By any standard Byrd has been a remarkable senator, a larger-than-life character whose exploits are legendary on the Hill, if less well known to the world beyond.

From his early days, he became a protégé of Lyndon Johnson's and learned retail politics. He was rarely in evidence on big issues, but always the man to see for small favors and perks, everything from finding new office furniture to keeping members informed on the voting schedule. "From the very beginning of his days in politics," Hulett Smith said, "Byrd worked his way up by paying attention to what people wanted." He eventually handled such chores as assigning committee staff and controlling certain committee assignments. He also became a master of parliamentary procedure; he knew all the rules of all the fights, having read deep into volumes of Senate precedent that many of his colleagues didn't know existed. He delighted in detail; after all, this was a man who, a former secretary noted, would take outgoing correspondence and hold it up to the light to see if any corrections had been made.

In 1971 he called in his many chits. In a vote that was seen as the triumph of an insider over a glamorous national figure, Byrd beat Ted Kennedy for the majority leader's post. In those days, Byrd had grand ambitions, holding Lincoln as his model. Richard Nixon courted him and even talked him up as a possible Supreme Court appointee. But Byrd's love of the Senate won out, and he turned on Nixon when the president tried to encroach on the Hill. Byrd fought Nixon's attempts to gain control of the budget process and preserved the powers of the special Watergate prosecutor. Those who know him say he long considered the idea of running for president and he declared himself a candidate briefly in 1976 before the voters decided otherwise. Even then, as his politics began to moderate, his style was that of a nineteenth-century politician in a zoom lens age. "You've also got to remember that this was a guy who started his political career with a white sheet over his head," one Senate staffer remarked. "How much farther did he think he was going to get?"

He was the Senate Democrats' leader through their decline in the 1980s, enduring a growing chorus of grumbles that he wasn't the best front man the party could offer. Finally, in 1989 he decided to make a change. He'd also heard the grumblings back home that he hadn't done all that much for his state. Jennings Randolph, the other senator, had always brought home the public works bacon while Byrd tended to weightier matters. But Randolph had retired, and there was a perception that West Virginia was getting shortchanged. "I think he was frustrated in the leader's job and heard folks at home wondering why he couldn't do more," said Mike Willard, one of his former Senate aides. Byrd traded in his trunkful of favors for the job that had the least visibility and the most power: chairman of the Appropriations Committee. He vowed to take care of West Virginia.

He quickly became testament to the truism of Henry Adams: "Power when wielded by abnormal energy is the most serious of facts."

Byrd became, like Tip O'Neill before him, the new embodiment of the welfare state. But rather than sprung from the brow of Hogarth, Byrd was a creation of Dickens, a symbol of leaner, meaner times. Where O'Neill was a bluff giant who gregariously handed out goodies, Byrd was a pinched, reclusive miser who scraped up his own coins first and parceled out the rest one at a time. Oddly, the net effect on total spending has been about the same.

He has been uncorruptible and focused, never touched by a hint of scandal or personal gain. As his former secretary Evelyn Williams noted, "It has served him well that he's never needed to associate with those who have so much of the world's goods called money." In fact, he's been as much the preacher as ever, bringing a messianic zeal to the task of saving West Virginia with pork. "The Senate has always been a religion for him," one staffer remarked. "Appropriations became his reform denomination."

Like any evangelical, he lost no sleep over his convictions. The acquisition of pork coincided perfectly with his belief in the power of the purse. The duty to spend taxpayers' money belongs to the elected officials of Congress, not some appointed bureaucrat. And if Byrd decided West Virginia hadn't been getting its fair share, that was his choice to make.

But whatever the rationale, he's been brutally effective. Though there's no way to chart such matters, anecdotal evidence suggests that Byrd has acquired more pork in a shorter period of time than any member of Congress in history. It comes as no surprise, then, that to call Bob Byrd a saint in West Virginia is to diminish him. They think he's better than that.

You want miracles? "Children had never seen water come out of a tap until he provided the funds to bring water pipes to this area," said Evelyn Williams of Ravenscliff, a coal country hamlet west of Stotesbury. Elsewhere, he's stopped floods and cleaved mountains.

"He's done more good for the people of West Virginia than anybody ever," said Judge Hall with the finality of a not-guilty verdict.

And it's a state, the people who live there will tell you, that needs some good.

"There is a sense here that people are owed something," said Hulett Smith, the son of a former mayor of Beckley who went on to serve a term as governor in the 1960s.

To appreciate West Virginia's feelings, you need only contemplate the common sight of a woman bony and tough as an old chicken leading her withered husband slowly down the street by the elbow while he wheezes air through a gauze face mask into his coal-scarred lungs. Coal mining and its effects aren't the only metaphor for the state, but they are a damn good one. West Virginians feel they've been scraped raw by a couple hundred years worth of the fat boys in Philadelphia, New York and Chicago carting off their resources while leaving nothing behind.

A sense of inferiority and suspicion goes back to the days just before the Civil War, when the state split from Virginia because its inhabitants felt those country gentlemen to the East were spending all the tax money on themselves—and because those simple old hill people were silly enough to oppose slavery. In those days, timber was the favorite resource to haul from the state. When industrialization arrived and coal became king, the state boomed—but not its workers, who were exploited like mules. They had to practically start a revolution before anybody would pay them a decent wage. For a time they were fine, but in the last half century, the boom-bust pattern of the American economy returned with the fury of a berserk roller coaster, running up wages and hopes on a half-dozen occasions then sending them crashing deeper each time. For some reason, the folks who manage things here never seem to get it right even in the good times, forgetting, somehow, to build industry that's insulated from the swings of the business cycle. Like a miner with his jeans full of cash on Friday, it's gone by Monday—and all that's left is a headache. The cruelest joke is that over the past few years, coal production has been at an all-time high, but mining employment has fallen from a peak of 120,000 at the end of World War II to 30,000. The mine owners finally won the war by replacing men with heavy equipment in a technique to shear coal veins called long-wall mining. Unemployment in the coal counties such as McDowell and Wyoming is at more than twice the national average, topping 15 percent, although the state as a whole is close to average.

All Byrd wants is to reverse that history. Explained Bob Brunner, press secretary to Governor Gaston Caperton, "He wants to be the one to move this state from a place where everyone earned their living in a mine or under a chemical pipe or in front of a blast furnace to the information age where we have modern highways and work at jobs in front of computers linked to the rest of the world."

Brunner, who covered Byrd as a reporter in Charleston and Washington, echoes most West Virginians when he says he doesn't see anything wrong with Byrd's actions.

"Is what he's doing so bad? Take the FBI center. They needed one anyway. After it's built, the costs are lower here. People will stay on the job. You're talking about mostly data-processing clerks earning $20,000 a year. In Washington, that's nothing. Here, it's a career. You can support a wife and two kids and buy a house on that. They'd much rather be here than in the tire plant in Akron or the clothing mill in North Carolina."

Brunner, and just about everyone else in West Virginia, will readily tell you that the state has always had few federal government jobs, particularly military bases and weapons plants.

Then there's roads—a very sore point to bring up with any native. "There's an obsession with them," admits Brunner. "People see it as a lifeline. It's how kids get to school, people get to work, to the hospital. And we've never felt they were any good."

The first problem is that you need lots of them because people live so spread out. Despite the waves of industry that brought chemical plants and timber plants as well as steel mills, the state remains the second most rural in the nation, with almost two thirds of the 1.7 million population living outside urban areas. Second, they are ungodly expensive to build; not only is the terrain terrible, but the creases people tuck themselves into can be dauntingly remote. Third—and this goes back to the old inferiority—people here think they're way behind the rest of America when it comes to roads.

The same sort of thinking applies to rivers. Things just aren't that simple to fix in West Virginia. Bill Byrd, who edits *The Beckley Herald* and is not related to the senator, remembered when he first went to the southwestern end of the state to cover the flooding at Williamson twenty years ago. Although his family has roots in the northern part of the state, he spent much of his youth elsewhere.

"I'd never been down there. I was at a meeting where they were talking about how the Tug Fork kept coming over its banks and filling up the town. I remember thinking, why not just move the people out? Move the town. I asked someone. But they told me, 'You can't do that. Everybody in West Virginia lives along rivers and creeks because that's where the only flat land is. And sometimes creeks flood. Are you going to move everybody?'"

Questions like that made David Greenfield uncomfortable. As editor of *The Charleston Daily Mail,* he occupied the other end of pork's political spectrum from Bill Byrd: a rare conservative who found himself a natural, if reluctant, adversary to Senator Byrd's big-spending ways.

"We have difficulty reconciling what he brings to the state against our sense that this kind of spending has to stop," Greenfield said, choosing his words like finger holds on a cliff face. "Operating under the current system, we can't blame him for getting what he can. We tend to look at projects on a case-by-case basis. The FBI fingerprint lab may actually save taxpayers' money. We've criticized him on the wildlife center. The two-hundred-million-dollar Stonewall Jackson dam was way out of line. We think the whole highway bill is too expensive. But it's considered totally unpatriotic to criticize Byrd.

"People assume the Senate Appropriations Committee chairman has the right and the ability to take his share. They think he's outsmarting everyone up there in Washington, and they admire him for it. While they may be proud in West Virginia, they're not above taking a good dose of help."

Greenfield's discomfort would be amplified by anyone not actually living in the state. While there must be plenty of fine people there, anyone who's spent time in West Virginia could be tempted to ask some intemperate questions. Such as *If a bunch of stubborn hill folk want to live in a godforsaken place with no means of support, no decent roads and the certainty that once every few months the furies of nature will descend on them like the plagues of Job, all because they like to hunt squirrels in their front yards, why the hell do I have to subsidize them?* Or, more simply, *Show me where in the Constitution it says everyone's got a right to a four-lane highway that costs more than the gross domestic product of Mongolia.*

But one refrains from that sort of question in our enlightened society. What has been substituted are the sort of dry economic queries that find their way into reports that serve as drink coasters for harried Hill staffers. Questions like *Can this money make a difference? Is West Virginia getting more than its fair share compared to other states with equal needs? Why are we spending more and more money on a state where people are leaving at a rate of 20,000 a year?*

Not that it has mattered. Asked or not, the reality is that what West Virginia has gotten has been based on the power and the will of one man: Robert C. Byrd. His mastery of the Senate has been awesome, evoking legends like Daniel Webster and John C. Calhoun. His maneuvering in budget matters proves that he has the ability to create change—as few in Congress ever can. But by any sort of broad political standard, he has chosen to use those skills and experience for trivial ends. His legacy will be one of pettiness, but worse, in his own way, he may have ruined the process he reveres. That there is a colossal financial mess facing the country is not open to debate. Yet Byrd, with his vast powers, offers no solutions of his own. He simply carries out his role as spender in chief and does it with frightening efficiency. You can look at Byrd as blameless, as many on Capitol Hill do, a force of nature playing his appointed role in the system. But clearly he knows better. He studied to be a statesman and has acquired all the tools. But when it comes time to use them, he proves himself to be just a semi-skilled local pol hiring himself out cheap.

Whose fault is that? The question is a crucial one. And certainly you could look for an answer among all the great political seers who are currently shaking their heads about the failures of American democracy. Or, you could start with one Andrew "Trap" Underwood, a resident of Crab Orchard and a longtime friend of Byrd's. Sitting in the living room of his home on Wilcox Street overlooking Robert C. Byrd Highway, with the daytime game shows turned up loud to compensate for deafness caused by half a lifetime working a coal-cutting machine in a three-foot-high tunnel, Trap tells some homey old stories about campaigning with "Robert," about fiddling and teaching him to drive, about trying to convince the Republican railworkers that Byrd was on their side, and about the hard times in the coal camps.

Needless to say, he thinks the world of the senator. "Smartest man I ever met," he said. "And a good man. He's had his hand in just about anything we've got around here."

But he doesn't see his friend much anymore. Byrd only comes back maybe once a year. So he wonders if a visitor might deliver a message. What Trap wants to ask his old pal Senator Byrd, the legislative giant, the most powerful man on Capitol Hill, is this: Can I get better mail delivery?

"If you see him, ask him if he can get the darn Post Office to carry the mail up here to Wilcox Street. They make us walk down the hill to get it now."

That's all, at least for now. And maybe that's all that any voter wants from his politicians. No grand visions of making the world a better place, no reshaping the community of man. Maybe he just wants a very personal sort of government—a service bureau, really—that provides some of the simple pleasures of life *free of charge*. On the one hand, it seems natural. On the other, kind of greedy, petty and cynical, breeding—what else?—a government of greed, pettiness and cynicism. But there's nothing new here. As the consummate cynic H. L. Mencken used to say sixty years ago, "Democracy is the theory that the common people know what they want—and deserve to get it good and hard."

And there in the living room of a retired coal miner's modest home is the tension of democracy. Personal wants aside, we're all in the pot together. So just because Trap Underwood needs Bob Byrd, do we all have to get him so good and hard?

# 11

# THE BOAR WARS

O

N A WARM, BREEZY AFTERNOON IN MID-JUNE OF 1991, UN-
der a cloudless blue sky, a dozen men in suits stood on the lawn
behind the Capitol in front of TV cameras. The gusting wind
mussed strands of hair carefully combed over bald spots and top-
pled cardboard charts as the men waited for television technicians
to tell them when the equipment was ready to roll.

This was, after all, a photo opportunity, a chance to win a tiny
moment of video immortality by offering an attractive backdrop to
some news director starved for "visuals" out there on the great sat-
ellite pathway that joins us as a nation. And certainly the pure white
dome set against the summer sky made a stunning picture—though
as Washington photo ops went, this one had a C-list talent pool.
With one exception, there was a bunch of no-name backbenchers
standing around the clump of microphones and self-consciously
straightening their ties. There was Harris Fawell, a lean, white-
haired former Illinois judge; Bob Walker, a somewhat eccentric
Pennsylvania congressman who had waged a long, lonely war
against pork; Chris Cox, a young former Reagan administration aide

who represented Orange County, California, and had decided that pork was an issue with some juice to it; Mel Hancock, who fancied himself a fiscal tightwad from the Missouri Ozarks; Tim Penny, an intense Minnesota farm boy with a zeal for untangling the budget; and Bob Smith, looking like the high school history teacher he once had been in his baggy blue blazer, gray slacks, blue button-down shirt and red tie. The exception was John McCain, whose celebrity was unwanted. The senator from Arizona had become a household name as one of the Keating Five, the senators who had performed various favors for Charles Keating, Jr., the sleaziest of the sleazeball savings-and-loan con men. Oddly, McCain had done little for Keating beyond putting in a good word here and there; his crime was that he was the tycoon's friend, which cast serious doubt on his social judgment but left his integrity mostly intact.

With a few others, this ragged band made up the remnants of the Porkbusters. The initial outrage that followed the 1990 budget deal had cooled somewhat, and for a variety of reasons, about half the congressmen who originally backed the notion of a bill to slice out some of the pork from the fiscal 1991 budget had dropped out of sight. Even Dan Coats, who'd come so close with the Philadelphia shipyard vote, was nowhere to be seen. But the hard-core reformers had persevered, and after hundreds of hours of staff work, the Spending Priority Reform Act of 1991, otherwise known as the "Porkbusters Bill," was ready to be introduced. The response was underwhelming.

As a group of bored Capitol Hill reporters rolled their eyes at the anticipated futility of this venture, Smith began with the mantra of the fiscal conservative: "As Senator Everett Dirksen once said, a billion here, a billion there, and pretty soon you're talking about real money."

What the Porkbusters had come up with was an even billion dollars spread over 325 projects. They were asking Congress to stop all of them and return the unspent funds to the national Treasury on the grounds that the projects violated all sorts of congressional rules, to say nothing of common decency.

Topping the list were some of the year's pork hits: the Lawrence Welk Museum, Steamtown USA, the Hatfield-McCoy feud study, the memorial to William McKinley's in-laws and the study of "the handling of animal manure and the development of resolution techniques to address conflicts between producers and the general public."

"Who is kidding whom?" Smith wondered. "If you asked the American people if their tax dollars should be used to finance these projects, they would probably hit you over the head with their pocketbooks."

Not that everything is quite so ridiculous, Harris Fawell cautioned. Pork, when you pry into it, is more complicated than it seems.

"Pork is subjective, and we've tried to be fair," Fawell said. "There are some projects we can all agree on, and some that are going to be more controversial. Maybe we can agree that funding a Cleveland theater project from Section Eight low-income housing money is wrong, but there's money here for Children's Hospital in San Diego. On the face of it, how could you object?"

Who could argue with elderly housing rehabilitation in New Orleans or a drug-abuse center in Cleveland?

"They are not all bad projects," Smith conceded, "but they are all unfair. Maybe there's nothing wrong with money going to a children's hospital in San Diego, but what about all the other children's hospitals in the country? Everything in this bill is here because somebody broke Congress's own rules to put it in. It reflects the fact that we've got no sense of priorities in how we spend money. Maybe these projects are needed, maybe not, but we know that they got in through political power, not merit."

The bill had a broader purpose, they said.

"This is a modest attempt to call attention to a serious problem," Smith continued. "The federal budget process is broken."

Their ultimate aim was to spark some kind of process reform such as giving the president the power of line-item veto, meaning he could strike out single spending items and force Congress to override him instead of having to veto an entire bill to get out a paragraph or two. Or maybe they could prompt Congress simply to enforce its own rules, which would technically prohibit most of the monkey business needed to get pork into place.

"If a project is worth it, we should be willing to vote on it," Smith said.

McCain said their effort had taken on greater urgency when considered in the context of a federal government that is bleeding red ink. "In the next year or two, we're likely to spend more on interest than on national defense. If you said that ten years ago, people would have called you crazy. But here it is. If members of Congress don't support this legislation, then they're part of the problem."

The bill itself was a remarkable achievement. The Porkbusters—or more precisely their staffs working with several taxpayer lobbying groups—had done an exhausting job of setting out a very strict pork test and seeing that each project on the list met it. The fifty-six-page bill contained the purest pork ever discovered by man, Grade A connoisseur's pork that, for those who know how difficult it is to find this stuff, was a marvel to behold.

"I wanted it to be unchallengable," said Smith.

The tests were these:

- Had the spending item been authorized by the proper committee in Congress?
- Had it been the subject of hearings?
- Had it been added during a conference committee even though neither the House nor Senate bill had contained it?
- Had it been awarded competitively?
- Had it been "earmarked," that is, had a government agency been told to spend money on a specific project?
- Did it bear any relationship to the agency that was supposed to pay for it?
- Was it of purely local interest with no national or regional merit?

A project had to meet three or more of these tests to make it into the bill.

Staffers such as Tom Hodson of Smith's office and Fawell's aide Kristin Jacobson had worn their eyes bloodshot tracing the history of thousands of items that often appeared as cryptic paragraphs in the final budget bill. They deciphered how each one had gotten there by hunting back through committee reports and legislative language.

The billion dollars they came up with was by no means comprehensive, and the strictness of their definition left out all sorts of spending that could reasonably be defined as pork. But the precision of their research left no doubt that they had isolated the essence of pork. As such, it served as a sort of laboratory sample that, under analysis, might reveal some broader truths. For instance, just by assaying the sample, it was possible to establish a rough breakdown of the various types of pork.

*Rotten pork.* About 40 percent of the pork was goofy stuff that ought not to have been funded—the sort of projects that get a quick chuckle from most people but in older conservatives causes a sharp rush of blood to the brain that can result in strokes. Among the other stinkers that made the list were things like the project to develop the Hawaiian handicrafts industry, a second visitors' center for Fort Larned in Kansas, the ongoing Arkansas catfish farm empire, Oregon's new seafood consumer center and the wave of cultural spending on arts and entertainment centers in places such as Newark, Cleveland, Philadelphia, Miami and Lynn, Massachusetts.

Universities seemed to be a prime source of excess, including such handouts as $3 million to rehab buildings at two Tennessee colleges; tens of millions from the Federal Buildings Fund, which is not allowed to provide for private entities but nonetheless gave to all manner of schools and hospitals, including in one of the more bizarre three-cushion billiard shots of the season, a grant to the Philadelphia Urban League to establish a drug-abatement research program at Texas A&M University.

In the category of pure waste, too, would go the blatant power play of the Philadelphia Naval Shipyard, typical of many cases where bureaucrats have clearly decided they don't want to spend money and Congress insists that they must.

*Greasy pork.* The next 20 percent was made up of projects that had some value even though they weren't critical and arguably were not the sort of thing the federal government ought to be doing—especially when the budget was so far out of balance. Roads were the greatest culprit here. Forget questionable interstate expansions and low-use highways to nowhere; in Iowa alone the feds were being told to rebuild the state road from Keokuk to Dubuque, then fix Fifth Street over in Waterloo and extend the highway in Ottumwa—and while they were at it, they had to tear down an old factory in that same Ottumwa as well as plan the economic revitalization for the lucky citizens of Sioux City.

Not that Iowa was the only place receiving special treatment. Among those getting a free federal shine were State Route 509 in Tacoma, Washington; Ninth Street in Provo, Utah; Lakeview Road in Stillwater, Oklahoma; and Leopard Drive in Texarkana, Texas. There was also money for things like public safety equipment for Lawrence, Massachusetts and bridge lights for Bay City, Michigan.

*Charity pork.* The next 20 percent were things whose purpose was harder to challenge because the underlying need was so apparent. Still, they flunked the pork test on several counts. Among these projects were things such as funds for a residential treatment center for chemically addicted battered women and children in San Bernardino—what ice-hearted bastard is going to cut that out?—low-income housing in St. Louis, a sports program for children living in public housing in Fort Meyers, Florida, and a wheelchair ramp for the health clinic in Colville, Washington.

Each item raised that fundamental debate of whether Uncle Sam should try to solve all the country's social problems or whether his main responsibility is to run a sound national economy. That debate ran all between the lines of the Porkbusters Bill. What could hurt, a few million dollars for an old folks' home in Iowa? But multiply that times a thousand similar projects, then go to the bank to borrow money to pay for them, then keep funding them year after year, and they could hurt plenty.

Then there was the less abstract argument: the government already had dozens of programs to take care of these very needs. Hundreds of billions of dollars were being spent annually on everything from food stamps to Medicaid to Social Security. Squirreled away in every corner of the budget were funds for women, children, poor women with children, battered women with poor children, children with children. Maybe there wasn't enough money, or maybe the needs kept growing to exceed the funds available. But there was supposed to be a system for dealing with these problems. The question the Porkbusters Bill asked is, Haven't we gone too far in letting powerful individuals cheat that system?

*Trophy pork.* The final 20 percent was for things the government was going to do anyway; they just got done unfairly, which further distorted the system. The success of the most skilled porkers tells everyone else that the guiding ethic on the Hill is stealth, cunning and power, not truth, justice and the American way. What is supposed to be the temple of civility and national interest becomes a seedy den of self-interest and political greed—because those are the measures of success. Some university was probably going to get a grant to research strategic materials, whatever they are, because that's the sort of thing the federal government is supposed to research. But did it have to be the Rochester Institute of Technology merely because it had a skilled lobbyist or a well-positioned congressman?

There's even a further argument to be made that subverting the process ruins it *especially* for those who need the help. Let's say there's a crisis brewing in the deterioration of the nation's highways. And let's say, as the Porkbusters Bill made clear, that powerful legislators in a handful of states like West Virginia, New Jersey, New York and Iowa manage to get what they need through the pork process. Where does that leave everyone else? The pressure that's supposed to make the system respond is artificially relieved. The same goes for housing, health care or any of ten dozen other social needs. If a few people can prosper by working around the system, then the system doesn't work. If drug treatment or tax reform or whatever is a good idea, by giving those benefits only to those who are clever enough or rich enough to know how to lobby for them, you lessen the chance of any meaningful change for everyone else.

Not that the press conference dealt with these issues in quite this detail. Or any of this detail. Washington press conferences are not for discussing ideas, only for presenting images. But the material was there for anyone who chose to mine it. In its own way, the Porkbusters Bill was a major accomplishment, a rare window into the world of government.

It also contained the seeds of its own destruction. Smith's fear was that it would drown in specifics. The strength of its precision could also be its downfall in that anytime you single out the actions of individual members of Congress, they'll react like cornered badgers. Which is more or less what happened.

The worst fate fell on John McCain, who hadn't done his homework. It turned out that there were several Arizona projects in the bill, and someone leaked to the press the fact that McCain had lobbied for them with the Appropriations Committee. Coincidentally, Arizona's other senator, Dennis DeConcini, was a member of that committee.

"McCain Attacks 'Pork' Projects, Then Finds He Backed 3 in State," the headline in *The Arizona Republic* read.

"It seems pretty weird," the story quoted DeConcini's press secretary, Bob Maynes, as saying with deft malice. "He appears to have done exactly what he is criticizing."

And the poor fellow handled it badly, sputtering and stammering and finally backtracking to say that they were, indeed, good projects.

The *Republic*'s editorial page, a bastion of conservatism, gave him what he had coming: "Had McCain attacked the process and even singled out those three Arizona projects as examples of extravagant spending, he could have made an important point. Instead, he was left defending his pet projects while criticizing everyone else's pork barreling. And that is precisely why Congress cannot get spending under control."

The *Chicago Tribune* mocked Dennis Hastert, one of the co-sponsors, for putting in a project supported by Bob Michel, the House minority leader from Peoria. Several months earlier, the *Trib* said, Hastert had asked the leader to help preserve funding for a government lab in his district. Now Hastert was trying to cut out the unauthorized funds Michel had wheedled to relocate a public housing project in Peoria. Though he's the Republican leader, Michel is a man who takes his pork seriously, routinely touting all manner of grants, studies and defense contracts in a series of press releases to voters back home. And Hastert had the nerve to question one of those? Some loyalty.

Even Smith got sidetracked when the New Hampshire press noted that his bill would cut a $1.7 million highway bypass study for Conway. Warren Rudman, the state's other senator and the coauthor of the Gramm-Rudman deficit reduction bill, had pushed it through Appropriations. Smith had to concede that he thought it was a good project, it just hadn't gone through the process properly. Rudman's spokesman smirked that *his* boss had no problem with the way it was done and that he'd continue to fight for funds for the people of New Hampshire.

The appropriators could be heard whispering *No one is clean. No one is clean.*

But other than these geek-show stories, the bill got little press. The reporters who serve as racetrack touts on the Hill had already written it off.

Sitting in his sparsely decorated office a few days later, Smith was undeterred. He knew he'd made some kind of impact because of the hostile glares and veiled threats he was getting.

"I've been told I'm tampering with the process. That I'm doing this at my own peril, that sort of thing." He wouldn't say by whom. Although he is a big man with a busted nose and a navy veteran with a tour in Vietnam behind him, Smith is a soft-spoken gentleman whose temperament fits with the decorum of the Senate. He isn't about to finger a fellow senator. He also has a respect for the process of government that he learned as a history teacher and president of the school board in Wolfeboro, a town of 4,000 on the shores of the summer haven of Lake Winnipesaukee.

But he said his work on the bill had made him more convinced than ever that something like it had to be done.

"Pork is about money spent by influence rather than merit. I'm out to change that. People throughout the country say they're outraged with this, but are they willing to do anything about it?"

His own experience had told him that voters are more concerned and more astute than many politicians are willing to give them credit for. When he ran for the Senate in 1990, the Pentagon was going to close Pease Air Force base in New Hampshire.

"I said, 'Good, they ought to close it. It's outdated. It's a waste.' My opponents in the primary and general election went after me for that. But the issue never caught on. I made no apologies; I explained to voters that I thought fighting to keep the base open was wrong, and they agreed with me. People will respond when you explain things to them. But I think too many politicians are afraid.

"Maybe we need to do something like they're doing with that base-closing commission. You should look at that. Get an outside body that's insulated from politics to make some spending decisions. Part of me would hate to see it, because we'd be admitting we don't have the courage to make hard calls. But we need *somebody* to set priorities around here."

His own priority was to round up some cosponsors for Porkbusters and bring it up for a vote. Time was critical. Whatever its chances for success, the bill had one potentially fatal problem from the start: the clock was ticking. After all, it had taken a half year just to figure out the pork in the 1991 budget. The cardinals were already half done with the budget for 1992. If Smith didn't get a vote soon, all the money would already be spent. Still, he was optimistic. It would be a few months before the ex-teacher would get one of the great educations of his life.

## 12

# STOP ME BEFORE I SPEND AGAIN

A STRANGE THING HAPPENED ON CAPITOL HILL ONE DAY IN the summer of 1991. Pork was trimmed and money was saved.

While the freight trains of the major spending bills were being loaded and coaled in the Appropriations Committee's private conference rooms, seven men held a series of painfully public hearings at which they decided to shut down a collection of useless military bases. Remarkably, they succeeded.

Their venue was the vast oval chamber of the House Ways and Means Committee on the first floor of the Longworth Building, the scene of so much fiscal bloodshed over the years that it was better thought of as a slaughterhouse than a hearing room. Here, under the watchful portraits of Ways and Means legends—including that greatest of all tax accountants and friend to bartenders and cheap blondes throughout Washington, Wilbur Mills—the carcass of the taxpayer had been slit and quartered for many years. Under the gold stars embedded in the ceiling of this very room, for instance, a series of unconscionable lies, half-truths and distortions about the state of the economy has been offered by an endless procession of grim but self-assured presidential advisers over the years—up to and most certainly including those of the current administration. *What recession, Mr. Chairman?* they've all more or less said.

Equally bad deeds have occurred just outside the great doors in the cramped hallway known as Gucci Gulch, immortalized in Jeffrey Birnbaum and Alan Murray's entertaining—no kidding—account of the 1986 tax reform bill, *Showdown at Gucci Gulch*. On the day of a key vote, they wrote, "A few of the lobbyists huddle round the back door . . . hoping for one last chance to make a pitch before the vote. The desperation in their voices makes it clear that big money is at stake. Their expensive suits and shiny Italian shoes give this hallway its nickname." What the lobbyists were hoping for was to have someone insert all manner of special breaks and loopholes into the law for the sole benefit of their clients, ranging from Texas drilling companies to Maine insurance firms to rich old ladies in Ohio. And for the most part, they have oozed their way to success. If you squint, you can still see some oily patches on the walls from those long mornings of leaning and waiting in 1986.

But the most unspeakable things have happened in the anterooms off the main chamber. Here, and over at the Senate Finance Committee, is the true home of tax pork, that elusive subspecies of the pork barrel that doesn't involve money going out, but rather money *not coming in*. Tax pork usually comes in the form of what are called targeted tax breaks or, in the slang of the Hill, rifle shots—so named for the precision with which they find their beneficiary. Most often the break is a favor to an industry or even a specific company or individual that gets put into the tax code because somebody made a special pleading to a member of Congress who had the power to change the law. And of course in each case, the beneficiary believes he has a great case as to why he shouldn't have to pay the tax—as does probably everyone in the country who pays taxes, the difference being that only a lucky few ever find a sympathetic ear.

But of course, one man's tax break is another man's tax bill. Every special break means a dollar not received by the Treasury and thus a dollar that either has to come from someone else or has to be borrowed. So each favor—and most years there are plenty of them—has to be paid for. Birnbaum and Murray write of the day Ways and Means chairman Dan Rostenkowski sat down at 7 A.M. and started calling key Congress members with a simple question: "What do you need?" By the end of that bloody day, he'd given away $5 billion in taxpayers' money. A total of $20 billion in special breaks was given out in 1986, which was then thought to be an all-time record. (But the 1991 budget contained $27.4 billion in special-interest breaks, according to an analysis by Citizens Against Government Waste.) "It was Santa's workshop in October," Congressman Tom Downey of Long Island told *The Wall Street Journal.* Santa's helpers were Rostenkowski and Robert Packwood, the top Republican on the Senate Finance Committee and a man with a limitless capacity for empathy with those earning in the high six figures.

These numbers are just estimates, though, since trying to decipher tax breaks makes the appropriations process seem like child's play. Two of the best investigative reporters in the country, Donald Barlett and James Steele of *The Philadelphia Inquirer,* spent 15 months tracking down just a handful of the thousands of special tax breaks layered into the 1986 tax reform act. Predictably, the members and staffs of the tax-writing committees in Congress, a cult of self-protective *Übermenschen* not unlike the cardinals, insisted that the breaks were secret. In other words, the public had no right to know how its money was being spent. Barlett and Steele had to travel all over the country and review thousands of pages of public records to piece together the meaning of deliberately vague language inserted into the bill.

This is the sort of wording they unraveled, the sort that is routinely produced by the Ways and Means empire:

"In the case of any pre-1987 open year, neither the United States nor the Virgin Islands shall impose an income tax on non–Virgin Island source income derived from transactions described in clause (ii) by one or more corporations which were formed in Delaware on or about March 6, 1981 . . ."

*Translation:* A man named William M. Lansdale, a pal of Ronald Reagan and California Governor George Deukmejian, wouldn't have to pay Uncle Sam about $4.5 million on some investments because somebody on the Hill did him a favor.

Or "The amendments made by section 201 shall not apply to any property placed in service pursuant to a master plan which is clearly identifiable as of March 1, 1986, for any project described in any of the following subparagraphs of this paragraph . . ."

*Translation:* A $500 million break for a Texas wheeler-dealer who wanted to build an oil pipeline and had lots of friends in Washington, including former Speaker Jim Wright and Senator Lloyd Bentsen.

But don't try this at home, kids. Sifting through a tax bill could make your eyeballs explode—as it is intended to do. Take it from Congressman Phil Crane, who once said, "Unless you are a Sherlock Holmes, you cannot necessarily know what all these references are alluding to." Starting with Crane, not many members of Congress are anything like Sherlock Holmes, though there are more than a few Professor Moriartys.

And like all archcriminals, they have evolved a keen rationale for their behavior. The explanation is that all these special favors—whether it's tax pork or any of the various other forms of give-aways—are the glue that holds a complicated piece of legislation together. As Birnbaum and Murray wrote of the giant 1986 tax bill, even the most hair-shirted congressional reformers bought into the scheme. "If ten or fifteen billion dollars in temporary transition rules would enable Congress to close several hundred billions of dollars' worth of permanent tax loopholes, then they were willing to go along." This is the dirty business of legislation, the pros will tell you, inadvertently confirming that your average member of Congress would not have voted for this revolutionary reform because it was good for the country, but only because it gave him the chance to slop a handful of constituents who were concerned that their profit margins might be slipping below 20 percent. Congress has as much as admitted that, with rare exceptions, it can't make the hard decisions about the country's future that it was designed to make.

So the hearing room of the Ways and Means Committee was awash in irony that day in late June when the members of the Defense Base Closing and Realignment Commission started tossing military facilities onto the ash heap of history—and did it in the bright light of day. To be sure, one could still hear cries of anguish; however, they came not from taxpayers but from members of Congress.

To untrained eyes, the spectacle was at once pathetic and alarming. Grown men with quivering lips seemed on the verge of throwing tantrums as they kept repeating the word "Outrage!" and making dire pronouncements about how "They won't get away with this!" as they were followed by packs of notebook- and camera-toting reporters from back home. The home-press nodded sympathetically and took down every bleat. As a rule, in cases where government money is at stake the vigilant press assumes its role as community booster and views its representative, whom it may have been pounding the day before, as the village champion. The congressmen respond by assuming a pose of anguished fury, indignant to the point of trembling that the government could, even for a minute, consider taking away *the fair share* of Dumb Fork, South Dakota, or Tumbleweed, Texas.

The worst practitioner that day was Arlen Specter, the Pennsylvania senator who was trying to protect—*surprise!*—the Philadelphia Naval Shipyard. A man with a dyspeptic expression at the best of times, that morning Specter looked like his liver was leaking bile.

"It looks like the Pentagon is declaring war on Pennsylvania!" he told any television camera that would listen. But, of course, war on Pennsylvania was not really what concerned this statesman and military strategist. The fragile state of the nation's security was what troubled him.

"I don't think these installations should be kept open as a matter of local economy," he propounded, to the disbelief of anyone within earshot and certainly to anyone listening in Pennsylvania. "The central issue is national defense. I don't think there's any way you can close it and maintain readiness."

Now why hadn't General Colin Powell, the chairman of the Joint Chiefs of Staff, thought of that when he recommended to the commission which bases should be closed? Sure, he'd just stage-managed the most brilliant military victory in U.S. history in the Persian Gulf, but why hadn't he consulted the former district attorney from Philadelphia when deciding how to realign the global force structure of the Defense Department? Did Powell think for a moment that Specter would be so parochial as to put the interests of Philadelphia ahead of those of the nation? And just because 1992 was an election year and the quasi-liberal Republican Specter was thought to be mighty vulnerable, and just because closing that shipyard could very likely mean that Specter would end up trying whiplash cases back in circuit court, did Powell think such pettiness could influence the Pennsylvania senator's clear, unshakable vision of how the U.S. military should configure itself to best carry out its role of maintaining national security?

Yes, Powell probably thought all those things. And so did the members of the base-closing commission, a panel set up to be independent of both the Pentagon and Congress. There was, in fact, no better testament to the commission's success than the pained expression on Specter's face. The commission was a bold experiment, and to the consternation of Specter and a couple dozen other Congress members, it was working.

One of the unwritten laws of American politics says that saving useless military bases is a mortal obligation of members of Congress. Over the years, they have been remarkably successful to the point that in 1991 there were about 5,000 bases around the country and a need for less than 3,000. In fact, many of those bases dated to defense plans mapped out during the Indian wars of the nineteenth century, Powell told the commission. In other words, the nation continued to be well protected against a sudden uprising by the Sioux Nation, should it choose to come charging off the reservation, but seemed less able to handle the need for a lean, efficient military that did not suck the blood out of the economy. Or, as Powell put it with martial understatement, "This is not a rational structure." Fort Douglas in Utah had been built to guard stagecoach routes; Fort Monroe, Virginia, moat and all, had been built to hold off the British in the War of 1812. Both were still operating. It's been estimated that closing unneeded bases could save the Pentagon $5 billion a year—and that was before the Soviet Union decided to slit its wrists.

But the greater the argument for closing bases, the more Congress resisted. Through fancy footwork by sly legislators, it had become all but impossible to close a base in the last decade. The man to thank for that is Senator William Cohen of Maine, who served in the House in the 1970s, when the Pentagon said it wanted to close Loring Air Force Base, a bomber field at the northernmost tip of the United States that had lost its reason for being in the age of long-range bombers and intercontinental missiles. With its miserable weather and mounds of snow and ice, Loring might have been a poor excuse for an air base, but it was *Maine's* poor excuse for an air base. Cohen was duty bound to save it.

A respected congressman who had helped shape some important environmental legislation, Cohen made a pact with the Devil and used those same laws to thwart the Pentagon. In a masterpiece of obstructionist legislation, he teamed up with Speaker Tip O'Neill, a man who never saw a government dollar he didn't want, to push through a bill that said that before the Department of Defense could close any base, it had to carry out a time-consuming, costly environmental impact study. And one of the impacts to be studied was what effect the base closing would have on the local economy. Given the well-trodden paths of appeals and court challenges available to anyone in disagreement, it would take many years before a base could be shuttered. No studies would have to be conducted on what effect keeping the base open would have on the *national* economy.

The success of Cohen's initiative can be seen by a simple statistic: from 1977 to 1989, not a single major base was closed.

Of course, that period coincided with a time when defense spending became the greatest pork barrel in history. What were a few hundred useless bases when the party was awash in hundreds of billions of dollars in contracts for weapons systems, some of which we actually needed?

"Many members look on the defense bill the way Jimmy Dean looks at a hog," Congressman Richard Armey noted in 1987, at the height of the feeding frenzy.

Defense became *the* political feast of the 1980s. Fueled by Ronald Reagan's conviction that we would spend the Russians into the ground—you have to give him his due on that, it probably worked—everyone got in on the spending spree. In few instances in American history have legislators been so willing to cross ideological lines and violate their convictions for the sole purpose of bringing government money to their districts. Thus you had the unlovely spectacle of people like Senator Carl Levin, a nice liberal Jewish boy from Detroit, slobbering all over the M-1 tank—made in Michigan—and insisting that the nation's security depended on having lots of them. Or the mostly liberal Connecticut delegation, which was particularly pathetic when it came to anything having to do with submarines—made in Groton, Connecticut. At one point, Sam Gejdenson actually voted against funding the nuclear-tipped missile that was the main reason we were building the Trident submarine but *on the same day* voted for continued production of the submarine itself. In one of the great leaps of pork-barrel logic, he explained that if we had the submarines, we could fool the Russians into thinking they were loaded with missiles. The wildly expensive Star Wars project was sustained not because most members believed in it but because it provided research contracts for hundreds of congressional districts. The B-1 bomber, a fiasco of an airplane, was the product of a masterfully cynical plan to build its components in enough congressional districts to assure its continued funding.

No one ever tried to assess just how much of the trillion-dollar buildup might have been pork. But even using a low pork coefficient of 10 percent—and everything in Congress seems larded with at least 10 percent pork—that's $100 billion in extra waste over the decade. But that's probably a modest assessment, since the spending frenzy has distorted the entire process of funding the Pentagon. What has happened is that the lust for pork has made each member of Congress a "defense expert" on the handful of Pentagon contracts in his district. "You have 535 individual program managers," Sam Nunn once noted, each intent on micromanaging his piece of the pie, which usually means a contract in his district. So the logic of pork has taken over Pentagon spending: any project that has a member of Congress defending it is, by definition, a good project.

The pressure to spend was summed up one day by Toby Moffett, a Connecticut congressman, who cried, "We are all hooked on this like a bunch of addicts. . . . We need help!"

It was the plea of the weak-willed sociopath, known to psychiatrists and priests everywhere: *Stop me before I sin again.*

Dick Armey thought he had a way to do just that. An acerbic former economics professor who was elected to the House in 1984 from a prosperous suburb of Dallas, Armey was convinced that government waste was sapping the economy, that government was a bad provider of most services and was best kept to a minimum. His intellectual heroes were conservative economists such as Milton Friedman and James Buchanan, and his mission was to cut spending. He quickly became a forceful, if often unsuccessful, presence. He won notoriety by sleeping on a pull-out couch in his office for several years to demonstrate that he didn't want to become a creature of Washington. A partisan warrior, he loves to nettle the opposition, down to calling them the "Democrat Party," because he says they are so controlled by special interests that "there's nothing democratic about them."

Winning approval of the base-closing commission was certainly the biggest success for Armey, and probably for any other reformer in recent memory.

"After I had been in Congress a few years, I realized the key was that the typical congressman doesn't really care if the *base* survives. He just cares if *he* survives."

So the trick was to insulate members from the tough decisions. Forget what the textbook says they're supposed to do. The reality was that they couldn't. So work around it.

The idea for an independent panel came from the Grace commission. Armey tailored it to meet political necessity by making sure the president couldn't abuse the process to punish certain members of Congress.

One of the motivations behind the Cohen-O'Neill base-closing blockade was the legitimate fear of all members of Congress that the president will bash them over the head to get something he wants. Whatever their party, they worry that the White House can manipulate the closings to its own ends.

"Pork is power," Armey once wrote, "both the ability to distribute it and the ability to deny it. If the executive branch has unrestricted freedom to close bases, the argument runs, it would have a potent political weapon in its hands to retaliate against anyone who defies the president on key legislation." Armey recalled the lingering memory of Lyndon Johnson telling the town fathers of Amarillo that if he didn't carry their district, he'd shut down their air base. He didn't, and he did.

Armey's plan was to have a bipartisan commission appointed by the president and confirmed by the Senate. The Pentagon would then submit a list of recommended bases to close. The commissioners could add their own bases as well. Then there would be hearings at which citizens and members of Congress could argue to keep a base open. The commissioners would decide which bases deserved to be closed. Congress had to vote yes or no, but only on the entire list. No special pleadings. The same for the president. He had to sign off on the whole list, or veto it.

The plan seemed to keep the various Washington interests at bay, and it also afforded the political protection members would need. Armey understood that it's the nature of politics that many things are done for show. Winning and losing are not everything, but appearances often are. The commission was like a dramatic foil that members could seem to oppose, thus showing the voters back home they were fighting on their behalf. In a wonderfully blunt assessment of why the base-closing commission would work, Senator Phil Gramm of Texas explained that after the commission did its dirty work, "I can go out and lie down in the street and the bulldozers are coming and I have a trusty aide there just as it gets there to drag me out of the way. All the people in Muleshoe, or wherever this base is, will say, 'You know, Phil Gramm got whipped, but it was like the Alamo. He was with us until the last second.' "

Armey also discovered that once bases are closed, the surrounding communities are usually better off. One Pentagon study following up on 100 base closures found that there had been some initial pain, but that the towns affected had gotten ready-made industrial parks, school facilities, airports and factories. A total of 45,000 more jobs had been created than had been lost by the closing. Those communities that had taken up the challenge and had tried to develop the base had usually prospered.

After a year of trying, Armey sold his idea to Congress in 1988, proof the members aren't irredeemably greedy. They'll often do the right thing, as long as they're protected.

A short list was tried in 1989, and it seemed to work. Things fell apart in 1990, largely because the Pentagon targeted mostly bases in Democratic districts. After some modifications to the process, the Pentagon came up with a more balanced, longer list in the spring of 1991.

Chaired by James Courter, a former congressman from New Jersey, the commission traveled around the country to hear testimony, winding up with a marathon weekend session in Washington. Virtually everything the commission did except for its final deliberations was in public session, a frustrating development for Washington insiders used to the privacy of closed-door meetings. There was no opportunity for lobbying or deal making. There were also very few staff members to act as a buffer and to advocate special pleadings. The commissioners listened to the merits of everyone's case and made their decisions. By Washington standards, it seemed almost un-American.

Naturally, according to the testimony the commissioners heard, there were *no* unneeded bases. Or, more precisely, there were certainly unnecessary bases, just not *our* particular base. "We support the commission's work, it's just that when it comes to this facility . . ." was heard over and over. Despite the fact that the country had won the war against communism and that the military was grossly oversized, it seemed we still needed every single base in the United States, if you were to believe the earnest testimony of Congress members and community leaders. It was amazing to see the number of people who had such detailed knowledge of the nation's specific military needs, as if somehow strategic doctrine had become the hobby of millions.

All of which contrasted with the simple recommendation of Colin Powell, the guy who had written the doctrine.

"I ask you to be vicious in closing bases," Powell told the commission. The word was well chosen. Powell knew how wasteful the bases were. At a time of shrinking resources, the greatest danger was that professionals such as himself would be hampered by politics in reordering their priorities. Powell knew that instead of letting him carve the military down to a well-muscled force, the politics of pork would try to force him to maintain a vast, flabby machine with airfields and armories and munitions plants in every godforsaken corner of the country. And since his overall budgets were certain to decline, what he'd be left with was a stretched-thin, weak force—an army designed by amateurs. Viciousness is the quality you need to win wars, and it's the quality you need to cut budgets. There is no nice way to do either, but the alternatives are immeasurably worse.

When the commission announced its final decisions, it hadn't been vicious, but it had been tough. Major bases would be closed, saving about a billion dollars annually. Included on the list were the Philadelphia Naval Shipyard, Monterey's Fort Ord and the Presidio overlooking San Francisco Bay, Fort Benjamin Harrison in Indiana and Loring Air Force Base in Maine. The pain seemed to fall equally on Republicans and Democrats and not too heavily on any one region.

There was remarkably little protracted whining. There was some posturing, to be sure, but for the most part members of Congress issued press releases that said, "This is an outrage, but we must move on and decide how best to deal with the change."

There was even some heroism. Tom Campbell, a congressman from the San Francisco area who lost a large base, said, "The deficit will never go down unless all of us give up some parochial interests. . . . I do not believe in the idea of 'balance the budget, but don't touch my district.'"

Of course, that message didn't get through to Arlen Specter, playing the oldest of the old-boy roles, who vowed to fight the shipyard closing in court and to try the case himself.

Still, while the commission did its job, one could also say that the process was remarkable for how little it accomplished. Of 5,000 bases, 36 were closed. If the military is to shrink by between 25 and 35 percent in the next five years, that means that roughly 1,800 facilities should close pretty soon. One part of the original plan was scrapped entirely: the scheme to close many of the regional offices of the Army Corps of Engineers and save $100 million. This was the same idea that the Appropriators on the Big Pork subcommittee had already done their best to short-circuit. "We knew we'd have to dogfight with congress if we tried to close the Corps offices," one member of the commission noted.

But for now, Dick Armey's willing to take what he can get. Sitting in his office, he allowed himself a brief smile at the commission's success. In the world of pork, it had to be considered one of the great victories in history.

"It worked okay," he agreed with a casual kind of cowboy humility that might even have been genuine.

But could it work elsewhere? If the principle of saving Congress from itself is so sound, why not apply it to other areas of waste?

Armey hadn't considered this.

"I sold the base-closing commission for a very specific purpose, and I did it one on one with members. They bought it because they know there's a problem, but they were also convinced that I wasn't doing it to promote some sneaky interest for myself. I had to make them understand that I had no particular list of my own and I wasn't trying to save anything. That's the way things are done up here.

"Sure, maybe you could use this idea to cut big spending areas such as entitlements. I mean, the concept could work. I just don't know if Congress would buy it. You're asking them to give away a lot of authority. And I don't know who'd try to sell it."

So it's not impossible to deal with pork after all. Just improbable.

# 13

# WHOOPS!

THIS MEETING MIGHT ACTUALLY HAVE HAPPENED.

One early morning in mid-July Richard Darman, freshly shaven and slicked back for business, strode into the Oval Office with his chin thrust out confidently but his mouth straining to hold on to a weak smile.

"Good morning, Mr. President."

"Oh, hello, Dick. Nice to see ya. Have a seat here."

The president had his reading glasses on and was frowning over a blue-bound report on his desk.

"Now, Dick, tell me about these, ah, new budget numbers your fellows have cooked up over there. I . . . I just don't get it."

"Well, Mr. President . . .

"Thought that deal you and Sununu worked out was supposed to make this deficit thing go away. But now it's back. Bigger than ever. This says three hundred fifty billion dollars for 1992! Lotta money there, Dick. Election year coming up."

"Well, yes, Mr. President, there were some technical problems with the numbers, some of the economic models, the, ah, Treasury

folks . . . computers . . . income shortfall . . . Medicaid cost re-imbursement formulas . . . basically technical reestimates."

"But darn it, Dick, that's a, whoa, big number here, ah, let's see, seventy-billion-dollar mistake. And this chart here. The deficit one. Lines're supposed to go down. Got them going up. No good. People are gonna think we don't know what we're doing. I mean, Red Ink City."

"Well, sir, you know, as David Stockman said once, 'None of us really understands what's going on with all these numbers.' Heh, heh. You don't remember that?"

Bush leaned forward, his eyes narrowing and his face seeming to draw together until it looked like the blade end of a hatchet. Darman shifted in his chair, uncrossing his legs and putting his moist palms onto the knees of his suit pants.

"You mean Mr., ah, Voodoo Economics? Let me tell you something about Mr. goddamned Voodoo Stockman. Had some damn big ones, deficits, too, didn't he?"

In private, the president was far more profane than his public image would suggest, especially when he became agitated.

"The biggest problem since the end of World War Two. In 1983 the deficit was 6.3 percent of gross national product. That's the best way to measure it, compared to the size of the whole economy. That was when people really started to panic." Like Darman was panicking at that moment.

"And where did it go after that?"

"Down."

"Where's it been going since we've been in?"

"Up."

"Where the hell will we be in 1992?"

"About 5.8 percent of GNP. That would be the second highest since World War Two. Assuming, of course, that we manage to hold the line at $350 billion . . ."

"Holy shit, Dick, you don't mean this, ah, deficit thing could get worse?"

"Uh, the folks at the Congressional Budget Office are already looking at three hundred sixty-two billion. And, well, you know, this recession doesn't help much. We'll do everything we can to keep it under four hundred billion."

"Four—my God! Little angry here, Dick. You knew we were fucked up in this recession—steep one, don't understand where the confidence thing has gone, people should buy stuff—you knew that when you came up with the first set of figures. We all did."

"I don't think we could ever have sold that deal if people dealt with real numbers. Remember, sir, you told me, 'One word: Get a deal. Period.' "

"I said that? That's three words. Or four. Sounds like Quayle said it. All right, if you say I said it. Sure, sure. But what about all these goddamned caps and firewalls and all that crap you and Sununu told me you put in there?"

"Mr. President, those were to keep the lid on spending. If income drops off, well, there's just no mechanism to take that into consideration. You remember we told you that we got rid of those Gramm-Rudman targets. The ones that made us cut spending automatically if the deficit started going up. We didn't like those much, and the boys over on the appropriations committees just hated them. And then we sort of decided not to put caps on the entitlement spending, because we all thought that was political dynamite. Republicans, Democrats—we all wanted to stay as far away from that as we could. You don't want to go fooling with the old folks' checks. So as it is now, something like Medicaid or food stamps can go through the roof and nobody's responsible for stopping it."

"So you're telling me the budget is what? Out of our control?"

"Pretty much, sir."

"Shit."

The president's face seemed to melt from vertical to horizontal as the hatchetlike frown sagged into a pursed-lipped scowl. He was thinking, but he didn't know what to think. This was an economics problem, and he didn't know what to think about economics. So he thought about politics.

"Isn't the doo-doo gonna hit the old fan-ola when we make these numbers public?"

"I don't think so. I'll just send a note over to Congress. I mean, they're in on the deal, too. They won't beef."

"Okay, Dick, if you say so. But I gotta tell ya. You know, kinda feel like Reagan here. Little in the dark. Little unclear about this numbers mumbo jumbo. Gotta bad feeling. You're sure it's not a problem?"

"Trust me, Mr. President. Besides"—Darman grinned for the first time that morning—"as a great man once said, 'None of us really understands what's going on with all these numbers anyway.' "

Darman left the president laughing.

. . .

The previous scene has been shamelessly invented, but the substance and the numbers are correct—which is the opposite of the way things often work at the White House. Sometimes in Porkland you have to let your imagination wander in order to grasp essential truths.

Darman really did make a colossal boner in estimating the 1992 deficit and was forced to 'fess up in a press release on July 15. And Darman really did send a report to Congress that said, "The budget reforms enacted in 1990 have been working." He blamed the new numbers on "technical reestimates," presumably made by some computer geeks at the Treasury Department. As expected, Congress said almost nothing. And Darman had to have told Bush, whose reaction remains a mystery.

One nerve was struck, however. Darman's growing number of conservative critics became apoplectic, finding proof that the deal had been a sham all along, and began to allow their own imaginations to contemplate if the problem wasn't really with Bush himself.

The mistake—if it was a mistake—was so outrageous that one needler even brought the debate to a new level by suggesting that Darman should be criminally prosecuted. If Exxon can be indicted for its oil spill and Mike Milken can get sent up the river for securities manipulation, argued economist Paul Craig Roberts, "then surely the signatories to last autumn's budget agreement can be indicted, for no greater fraud has ever been perpetuated on the American people." Writing in *The Wall Street Journal*, he said Darman knew he was putting out phony forecasts during the deal making, particularly by denying that the recession would eat up the new tax money.

More typical in his criticism was Marc Wheat of Citizens for a Sound Economy, who concluded simply, "The fiscal situation is completely out of control."

The actual damage was that, in return for a tax increase, the deal had promised deficit reduction of $500 billion over five years, but what Darman's midyear revision said was that the deficit would actually go *up* by $500 billion. Even giving him a little wiggle room and rounding off a number here and there, the trend line was inescapable. And the hardest thing to figure was this: how were the Bushmen possibly managing to exceed the giant Reagan 1983 deficit—the result of a badly botched plan born of can-you-top-this tax cuts and a wild boost in defense spending—at a time when they were *raising* taxes and *cutting* defense spending? The deficit balloon of 1983 was a huge screwup that the Reagan folks had scrambled to repair, and to some extent they had by 1989. Yet Bush, who had become the biggest-spending president since World War II, saw a similar deficit as business as usual.

What all this had to do with pork was twofold. First, pork helped explain the deficit. And second, the deficit helped explain pork.

While pork played a role in the fateful deal, it wasn't the sum total of the deficit problem. The deficit dollars were too big and the pork dollars too small to say that one caused the other. But what the midyear mea culpa illustrated was the *pork mentality* and how that played a disproportionate role in the swelling deficit. The culture of pork was the I'll-get-mine-and-damn-you philosophy that seemed to pervade government thinking, and probably voters' thinking as well. What became clear in July was that the house that pork built was coming apart because of how it was made. Darman had cut the deal not with Leon Panetta or Richard Gephardt or any of the more thoughtful members of Congress who agonize over the long-term health of the economy, but with Byrd, a man whose horizon extends from the beginning to the end of a spending bill. Byrd got his pork up front and the cleverer-than-thou Darman got had. All of Darman's intended savings were "down the road," but down the road would never come. The deal would disintegrate by then. Once again, Darman's deal was a Porkland special: the kind you make with other people's money. "I pay you today on the chance I may get something back in a few years"—that was basically the way the savings-and-loan crisis had gotten started.

At the same time, those deficit numbers that came gushing out of Darman's office that summer created a powerful argument against pork itself. All pork, and all government spending, needed to be measured against the skyline of Red Ink City. To be sure, Byrd, Whitten and others would say it measured up just fine. They'd say there was no such thing as pork, that it was all necessary local spending, that we'd been holding it down for too long and that, yes, we should borrow to pay for it because only through these kinds of projects could we make America great again. But others would say it was ludicrous to spend on anything but essential services until we could get the deficit back under control.

So what much of the debate over pork came down to was, How much do you think the deficit matters? If it doesn't matter, then why fret over all these nonessential programs? But if it does matter, then pork and the pork mentality are at the heart of the problem of why Washington can't stop spending.

Talking about the deficit is like talking about global warming. It makes people leave the room to freshen their drinks or start changing the channels in search of a college swim meet. Anything. The subject is hard to understand and abstract to the average person's everyday life.

"We've reached a point where any amateurs are precluded from looking at the budget because they don't even know what numbers to use," said John Makin, an economist at the American Enterprise Institute.

"The budget numbers are becoming increasingly divorced from those that can be understood by the average person," cautioned Alan Schick of the University of Maryland. "We will pay a high price for not being able to open a book and have the numbers tell it like it is."

In other words, the deficit has become the arms control debate of the 1990s. And like nuclear weapons, it may not see a solution until the average citizen gets hysterical.

He'll get no help from the professionals. The view of those who crunch budget numbers for a living can be summed up this way: The deficit is a problem; the deficit is not a problem. Is that clear enough?

There are a dozen theories about whether the deficit matters or not, all put forth by people who are tenured college professors, lifetime government employees or fellows at think tanks. At press time, a majority seemed to say that while troublesome, the deficit isn't that big of a deal—although, if somebody were to cull the views of these soothsayers into an Index of Leading Economic Babble, it would surely show that as the deficit numbers continued to rise, so did their level of concern.

On the other hand, there's the Common Sense Theory of the National Debt, which says, If it's such a good idea to spend more than you earn, why aren't we all rich? The notion here is a simple one, based on the intuition of people who do not have doctorates in economics but somehow still know that *it's got to be goddamned crazy for a person, a company or a government to spend money it doesn't have year after year after year!* And if you had to bet on the common sense of the occupants of your average airline waiting room or a roomful of Ph.D. economists, where would you put your money?

Still, there are a few things worth knowing about the national debt before you make up your mind.

The deficit is the amount the government overspends each year. It's the difference between what comes in, mostly from taxes, and what goes out.

This gets added to the national debt, which is the accumulation of all the deficits that were never paid back.

By the end of 1992, this total debt will be somewhere around $4 trillion.

Even if you were to balance the budget tomorrow, you'd still have to pay interest on the national debt and—someday—pay it off.

The fastest-growing part of the budget is interest payments on that debt, and by 1993 we may spend more on interest than on defense.

If you're an American citizen—man, woman or child—your share in 1992 is $16,000.

Probably no badly shaved guys named Vinnie and Bats wearing overcoats in June will ever come to your door to collect it. However if the clean-shaven agents of the IRS *were* to collect from the average taxpayer—he's a cop, she's a part-time bookkeeper, two kids, forty-six grand a year, three-year-old Taurus in the driveway—their share would be about $64,000. Imagine that letter? "Dear Mr. Sap, This is to inform you . . . your share . . . in addition to your usual tax liability. Please pay promptly to avoid penalties."

As it is, these average taxpayers coughed up $12,984 to the feds in 1991, according to a study by the Tax Foundation. Interest payments on the national debt claimed $1,808 of that. It'll grow every year.

While there is no scientific proof of this—economics is not a science, whatever anyone tells you—the deficit may be one main reason why many Americans are finding their paychecks moving in the direction of the average Malaysian factory worker's.

One theory is that the money the government borrows "crowds out" money that would otherwise go to private investment. That interest payments eventually become burdensome on the government budget. And that paying that interest means taxing the middle class to transfer funds to the rich.

An area this may be immediately apparent is in mortgage interest rates. As the Federal Reserve Bank slashed short-term rates in 1991 and 1992, long-term rates stayed surprisingly high. One reason is that the government needed to borrow so much money that it had to keep offering investors higher rates. Thirty-year mortgages are closely linked to thirty-year Treasury bonds.

The other theory is, So what? Government spending creates jobs and spurs private investment. And as long as you can pay the interest, who cares how much you owe? Ultimately, these theories say, you owe it to yourself.

These conflicting arguments are centuries old.

Adam Smith, who practically invented capitalism, said two hundred years ago, "When national debts have once been accumulated to a certain degree, there is scarce, I believe, a single instance of their having been fairly and completely repaid." He said the result was that they "enfeebled" the economy.

George Washington struggled unsuccessfully to pay off the government's debt from the Revolutionary War.

Thomas Jefferson was a fuddy-duddy fanatic on the subject. He called public debt "the greatest of the dangers to be feared" and thought it was unfair to transfer the debts of one generation to the next. As vice president, he once tried for an amendment to the Constitution that would "take from the federal government the power of borrowing." And as an old curmudgeon, he cautioned, "We must not let our rulers load us with perpetual debt. We must make our election between economy and liberty, or profusion and servitude."

Things hadn't changed much when Abraham Lincoln offered the prevailing wisdom of his tightfisted day in 1843: "As an individual who undertakes to live by borrowing soon finds his original means devoured by interest and next to no one left to borrow from, so it must be with a government."

In the early part of this century, John Maynard Keynes, the economic guru of the century, proposed the theory that government spending, even deficit spending, was good for the economy because it primed the pump and created new business activity.

His greatest disciple became Franklin Roosevelt, who decided to try to spend the country out of the Great Depression (although most analysts believe World War II did this and not the New Deal). FDR ratified what some think is the modern myth of government debt when he said in 1939, "Our national debt, after all, is an internal debt owed not only by the nation but to the nation. If our children have to pay interest on it, they will pay that interest to themselves. A reasonable internal debt will not impoverish our children or put the nation into bankruptcy."

Every presidential candidate since FDR has campaigned on a promise to balance the budget and control the size of the debt, Lawrence Malkin notes in his book *The National Debt*. Some even succeeded. Harry Truman ran four surpluses; Dwight Eisenhower, three.

Lyndon Johnson sparked the modern era of debt when he coupled his sneaky Vietnam buildup with his Great Society welfare programs in 1968, but the next year he managed to run a slight surplus, the last in history.

Richard Nixon was a surprisingly big spender for his day; Jerry Ford was mighty careless with a dollar; and Jimmy Carter was relatively prudent.

But all the spending of all the thirty-nine presidents hardly mattered until Ronald Reagan took office. The nation's total debt accumulated over two hundred years almost tripled in eight—from just under $1 trillion to $2.8 trillion—thanks to the man who was the most conservative president of the century and a politician who made chopping government spending a centerpiece of his rhetoric.

Remarkably, even Reagan is being exceeded by his understudy, George Bush, who so far is in a class by himself. His first, and perhaps only, four years will add at least another $1.2 trillion.

There are several possible explanations for Bush's behavior. Maybe the deficit really doesn't matter, and he knows it; maybe it's out of his control; or maybe, when it comes to the admittedly hard, frustrating work of trying to rein in the government, Bush will simply be known as the wimpiest president of the century.

Whatever the reason, Bush finally became aware of the problem in the fall of 1991, when the recession persisted and he suddenly found that the deficit had boxed him into a corner. Cutting taxes and increasing spending, the classic remedies that have softened the pain of recessions for fifty years, were no longer available.

Bush's second problem with the deficit was in his future. Like your charge card, the government has a debt limit. Unlike your card, it can raise the limit whenever it wants. As part of the budget deal of the fall of 1990, Congress and the White House conspired to raise the limit so high (to $4.145 trillion) that they wouldn't have to do it again until after the 1992 elections. But the soaring debt for 1992 may force them to do it anyway—just before the election.

The actual number of dollars in the budget deficit matters less than how it compares to the size of the gross national product, or the total amount of all the goods and services produced by the economy. It's the same principle that says that when you have a higher salary you can afford a bigger mortgage.

In 1992 the deficit is likely to be more than 6 percent of GNP, the highest level since World War II. Only Italy, among major industrial countries, has a larger budget deficit as a share of GNP than the United States.

Some economists argue that the real problem with deficits is the accumulated interest that has to be paid. Even those huge World War II debts cost only a very small part of overall government spending. But because of all the debt built up over the past decade, interest payments are now 15 percent of the budget and growing.

There was a time when we—that is, the citizens of the United States—used to own all the debt. But not anymore. Foreigners now own about 20 percent of it.

Interest payments on the debt also don't exactly go to "us," they go to a select group of people who can afford to own government bonds. That's about $200 billion that flows from the taxpayers' pockets to the pocket of whoever it was who lent the money, say, Japanese insurance companies, investment funds made up of German doctors, millionaires from New York and all sorts of American pension funds run for the benefit of the average working guy.

Borrowing money is an expensive way to do anything. Compound interest works both ways, which is why credit card companies are rich. Ask anyone who has run up his Visa balance and now struggles just to make the monthly minimum payment. Forget any hope of paying off the principal.

If you spend a borrowed million dollars on a boondoggle in Mississippi and interest rates are 10 percent, it costs you an extra $100,000 this year, $110,000 the year after, $121,00 the year after that and so on to the point that after ten years, the project has cost about $2.6 million.

Over ten years, the real cost of a supposedly $80 million project such as the famous Steamtown will be close to $200 million. And we'll still be paying interest after that. It's sort of like the Christmas Club from Hell.

Even those economists who aren't troubled by the deficit are quick to point out that it makes sense to run a high deficit only if you are spending the money for essential purposes—that is, investments that will help you in the long run.

There are rational arguments to be made that not all borrowing is wrong. Take the defense buildup of the 1980s. Excessive as it was, it worked. The Soviets caved in. Isn't that a benefit that the next generation and even the one after that should legitimately pay for?

But if it's not essential spending, then the people who are loaning all that money to the government should be loaning it elsewhere—such as to private businesses, which could use it to expand.

More than one third of all the money borrowed in this country is borrowed by the government, and the percentage keeps rising. Of new funds borrowed in 1992, an astonishing 70 percent is expected to be borrowed by the government.

So one way to look at pork-barrel spending is that in order for Bob Byrd to put up a new federal building in West Virginia, taxpayers from all fifty states will have to send quite a few bags of money to some fat Japanese banker in Osaka rather than keep it in a bank account where it could be used to make a loan to a local factory owner.

Another way to look at it is that the low savers among us are paying rent to the high savers for the privilege of allowing Mr. Byrd to be reelected.

This is called a transfer of wealth, and, given the direction in which it's being transferred, it's something the Democrats have traditionally opposed.

One fundamental test of pork, then, is to hold it up against the deficit. The key question: Would you borrow money to do this? If the question is, Would you borrow money to buy artillery shells to drop on Iraqi troops heading for Saudi Arabia, the answer might be "yes." If the question is, Would you borrow money to build bike paths for a wealthy suburb of Detroit, the average person might say "no." And if you asked, Would you borrow money to commemorate William McKinley's in-laws, if you put it that way, you might be chased out of town. Or voted out of office.

And that's why most everyone who makes his living in Washington is mighty relieved that no one in the rest of the country really understands what's going on with all those numbers.

## *14*

# LET'S MAKE A DEAL

**R**OOM 116 OF THE DIRKSEN BUILDING HUMMED WITH THE energy of a power cable one late-summer morning. Two dozen intense conversations were being whispered around the edges of a thirty-seat conference table while serious young men and women laden with paper pushed through a door, leaving in their wake a sea of plaintive faces. The supplicants were lobbyists representing everything from the space industry to garbage companies who, despite their six-figure salaries, craned their necks like ticketless gawkers at a Las Vegas fight hoping for just a glimpse of the action inside. In the next few hours, the problems created by months of pleading and badgering, of sly maneuvering, of promises and threats, of great expectations diminished by reality, of noble goals trying to thread through the reefs of pragmatism—in short, the competing interests of any major piece of legislation—would have to be resolved. A bill that satisfied the members of the House and the Senate was supposed to emerge, with all the differences worked out.

This was the mythical conference committee. Thirteen times

over the next few weeks, a cardinal from the House and a cardinal from the Senate, with their attendant monsignors, would sit across a hardwood table from each other, and roll up their sleeves and make a deal. Finally, the culmination of the spending process had arrived, the legendary last encounter when the masters of the game would slip in the eleventh-hour provisions. Time to read 'em and weep, to put up or shut up, to piss or get off the pot—to use all the many manly clichés routinely batted around the musky world of the Hill. Only, the first words spoken were by a woman.

"Close that door, and keep it closed!" came a big, raspy snarl from a short woman sitting at the center of the table.

There she was, perched on the edge of a spacious brown leather chair, her feet barely touching the floor and resembling, inescapably, Miss Piggy, the Muppet. Amazingly, seated directly across from her was the dour, slump-shouldered form of Kermit the Frog, her Muppet soulmate. Which made perfect sense because the friendly babble of Sesame Street made a better analogy to the proceedings than a tense game of Texas Hold 'Em. The secret of the Conference Committee, it quickly became apparent, was that there was no secret. Like other endeavors of the Appropriators, all the good stuff had been done before the meeting started. To be sure, there were a few points of contention—after all, Miss Piggy and Kermit fight, too—but rarely does anything change. And everyone stays friends.

The woman was Barbara Mikulski—"Madam Cardinal" to you, Buster—the tiny, tough-talking senator from Maryland and the only female member of the College of Cardinals. The gentleman with the comfortably drooping face was Bob Traxler, congressman from Bay City, Michigan, right at the angle of the thumb, and a man whose mealy-mouthed, midwestern twang belied a street-smart pol who knew how to keep the meat moving along the conveyor belt. And despite their vaguely comic appearance they were the right characters for the job, because the bill at hand was straight out of Warner Brothers' library of Porky Pig cartoons. It was a bizarre hash of a bill called "Appropriations for the Departments of Veterans Affairs and Housing and Urban Development and for sundry independent agencies, commissions, corporations and offices . . ." Those sundries included incidental items such as NASA and the Environmental Protection Agency, all of which had to exist under the same $81 billion ceiling. This was the ultimate test of the budget deal—and of the assumption that the cardinals would be forced to eat their young by pitting one favored program against another. It didn't quite happen that way.

Of course, none of this political drama would be readily apparent to, say, an average citizen who happened to wander into Room 116 of the Dirksen Building—not that they'd let an average citizen in, you understand, this being very high level business that could not be cheapened by the festive atmosphere of a gaggle of taxpayers wearing "I'm with Stupid" T-shirts. No, this was important work, sausage making if you will, that would seem confusing and even upsetting to the nonprofessional. There is a long-standing theory of government that says citizens should be shielded from such spectacles.

True enough, if a genuine citizen managed to get on line behind the reporters, the lobbyists, the Hill staff and the spies from every corner of the bureaucracy and by some magic managed to win one of the few seats in the small room, he'd probably be . . . well . . . confused and upset. What you could observe with the naked eye wasn't much. The public business sounded something like a dockside fish auction.

"Okay," Mikulski began, "Amendment number one, HR; number two, insert $13,512,920; number three, HR, insert $8 million . . . number seventeen, eighteen and nineteen, SR.

"Let me see here, Items J, K, L, HR. Items A-B, A-C, A-D, SR . . ."

And on and on in a rapid-fire rasp. A dizzying procession of letters, numbers and gigantic amounts of money. People around the room busily scribbled down her every grunt. What it translated to was whether the House would "recede" (give in to the Senate), or the other way around. "HR" means "House recedes"; "SR" means "Senate recedes." Often a dollar figure was changed, representing some sort of compromise between the two versions.

Which isn't to say that the coded lists Mikulski raced through were insignificant. There was much at stake. But to understand it, you not only had to be able to read between the lines, you needed to be able to see the molecular structure of the paper. Only then would the political architecture of the bill become apparent.

For instance, when Mikulski came to the section on NASA, a collective groan filled the room, a groan that made sense only if you had a scorecard. NASA, too, is a pork haven, but a prickly one. Unknown to the average moon-faced couch potato watching his two hundredth lift-off flaring in full color from his Trinitron, space exploration has always been as much about pork as about science. From its earliest days, the space agency has been guided by legislators who got massive contracts in their home states in return for support. The result has been an awesomely expensive space program that's produced scientific benefits of questionable value—at least when you consider the price tag. But from *The Right Stuff* exploits of the Mercury astronauts to the moon landing, NASA's always provided great public entertainment. And the giant NASA bureaucracy and its many supporters in *Fortune* 500 boardrooms across America hoped to continue in just that same vein, particularly if the large, ungainly item in the middle of that year's appropriation bill was any indication.

Sitting there like a China White boar a week before market was a $2 billion charge to start building a space station to orbit the earth. This had been a NASA dream for many years, and it was about to come true. Not that some people didn't view it as a nightmare. Like, for instance, *every* other scientist in America who was not getting some sort of NASA funding. It was called Space Station *Freedom*, and like the man used to sing, it would be anything but free. The $2 billion was just a down payment; completion by the year 2000 was supposed to cost $40 billion; the project over its entire life, about $120 billion. This, coming in a bill that was supposed to fund the rest of NASA, as well as public housing, veterans' affairs and the EPA. This was what Dick Darman had dreamed about when he conceived the budget deal: tough choices. Let Congress decide: does it want a space station or more public housing? We can't afford both. (Somehow the choice never comes down to apples and apples, such as, do we want a space station or a superconducting supercollider?)

Earlier in the year, Traxler had made his choice; he had opposed it. Bush wants us to make tough choices? he reasoned, Then I'll *make* tough choices. *Freedom* goes out because it's a scientific geegaw with no real purpose but to show off. The call didn't seem to be a hard one. For years, a parade of dozens of top scientists had been coming to the Hill to testify that the space station made no sense. Their testimony boiled down to this: the thing's damn expensive, and *nobody knows what it's supposed to do.*

Along with the supercollider, the space station was one of the worst examples of technology pork, a trend that had many scientists genuinely concerned. Big science was starving little science.

The open-ended, multi-billion-dollar boondoogles were draining all the funds that might once have gone to promising young researchers working in a university laboratory late at night. And many scientists felt that seeding hundreds of small projects would ultimately produce far more useful discoveries.

Space was particularly bad. The folks who brought you the first man on the moon, which felt good but probably wasn't worth the money, had done precious little since. As writer Greg Easterbrook has pointed out in a withering criticism of NASA in *The New Republic*, "Every year the United States spends more to accomplish less in space." His argument, and that of other critics, is that NASA is a badly managed, bloated bureaucracy that gave us the defective Hubble telescope and the *Challenger* disaster. And pouring in more money can't be the answer. Does the shuttle really do anything that a rocket with a payload couldn't? At a time of copious red ink, what's the point? Are we going to beat the Russians? Cut the trade deficit? Cure cancer? None of the above. Maybe someday a trip to Mars will make sense, but is it worth going deep into hock to do it right now?

Yet big science succeeds because it is pork driven. The validity of the idea never enters into the debate. You start with a scheme to build something—anything—and then build a constituency solely on the basis of jobs. Remember, you're dealing with members of Congress who don't know a microgravity experiment from a microwave oven (as Easterbrook pointed out, there is more peer review and scrutiny of some unknown researcher applying for a $50,000 National Science Foundation grant than there is of the space station). Then you sneak your way to the too-big-to-butcher point and say, "My fellow members, are we to throw away all this money we've already spent? Money, I might add, that has benefitted so many of your districts."

Traxler, who surely had played that game on other matters, decided for whatever reason—no, the appropriators are not always cash-sucking vampires; they sometimes make decisions that could be considered in the public interest, although maybe just by coincidence—to kill the space station. He simply took it out of the bill. The funds would go to other purposes.

But guess who wanted it back in? Goaded by Rocket Richard Darman, who once said that since childhood he's believed that humans will live on other planets, the president of the United States put his foot down and said, "We're gonna spend that money the way I want it spent!" And he proceeded to demonstrate that when the president really wants something, he can usually get it. He worked the phones, brought in astronauts and NASA officials to buttonhole members of Congress and let loose wild packs of defense industry lobbyists from places such as McDonnell Douglas, Boeing, Martin Marietta and IBM. He also had a secret weapon.

When the going got tough, none other than Dan Quayle got going. He is chairman of the National Space Council and had originally been opposed to the space station. A blue-ribbon report he'd commissioned had put *Freedom* last on the list of space priorities, and Quayle's own staff thought their boy could show some spine if he went against it. But according to a profile of Quayle in *The Washington Post*, under bullying by Darman he came on to lead a victorious lobbying effort. Thus Quayle's greatest legislative accomplishment in four years in the White House involved the complete collapse of his own convictions. But pork does that to folks.

True to form, the House vote, too, had nothing to do with science and everything to do with pork. Aside from Bush, the most potent ammunition in the space station battle came when NASA went the ultimate sleaze route by distributing a map showing all the districts that were getting space station contracts. Thirty-one states were supposed to benefit from the project. The brochure was labeled "Businesses Getting Buck$." Predictably, yahoos who couldn't tell a space station from a filling station were soon clamoring for it. The president won the vote 240 to 173—and lost a substantial piece of his moral authority.

"Once it was clear that the president was wheeling and dealing on the space station," said a Senate staff member who worked on appropriations bills, "the attitude was 'The store's open.' "

So no one who knew the score was surprised when, at the conference committee, both Mikulski and Traxler behaved as solemn converts to the president's one true way. Mikulski said she had been to the mountaintop and had heard from *the president himself* just how important the project was. Well, that was good enough for her. Traxler at least had the decency to be sheepish, as he said, "I find myself now defending the space station—contrary to where I was three months ago."

To the novice it may have appeared that the appropriators had lost. But appropriators, especially cardinals, rarely lose. The VA/HUD bill quickly became a pork bonanza for both of its chief clerics, as well as a few other key members. Mikulski got a $40 million down payment on a $200 million Christopher Columbus lab to study the oceans from downtown Baltimore; she robbed a new geriatric research center from Veterans Affairs; and she was assured of numerous space station contracts for Maryland, which already has the Goddard Space Flight Center.

Traxler took home a $30 million center to study NASA data; $20 million for an EPA training center; a rehab of the Saginaw veterans' hospital and six new HUD projects, including a conference center and hotel in his hometown of Bay City and a new building for nearby Delta College.

Bob Byrd got his usual tip, totaling about $50 million and including some science programs for Wheeling Jesuit University and an order to buy land next to the Beckley VA hospital, which caused VA officials in Washington to cower in dread of what he planned to build there. Up popped a new rocket engine factory worth $300 million for Jamie Whitten's district and hundreds of millions more for appropriators such as Jake Garn, Phil Gramm and Frank Lautenberg.

All that was left was to figure out how to pay for it. But the alert staff had solved *that* problem, as well. The Senate version had planned to cut some housing for the elderly and environmental programs—we've got to keep our priorities straight, after all. But someone discovered an accounting gimmick that put an extra $1.2 billion onto that year's books. They jumped on it. Traxler admitted, "This just puts off the ultimate day of reckoning," by which he meant the space station would cost even more the next year. But by then, it would probably be too big to butcher.

The housing portion of the bill became an absolute slop with page after page of "special-purpose grants," programs that had little to do with either housing or urban development. It was the booty bag for the appropriators, and all those who had been good little boys and girls got something. There were "business outreach centers" in New York; a rural health insurance program in Mississippi; water treatment for Homer, Alaska; a new road to the airport in Provo, Utah; a "technology incubator" to create "manufacturing jobs in rural areas" of North Dakota; a rehabbed auditorium in Ypsilanti, Michigan; and new recreational facilities for Biscayne Park, Florida.

Now remember, HUD is always referred to in news accounts as "the scandal-plagued agency," from its days when Ronald Reagan's pals used it as *their* personal candy store, handing out no-bid loans and grants for useless housing projects, shopping centers and office buildings. Congress went into a frenzy of indignation. Hearings were held, scoundrels were decried and, yes, a special prosecutor was appointed. Congress even came up with new guidelines setting up a strict review process for spending money. And it stuck to those guidelines for exactly one year until, with the fiscal 1992 bill on the table, it just couldn't control itself anymore and violated all the guidelines it had just established. The difference was that since it was Congress, the action was perfectly legal. What some Republicans may go to jail for, the Democrats were happily stuffing into their mouths.

This wallow was not without cost. HUD had its problems, but it also had a purpose. A lot of people in this country have pretty lousy housing, and there's some evidence that the government just might be able to help. Of course, most conservatives would tell you that on its best days, HUD is about 80 percent pork, just blantant giveaways to urban voters for ill-defined programs, which are then wasted or stolen. But one conservative who thought the government could influence change happened to be Jack Kemp, the secretary of HUD. Whatever you think of the ambitious former National Football League quarterback, he's a man with a coherent philosophy of government and innovative ideas. Some of his most interesting ideas have to do with trying to make tenants in public housing care more about their homes. Good conservative that he is, he looks for ways to create a greater sense of responsibility. It did no one any good to have all those folks sitting on their balconies in lawn chairs throwing chicken bones over the railings. Kemp's proudest program was called HOPE, and it was an experiment to let groups of tenants buy their homes from the government and, with luck, do a better job of maintaining them. He also wanted some tough new rules to make local housing authorities more accountable for Uncle Sam's money, including a demand that local governments contribute matching funds to new projects.

Except for a few dollars for HOPE, all of Kemp's initiatives were cut out. The members of Congress who had presided over the public housing mess for three decades and knew full well why it didn't work chose the old-school course of handouts. But not because Congress had hearings and made a rational decision to reject Kemp's ideas. Just because Mikulski and Traxler wanted it that way.

The Department of Veterans Affairs was another sacred pork

hunting ground for many years. Concede at the top that caring for veterans is an important responsibility. Concede as well that anything the government spends $30 billion a year on could be done for a lot less. An estimate by high-level sources in the VA itself is that pork costs about $3 billion a year. But more than that, VA officials say that congressional meddling has helped create an awesomely inefficient medical care system that is often hard pressed to do the right thing for its patients. "Try running a $15 billion corporation with 535 board members," grumbled one VA official. About half of the VA's money goes to various benefits programs, primarily pensions. The rest goes to a health care program that takes care of only 10 to 20 percent of veterans—since most have their own private insurance plans and prefer their own hospitals—but still comprises 172 hospitals and almost 500 other facilities staffed by 200,000 people. Thus the VA has a presence in most communities in the country—and just try to get it out.

Despite a steady decline in the veteran population, the VA hasn't been able to close a hospital since 1965. In recent years, it's tried to close a half-empty facility in Walla Walla, Washington, and another that sits on an earthquake fault line in central California. Both moves were stopped by Congress. At a time when private hospitals are scrambling to cut costs by specializing in certain services, the VA is forced to be all things to all people. When the VA tried to cut out a third of its heart surgery units, including those with an unacceptably high death rate, Congress stopped it, despite numerous studies that showed that fewer units would result in better care and fewer deaths.

"Anytime we try to make the smallest changes, we're stopped by Congress," said one VA official, pleading anonymity because of his pathological fear of congressional retribution. "We need no new facilities and should close a lot. But that can't happen."

In Maine, the department wanted to reassign ten people to New Hampshire to consolidate an office. Senator Bill Cohen held it up. A private hospital in Portland wanted a sky bridge connecting it to the VA facility, so Mark Hatfield got it for them. West Virginia has four VA hospitals and only 40,000 veterans who would ever use them. Boston has two hospitals only six miles apart.

"It's not just money, it's quality of care," the VA official said. "If we could do it our way, we could do it better. As medicine becomes more specialized, we're still a department store, because Congress forces us to do it that way."

The 1992 budget would be no departure from that well-worn path. And as always, the worst behavior was that of the cardinals. For instance, the item that was burning up VA administrators that year was Bob Byrd's insistence that they expand the hospital in Clarksburg because too many patients were being treated in Pittsburgh.

"We're talking about less than a two-hour drive to one of the finest VA centers in the country and a first-class private medical community," the official fumed. "Pittsburgh is a great medical center. But Byrd's telling us we've got to re-create that level of care in Clarksburg?"

Leading by example, Traxler told the VA officials they would have to build 500 beds, not the 400 they wanted, in a new Detroit hospital. Actually, they didn't want *any* hospital beds, figuring that a much cheaper nursing home was all that was needed in Detroit, yet another region with a declining vet population. "So we'll spend forty million dollars on beds we'll never use," the VA official said. That was to go along with the parking spaces they wouldn't use in the 1,500-car garage Congress told them to build.

Mikulski was equally brazen. After a review board of doctors decided that Baltimore was not the best place for a new geriatric research center, Mikulski decided they were wrong. What do doctors know? Baltimore gets it. When her spokesman was questioned about this by *The Washington Post,* he as much as responded, *"Moi?"* Actually he said, with a straight face, "She doesn't play that game."

All this happened with hardly a cross word spoken that morning. In a matter of a few hours, the conference was over. Minor tailoring had been done, a few compromises had been made. They must have been good compromises because when the bill finally emerged, only Jack Kemp was upset. He called on Bush to veto it, presumably thinking that this was consistent with the president's stated hatred of pork. There were grounds just on the excess of that unseemly commodity alone. "They went too far," Kemp raged. The pork had the added effect of forcing out the new programs that were also in keeping with Bush's stated love of conservative reforms. Kemp wrote that the HUD portion was a return to "the failed scandal-prone housing programs of the past." But of course Bush had just gotten his own failed, scandal-prone program tucked in, so everyone in Washington but Kemp thought the likelihood of a veto was nil.

When the veto didn't come, Kemp blamed Congress. He told *The New York Times*, "The Appropriations Committee is the most powerful committee in the history of the democratic experience." But he missed the point. This time it wasn't just the appropriators. When the president gets into a fray like this, it demeans him and strips him of his credibility as the last check on spending.

Is the space station really that important? Especially when you put it up against the deficit problem? Is it worth sending such a signal? Bush said yes.

In the end, nothing could go wrong because, as one Appropriations staffer put it, "Pork was the glue that held that bill together."

*15*

# THE EMPIRE
# STRIKES BACK

THE POWER OF PORK WAS FRIGHTENINGLY APPARENT TO ANY-one observing the business of the Senate early one afternoon in mid-September. Among those most impressed was Bob Smith, the junior senator from New Hampshire.

In this, his first season as a fiscal hound dog, Smith was learning that hunting pork is not unlike hunting ducks. Think of an appropriations bill as a flight of five hundred Canada geese. Since dawn, you've been sitting in a duck blind, cold and damp, waiting. You can hear their honking cries in the distance, but you can't see them. You cradle your shotgun and wait. Suddenly, they're over-head. For a moment, they blot out the murky sun. Five hundred green-banded line items, any one of which deserves a pellet through the head. But they're moving so fast! You've got to antic-ipate, to lead them. You aim and fire. Maybe you get one. But by the time your dog flops into the water and pulls one of the bodies out, the rest are long gone.

So it is with money bills. You know they're coming, but they're invisible until the last possible moment, when they roar out of a committee room, all two or three hundred pages worth of obscure language and legislative complexity, and rush straight to the floor, demanding to be acted upon immediately. If you're able to pick off one or two particularly slow-witted items, you're lucky. But the rest of the bill will soar blissfully south for the winter.

Smith got a bit of luck when his aide Jeff Merrifield sniffed what might be coming in the transportation appropriation bill. Through the Hill gossip circuit, he'd heard that the $14.4 billion bill, which funds such monoliths as the Department of Transportation, the Coast Guard and the Federal Aviation Administration, was loaded with a series of choice projects doled out to the heavyweights on the subcommittee, notably the chairman, New Jersey's Frank Lautenberg; the senior Republican, New York's Alphonse D'Amato; and, of course, Senator Byrd.

On Friday, September 13, Merrifield told his boss that the bill and its accompanying 207-page report had been passed by the committee earlier in the week, but that as usual the paperwork wasn't available to anyone not on the committee. A vote of the full Senate was scheduled for that Tuesday.

Smith wasn't in the best of moods. His colleagues had received his Porkbusters Bill with all the enthusiasm of a grand jury subpoena. In three months of trying, Smith had attracted exactly two cosponsors, John McCain of Arizona and Hank Brown of Colorado, both of whom had been on board from the start. Quixotic behavior is not unknown in the Senate, but Smith knew that if he took the bill to the floor and got only three votes, he'd be seen as a major league fool.

On the House side, Harris Fawell had gathered an equally disappointing twenty-seven cosponsors, though it hardly mattered since, as predicted, the bill had been referred to the Appropriations Committee, whose chairman would surely rather switch parties than release it to a vote. And worst of all, the White House was providing no support. Smith had sent his list of pork projects to Dick Darman's budget office with the hope that the president would ask Congress to strike them out through what's called a recission amendment. The White House had said no, making it seem clearer than ever that Darman really had cut a deal with Byrd to leave pork alone.

Smith needed something to rekindle the Porkbusters' flame. Maybe a quick win on the transportation bill would be the spark.

Each year, transportation is fertile ground for pork hunting.

Projects come with multi-million-dollar price tags and can be funded for years at a time. A road or a rail station is a high-visibility undertaking, and because the federal government pays such a huge part of the cost—90 percent for interstate roads, at least 75 percent for local roads and rail systems—it can seem like a gift to the folks back home. Never mind that this illusion of "free money" causes an irresistible temptation to fund projects that aren't needed or, once built, can't be maintained.

Take, for instance, the rail projects funded with grants from the Urban Mass Transportation Administration. Everyplace that thinks of itself as a city wants one, but in only a very few densely packed urban areas does mass transit make sense. Still, there's a pot of money, so projects costing billions get built as long as they have patrons who know how to get the money. A study by UMTA found that a much-touted line in Jacksonville, Florida, attracts only 1,000 riders a day and serves as "a shuttle from a large parking lot to downtown." Miami's downtown people mover has been a costly bust. Both projects bear the fingerprints of William Lehman, chairman of the Transportation Subcommittee in the House. Portland, land of Mark Hatfield, is building a rail line that will cost the government $20 per commuter trip and includes a provision that the federal government help in the development of a shopping center in order to give the line a place to go *to*. Towns like Austin, Texas, and Salt Lake City, Utah, have systems under way with $20-per-rider costs (UMTA thinks about $6 a ride is as high as subsidies should get), not because they have dense populations but because they have appropriators Phil Gramm and Jake Garn. But the best is Buffalo, where, thanks to Al D'Amato, an extension to its unsuccessful light-rail line is being built that will cost between $46 and $67 per trip—which is to say, it would be cheaper to have limousines pick up commuters at their homes and drive them to work.

David Stockman, Ronald Reagan's former budget director, writes of the time he decided to take on transportation pork, reasoning that so much of it was way outside the scope of what the federal government was supposed to do that he'd be able to win the day with common sense. He called transportation spending the best "single clear-cut case of what the Reagan Revolution required." But when Stockman met with Secretary of Transportation Drew Lewis to discuss his plan, Lewis "turned completely white . . . I was proposing to touch off a political firestorm by disrupting the flow of $14 billion per year of federal gravy to governors, mayors, contractors and unions." Lewis's pallor was prophetic. When cuts were proposed, some of the fiercest opposition came from within Reagan's own party. Liberals such as Arlen Specter and conservatives like Al D'Amato teamed up to thwart any attempt to cut funding.

"In the end," mused Stockman, "the transportation sector of the pork barrel never even knew the Reagan Revolution had tilted at it."

With Jim Miller heading OMB, Reagan tried again in 1987 when he vetoed the pork-rich highway bill. In a rare defeat for Reagan, Congress rose up to override his veto.

This year was no exception. With overall spending on transportation up a healthy 10 percent on top of a big increase the year before, the transportation bill was sure to be a productive place to look for pork.

When Merrifield finally managed to get a copy of the bill late Monday morning, he wasn't disappointed. As he and Tom Hodson, Smith's pork expert, began to pick their way through it, they found all sorts of choice morsels that had suddenly appeared in the report accompanying the bill. These were projects that for the most part hadn't been requested by any of the state or federal transportation professionals who are supposed to know about such things as where highways belong. There were grants to study "airway sciences" to colleges like North Dakota State, Northeast Louisiana and Middle Tennessee State. There were grants to study automated, or "intelligent," highways—which curiously were mostly in New Jersey, whose greatest claim to intelligence seemed to be Lautenberg and Robert Roe, the congressman who headed the House Public Works Committee. North Miami got new bike paths courtesy of Bill Lehman and, far more expensively, got even more money for the failing people-mover system. Meanwhile, up the coast, Jacksonville got many millions more for what's come to be widely regarded as the most wasteful mass transit system in the country. Across the country, Portland, which falls under the protective wing of Senator Mark Hatfield, the top Republican on Appropriations, got a down payment on its billion-dollar rail line to nowhere. Maryland's Barbara Mikulski, facing a tough reelection campaign in 1992, played Santa Claus for the Washington suburbs by scoring an extra $44 million in funds for that city's subway system—money the Washington Area Metropolitan Transit Authority hadn't even requested. And there were alternative-fuel vehicles for Tucson, Arizona, new bus shelters for Rutland, Vermont, and new buses for the resort community of Lake Tahoe, California. A million bucks in bad loans was generously repaid on behalf of several small private airlines such as Pocono Air and Dorado. In all, the bill probably had $1.5 billion in spending that could realistically be called pork.

But one section was particularly interesting. Merrifield and Hodson noticed that the demonstration projects, which totaled $387 million, mentioned only twenty-seven states. Almost half the country had been cut out of the goody basket. Then, when they added up who was to get what, they were stunned to discover that West Virginia was getting $182 million of the demo funds (including one project "to demonstrate methods of eliminating traffic congestion" in the bleak western part of the state and another to demonstrate that if you move a building full of bureaucrats to a remote part of the country—the FBI fingerprint center—you're sure as hell going to have to build a lot of new roads to get people there), followed by New Jersey and New York with $70 million and Arizona, Alaska and Iowa with another $57 million. That meant that about 80 percent of the funds was going to states that had one common element that had nothing to do with traffic congestion: a member of the Appropriations Committee. The rest of the country, which included Texas, California and, of course, New Hampshire, could go scratch.

Merrifield had an idea: what if you took the same funds and split them up by a formula based on fairness—say, taking into consideration such factors as population and highway miles in a given state? Remarkably, the Senate's Environment and Public Works Committee had just finished agonizing over such a formula in trying to decide how to divide up the government's gasoline tax money.

Using that formula, which the whole Senate had agreed was the fairest way to do it, Merrifield recalculated the $387 million and found, for instance, that instead of $182 million, West Virginia would get $4.8 million. In fact, all the big winners would be cut back and thirty-nine states would come out better.

"This is what we've been looking for," Smith told his aides. "Here's a case as clear as it gets."

Rather than argue that the funds were wasteful—which they were—he would simply ask to change the way they were being spent. "It's so simple. People aren't going to vote against their own interests. We're starting out with seventy-eight senators who win by changing the formula."

But it was Monday afternoon, and the vote would be the next

day. Smith needed language for an amendment, and he needed to make his colleagues understand what he was doing.

By the next morning, Merrifield and Hodson had compiled a simple chart that listed all fifty states and what they were getting in the existing bill compared to what they'd get under Smith's change. The list would be devastating if anyone bothered to read it, which wasn't a given in the routine press of Senate business. Dozens of bills were moving quickly, and every day brought a new crisis or two. Smith began phoning as many senators as he could find to lobby for his amendment.

At 11 A.M. D'Amato called his office and wondered, as Smith put it, "if I was going to be a nuisance and hold everyone up." That evening began Yom Kippur, and Lautenberg had made it known that he expected the bill to be cleared so he could get home to New Jersey. Smith was told that if he had an amendment, he better get it to the floor. He had fifteen minutes to make his pitch.

Smith rushed to his desk and asked to be recognized. He started contritely, just as Jimmy Stewart would have. In the eyes of the other senators, he was still a freshman, a hulking kid from an unsophisticated state.

"Mr. President, I apologize for any inconvenience to my colleagues," he began. "I have agreed to fifteen minutes of debate on this matter, although I would have preferred more time. I know many want to leave for the holiday."

He noted that the sixty-three projects he questioned had appeared, gosh, as if by magic. And the way the money had been split up was, well, just plain unfair.

"Why do we have an authorizing committee?" Smith asked with genuine wonder in his voice. "An authorizing committee is supposed to be the expert in the area. They are supposed to deal with the priorities.

"But I sit on the Environment and Public Works Committee, and we never reviewed any of these projects. Twenty-three states, including Texas and California, do not receive a nickel. Are the people in California somehow on a lower scale than the people of West Virginia? Or New York? Or New Jersey?

"Or the people of New Hampshire, are they somehow less American citizens? The state of West Virginia has approximately two million people; the United States of America has two hundred fifty million people. But West Virginia gets almost half the project money."

At that point, Al D'Amato, a lean and canny veteran from a very sophisticated state, stood up.

"Will the Senatah yield for a question?" D'Amato said in a voice that echoed the street-smart corners of Brooklyn.

"I only have five minutes," Smith replied cautiously. But he gave D'Amato thirty seconds. D'Amato needed no more. In New York they call him Senator Pothole for his minute attention to the gritty functions of government. If you want to talk foreign affairs, they say in New York, look up Senator Pat Moynihan, but if you want a visa, go see D'Amato. A man not burdened with thoughtfulness, D'Amato is a feral politician who understands the value of bringing home the bacon perhaps better than anyone else in the Senate—and never more acutely than now when he's been tarnished by an inconclusive ethics probe and faces a gauntlet of challengers for 1992. Country Bob Smith was not about to get in his way.

"Does the senator from New Hampshire know that there is $3.9 million for New Hampshire in the airways science program?" D'Amato began with the blandly innocent look of a boy who's just put a baseball through a window. "Do you know whether or not that was authorized?"

Smith didn't know what D'Amato was talking about.

"For Daniel Webster College," D'Amato helped.

"There is no money, no money—" Smith stammered.

Ah, but there was. His New Hampshire colleague Warren Rudman, a fiscal conservative to a point, had slipped in a fat plum for the obscure little college without Smith's knowledge. Laboratories, hangars, who knows what and who knows why, but it was right there in the report. Smith had missed it. Now he looked like an idiot as he had to face the ultimate appropriator's accusation: *No one's hands are clean.*

"I simply would like to point out to the senator," D'Amato bored on, "that in other areas of the bill, transit areas—"

"I'm not asking—" Smith interrupted.

"—Coast Guard—"

"I reclaim my time."

D'Amato sat down. Mission accomplished.

Smith took a deep breath and tried again.

"There is no money in this bill for the state of New Hampshire under the areas that I am contesting. *Nothing.*"

Just as there was nothing for Illinois, Ohio, Pennsylvania and on and on. Unless you wanted to go by Smith's chart.

"We are distributing it fairly rather than by simply raw, political, abusive power. That does not make me very popular with some of my colleagues to make comments like that, but that is a fact. I want to see process reform. I would not mind cutting all of this out, but I know that's not going anywhere. So let me make the point: the process is wrong. If you want to change the process, then you can vote yes on the Smith amendment and help your state."

Then Frank Lautenberg, a cardinal in good standing, rose to defend his turf.

"We will cut this debate very short," began the gruff, white-haired Lautenberg, who has the brusque manner of a CEO accustomed to people falling at his feet. Not surprisingly, he once was, having started with nothing, built a fabulously successful data processing company and spent $5 million of his own money to win a Senate seat.

"We are near the end of the bill, and the senator from New Hampshire suddenly wants to make the case of fairness and equity. At 2:30 in the afternoon, the senator suddenly wants to redefine the process."

Left unsaid was that Smith had first seen the bill twenty-four hours earlier and many of his Senate colleagues had not seen it at all. This is the second line of defense of the appropriators: *There's no time for this nonsense.*

"I want to respond to the argument about fairness. It is fairness when it is your turn, Mr. President. In Conway, New Hampshire, this committee provided eight million dollars over three years in 1988, 1989 and 1990 for the construction of a new bridge. At that time it was fair for New Hampshire, unless the senator wants to rescind that money. Maybe New Hampshire can pay us back the eight million dollars we then gave them."

The ultimate carnival trick of a politician is making you grateful for getting your own money back. Lautenberg was trying for a new level by making Smith seem guilty for taking it in the first place. But Smith was armored; he'd put this very same Conway project into his Porkbusters Bill, insisting that the $1.7 million installment for his state had come in through the back door and deserved to be cut out. Maybe what Lautenberg feared most was that he had finally met a senator who was truly clean. A terrifying thought.

"Mr. President," Lautenberg went on, "I will tell you, yes, this bill is fair. People come to the committee with projects, they articulate their needs, we make our judgments.

"We did not hear from the senator. He did not request anything of this bill. Now he has come to rewrite the bill in the full view of the Senate when the time is fleeting."

There it was in short order, *all* the defenses of the appropriators: Everyone does it. We don't have enough time to deal with this. We decide what's fair.

"Mr. President, I move to table the Smith amendment."

Smith had one more chance. Sounding something like the other Mr. Smith in the movie, he made his final plea.

"Mr. President, I would like to respond. I think I understand the nerve that is touched here when one tries to change the process. If we were doing the job so well in this country, the way we do business through the appropriations and the authorizing process, why do we have a four-trillion-dollar national debt? Why is it that the budget deficit is going up somewhere in the vicinity of three hundred twenty-five to three hundred thirty billion dollars this year?

"The point is, we are not doing it right and we are not doing it fair. That is the issue.

"Certainly I can understand the senator from New Jersey saying this is a fair matter because he gets forty-four million dollars out of this thing. I can certainly understand the senator from West Virginia, who gets almost half. That may be fair to the people in West Virginia and New Jersey, but it is not fair to people in Ohio, Idaho, New Hampshire, California, Texas, Florida and the other states."

He paused to looked at his colleagues, many sitting behind their school desks and actually paying attention for a moment.

"Stand up and say that the process is wrong. Have the courage to say it, and I guarantee you will stop this kind of stuff. You can change it. It takes fifty-one votes."

Smith sat down, and the clerk began to call the roll slowly in his well-practiced cadence.

"Mr. *Ad*-ams . . . Mr. A-*ka*-ka . . ."

But D'Amato and Lautenberg weren't finished. While the vote was being tallied, they were twisting arms furiously, because if the logic of Smith's amendment was simple to him, it was equally simple to the appropriators: this amendment was trouble. It went right to the heart of the appropriations process, which is based not on fairness but on power. Anyone knew that. The notion of spending the $500 billion the appropriators annually dole out based on some measure of fairness was a threat to their livelihood.

While Lautenberg worked the cloakroom where senators waited off the floor, D'Amato was buttonholing his colleagues right on the floor for whispered moments.

One staffer overheard him say, "If you do, you'll get burned."

Smith himself knew the stakes. Before the vote he had been told by a senator he won't name, "If you ever want to work with this committee again, you won't push this. You're doing this to embarrass us."

One senator stopped him on the floor to whisper, "They've put the word out. They want this one."

Smith knew that "they" meant the appropriators, from Byrd on down.

"Bob, this makes sense," another senator told him, "but I can't take on the appropriators."

What Smith had hoped would be a close vote turned into a rout with some senators—Porkbusters cosponsor John McCain among them—going so far as to change their votes against him before the tallies were finalized. His amendment failed, 84 to 14.

Smith came off the floor fuming. "The appropriators run this place!" he said. "Dammit, I didn't come here to serve them." His only consolation was that he had proved his point. The appropriators *were* the most powerful figures on the Hill, and no one was willing to challenge them.

Afterward in his office, he was calmer as he assessed what had happened.

"People look at this, and they say, 'There's a guy who took on Byrd and got his butt handed to him.' Well, I don't care if I got my butt handed to me. It's not an ego thing.

"What's going on in West Virginia is just an outrage. How long before people step up and stop it? Byrd is working the system, but the system is letting him work it."

The problem, Smith said, was that all the incentives in the Senate went to spending, not saving.

"People can get very comfortable in this place. If you play along, you're a responsible, good legislator. If not, they hold it against you. Everyone's polite, but it's made known that you can't be trusted. You're viewed as an outsider, not a team player.

"I've had members say to me, 'Just go along, put your paddle in the water and head downstream. Enjoy yourself and collect a nice pension in twelve years.'

"There's a temptation. But then I think to myself, how can I be a part of that and then go face Mrs. Brown in Wolfeboro, New Hampshire, and explain to her that her Social Security is only going up 3 percent because we've got all these other important things we've got to spend money on?"

Not long afterward, the Porkbusters Bill died an unmourned death.

"You can only push this so far before you run the risk of seeming like a lunatic," said one staffer. "A guy like Smith could lose his ability to do *any* business at all in the Senate."

Yet the New Hampshire freshman insisted he'd be back. "We'll try again next year," he said. "Maybe we'll be a little smarter."

A few weeks later a final version of the transportation bill emerged from a conference committee. It was a classic Capitol Hill compromise: everybody won. None of the 58 Senate pork projects or the 71 House pork projects was cut. The final bill had 129 pork projects.

The conference was also notable for an amazing debate about one of those projects. Houston Congressman Tom DeLay was fighting as hard as he could to *prevent* the committee from spending money on a giant rail project in his district. The people there didn't want a rail line, he argued, and besides, the city of Houston had no clear idea of how to spend the money; the city council was still squabbling over a mass transit plan.

But giving money back is a dangerous precedent. Frank Lautenberg said no. His colleague, Phil Gramm, coauthor of the Gramm-Rudman deficit reduction law, had told him Houston should get the money no matter what, and that was good enough for Lautenberg. DeLay was forced to accept a compromise and take $30 million, leaving a Michigan congressman named Bob Carr to throw up his hands in the middle of the conference committee and exclaim, "People are treating this like an entitlement. Nobody's due this money! It's only supposed to be there if there's a need for it."

Or if somebody who wants it is powerful enough to take it.

At that moment, it was clear that the meager defenses of the Porkbusters were down. There would be no serious objection to the Money Congress's business at hand that year. The time had come, as Shakespeare would have said, to let slip the hogs of Congress.

## 16

# HOG WALLOW

THE SECOND TUESDAY IN OCTOBER WAS ONE OF THOSE RARE, genuinely dramatic days on Capitol Hill. From early morning, the marble halls and cramped offices buzzed as television crews set up outside the building and reporters hunted members of Congress in search of quotes they could send off to a news-thirsty nation tuning in on car radios in Akron or CNN *Headline News* in Salt Lake City.

The reason was Clarence Thomas. The Senate was supposed to vote on his nomination to the Supreme Court that day at 6 P.M. But two days earlier, the seamy sexual harassment charges of Anita Hill had popped into public view, and all bets were off. In private offices across the Hill, fingers were being duly moistened and held up to the wind. Senators were shuttling to the floor to deliver anguished speeches in front of a packed press gallery. Telegrams and phone calls poured in. At one point an angry band of female House members stormed over to give the "boys' club," as they called it, a lecture.

The day was supposed to climax in a moment when the entire Senate would be seated at its desks as the clerk called the roll. Of course, it didn't. The Senate decided to call a time-out and study the matter further—thus the infamous Thomas hearings—so everyone went home, only to face the same vote two weeks later.

But while the Senate held the nation's attention, on the other side of the Hill the Money Congress convened its own session. Hardly anyone noticed, as was intended. In fact, aside from some slumbering high school students in the visitors' gallery and an occasional member who wandered onto the floor, the chamber was almost empty. Yet at the very moment that people like Dale Bumpers and Alan Dixon and the evil twin who had taken over the body of Alan Simpson ("She will be injured and destroyed and hounded and harassed . . ." Simpson graciously said of Ms. Hill) were expounding on Thomas and Hill, Jamie Whitten announced that he was prepared to entertain debate on the $52 billion agriculture spending bill—though, by the stern way he sat surrounded by most of the members of the House Appropriations Committee, it was clear he didn't intend to entertain much.

Farmers are important, he mumbled for the forty-third year in a row in his syrupy Delta drawl. They are the backbone of the country. They have it tough and they need government help. Any questions?

To those unaccustomed to his dense diction, the obvious question was, What the hell did he say? But those on the floor needed no translation. Several members of his subcommittee got up and offered high praise to the chairman for his fine work in getting this bill finished.

"I want to compliment the chairman, the distinguished gentleman from Mississippi, for his hard work, indeed, his untiring efforts . . ."

The cardinals and lesser clerics sat in such an array behind Whitten that you almost expected them to burst into Gregorian chant.

The only dog in the manger was Dan Burton of Indiana, who got up to protest a grant to the University of North Dakota, supposedly for agricultural research but actually to build a new road to the new football stadium.

"I don't want to be the person to throw cold water on this friendly discussion, but there does appear to be some pork in this bill."

No one paid attention. Actually "some pork" understated the case; there were a couple of Iowa counties' worth of fully fattened Hereford hogs lurking in the stack of paper on Whitten's table, some of them dating back to the day Whitten had taken control of the agriculture subcommittee. But this day, Congress's attention was elsewhere.

Whitten turned matters over to his understudy, eighty-two-year-old Bill Natcher, who rattled through a series of Conference Committee agreements with the speed of a tobacco auctioneer. "Mr. Speaker, I offer a motion."

"The clerk will read the motion."

"Senate amendment number 176: page 59, line 5, strike out all after 'than' down to and including 'assistance' in line 7 and insert . . ."

"I ask unanimous consent."

"Is there objection?"

*Bang!*

"The motion is carried."

"Mr. Speaker, I offer a motion . . ."

And so on, in the singsong cadence of legislation that can be mesmerizing and soothing if you have a lot of time on your hands. The high school students in the gallery did, and they were soon lulled into a stupor. Real civics was happening thirty feet below them, and they didn't have a clue.

Finally, after the motions and the accolades were exhausted, Whitten called the question. A few more congressmen had gathered, most of them from farm states. Anything having to do with farm legislation in Congress takes place in a subculture of farm state congressmen. It often seems that few others care. Farm staters are a potent bloc who stick together for the most part and get what they want.

But lots of urban money also found its way into the growing octopus of the farm bill. Food stamps, school lunches, the heartrendingly named Women, Infants and Children feeding program—these were the growth areas of farm spending. Certain kinds of food, the kind with a particular constituency, were being bought by the government and sent to people who supposedly needed it. Other programs funded a farm bureaucracy that, while running out of farmers to serve, was being clever about acquiring new clients. For example, the Agriculture Department will spend $1 million to maintain a farm extension office in Washington, D.C., which has no farmland. They say it's to teach cooking skills to poor people.

That day, the strangely successful urban-rural alliance was apparent in one of those strangely American encounters. As Natcher handled the details, Whitten went for a stroll around the floor. At one point, he came upon the sleeping form of Charlie Hayes, an immense, lazy old union hack who came from a part of the South Side of Chicago where the only thing that grew was toilet bowl ring, and from a political school with a simple slogan: "Spend more." Hayes has been charted as a man who virtually never opposes the spending of federal money. As Whitten approached, Hayes started, as if the scent of meat a-cookin' had wafted into his nostrils. He shook his head clear and smiled as the Prelate of Pork leaned over and poked a beefy finger at a paragraph in the bill he carried with him. Hayes was getting something he wanted. And whatever it was, it cost money. They both nodded and laughed, and then the two fat hands—one attached to a black packing house worker, the other to a southern plantation owner's son—gripped each other.

A few minutes later, the bill passed by voice vote.

In the weeks after, the spectacle of the Thomas hearings and the venality of the House check-bouncing scandal would plunge Congress into a swamp of criticism and self-loathing. People on the Hill and off somewhat hysterically began to question the body's ability to function. But the methodical work of the appropriators would stand as eloquent, if quiet, rebuttal. Over the next six weeks, each of the appropriations bills would clear its hurdles and be sent to the president's desk for his signature. There would be none of the histrionics of the year before, when money decisions had been in the hands of people like Dick Darman and Dick Gephardt. This year, it was left to the pros.

So the appropriations bills rolled down the track like giant Union Pacific freight trains, car after car laden with all manner of spending programs, some good, some bad, some questionable. All moved with surprising speed, given their size. God help anything stalled on the tracks. There were cattle cars full of farm loans and grain hoppers mounded with crop subsidies, coal wagons piled with goodwill for the residents of Appalachia, flatbeds stacked with new roads and cheap logs, shiny steel tank cars awash in energy research grants, well-used boxcars bearing everything from housing for the poor to custom-tailored boondoggles for the rich and, finally, a seemingly endless express train painted an ominous olive drab and holding all the weapons needed to reduce the earth to a smoldering cinder. They came on relentlessly, *clack-clack-clack-clack*, carrying $534 billion worth of cargo. Who got it was dictated by a combination of power, favoritism, regionalism, self-interest, ego, friendships, animosities and influence trading. In other words, politics. In other words, it was a typical year.

And typically, it wouldn't have been Congress if the session didn't end in a blaze of midnight deal making. Odds and ends—and matters as big as the $151 billion highway bill and a $95 billion bank reform bill—were left to the last minute, enabling the swift and strong once again to pile on some extra freight.

For the last few days, much of Congress ran on a twenty-four-hour schedule. The final draft of the 450-page bank reform bill was finished at 4:57 A.M. on the Wednesday before Thanksgiving. This wasn't an appropriations bill, but it still had plenty of pork. In the wee hours, the bill's managers agreed to millions of dollars in special items, including handouts to several charities that had lost money when a New York bank failed and they were stuck holding deposits that exceeded the insurance limit. The latter was a payoff to Al D'Amato in return for his dropping a bizarre plan to slap a lid on all credit card interest rates. Similar deals were being cut on an hourly basis.

William Roth, Jr., the puckish senator from Delaware with the face of a Borscht Belt comic, summed up the frenzy with a poem he read on the Senate floor two days before Thanksgiving and the end of Congress's year:

> " 'Twas the night before recess and all through the land
> The economy was stagnant, employees were canned
> The Congress was wrapped up all tight in its words;
> At home angry voices of voters were heard.
> While lobbyists with smiles and special interests with grins
> Went off to vacation to boast of their wins."

By Thanksgiving morning, the season was over. The warm, sunny day found Capital Hill deserted. An army of members, staffers and lobbyists had gone back to where they had come from, not to resume work until February, after the president's new budget was presented. For better or worse, their deeds were done. All that was left now was to sift through the rubble and figure out what had happened.

Only now could one pry open the spending bills and see what had been done. That year, pork held less sex appeal than it had after the budget deal, so there were fewer newspaper accounts.

*The Washington Post* followed some of the pork trails, and *Congressional Quarterly* came out with an exhaustive 168-page special issue that detailed each of the money bills and stands as an impressive, nuts-and-bolts view of the spending process. The porkologists were less diligent, having been discouraged by their defeats. Margaret Hill and Tom Schatz at Citizens Against Government Waste compiled their annual "Pig Book," but other watchdogs were mostly silent.

Still, there was plenty to find. And though porkology is a new and struggling discipline—no known universities offer it, and federal grants are unlikely—by year-end one could slice open the hog's carcass and define his parts into more specific categories. The Porkbusters Bill had provided an intense but incomplete sample. Viewed with a more critical eye, the size of the hog residing inside the federal budget was vastly fatter than one might have originally assumed. Here was his anatomy:

**ROTTEN PORK.** This is the really awful kind, the putrid, obvious, laugh-out-loud kind, the kind that seems so brazen that an ordinary person could never imagine it being approved. There seemed to be less of it this year. The cardinals were testy after the prior year's embarrassments, particularly Lawrence Welk, so they cut down on the silliness. According to one source, the curia had decreed that a "laugh test" be applied to project requests, and anything that sounded just too downright stupid for words was going to get cut out. But despite their best intentions, a few whoppers slipped through, often because the cardinals can be their own worst enemies.

For instance, the world's most expensive railroad museum in Scranton, Pennsylvania, got another $13 million, thanks to Joseph "Steamtown Joe" McDade. This graveyard for old trains will siphon off about $80 million before it's through, and then will cost at least $6 million a year to operate. McDade was so confident that he had passed the "too-big-to-butcher" threshold that he called for public hearings before the Interior Committee to get Steamtown officially authorized once and for all. McDade, newly named the senior Republican on the full committee, which makes him something like the Vatican's rabbi, also celebrated by buying himself several other projects, including one of the strangest: a $10 million grant to the nuns at a tiny Marywood College in Scranton to study stress on military families. The college's president was so surprised by the grant that she told *The Washington Post* that she had no idea how she was going to spend the money.

Across the state from Steamtown, Cardinal John Murtha of Johnstown grabbed another $13 million in his continuing quest to rehab a bunch of shuttered factories around his district and call them a national park under the program he had named America's Industrial Heritage.

The most bizarre project was Ted Stevens's sty-in-the-sky, otherwise known as his plan to harness the energy of the aurora borealis. The latest installment was a $25 million supercomputer, which he got for the University of Alaska in Fairbanks. *Huh?* That's what most of the scientific community said when it learned of this scheme, which makes Star Wars look like a high school physics experiment. Stevens, a man who parades around the Senate with the air of a small-city mayor and who's persistently tried to turn much of Alaska into a porkable commodity, must also be trying to change his image into that of Mr. Wizard. Proving that a little knowledge is a dangerous thing, he somehow got it into his head that scientists could figure out a way to trap the huge currents of solar energy that create the northern lights effect. He had already used his position as the leading Republican on Defense Appropriations to grab $20 million, and this year he picked off his biggest slab: the supercomputer that many first-rate universities would die for and one that U. of A. will be hard pressed to utilize. Not that old U. of A. is unfamiliar with federal handouts. Stevens has put almost $60 million into the place in recent years, much of it for Poker Flat, a rocket launching facility that NASA doesn't want. And all this for a state that is the richest in the nation, thanks to huge rake-offs from the sale of its oil. Alaska has no income or sales tax, runs a surplus each year—$11 billion last year—and sends each of its citizens a refund check for around $1,000. But, as Stevens would say, there's always room for pork.

**POWER PORK.** This is the brazen sort of political spoilmanship. Only a handful of members can get away with it—though Congress being an oblique sort of place, there are no actual showdowns; most of the loot's carted off by wimpy guys operating late at night or when no one's looking.

Senator Daniel Patrick Moynihan offered the best example of the year. The brilliant, bombastic and hypocritical representative of New York is also the next best thing to a cardinal. He chairs the Public Works Committee, which authorizes all manner of big-money projects, including that year's biggest, the highway bill— not to be confused with the transportation bill. Because the money comes from federal gas taxes, the cardinals didn't get a shot at this $151 billion bonus baby; Moynihan hashed the bill out through a deal with his House counterpart, Robert Roe of New Jersey. The undertaking, to say the least, was pork heavy. Roe, a wisecracking, spend-'em-up Democrat from northern New Jersey, set the tone by loading on billions of dollars in special projects to keep himself and selected committee cronies happy. Moynihan, the bowtied former Harvard professor who likes to give lengthy speeches on the Senate floor even if no one listens, tries to present the image of one who treats the grubbier business of the Senate the same way he would treat a roach he discovered in his salade Niçoise. He often chides his colleagues for their pork tendencies. He vowed there would be none in the highway bill, and at one point during a testy conference committee session with the House, he threatened to make members march in and explain the purpose of their various "congressional projects of national significance," the year's euphemism for pork. Roe blanched at this heresy, and war could have resulted had not cooler heads in the Senate prevailed and calmed down the windy senator.

So it was somewhat surprising when, several months after the bill had passed, Walter Pincus of *The Washington Post* discovered that Moynihan had pulled a fast one and stuck his own huge piece of pork right into the middle of the bill. It seems he felt the federal courthouse in Brooklyn was too crowded and the General Services Administration was dragging its feet in putting up a new one. Moynihan solved the problem by putting a $450 million paragraph in the highway bill that had the effect of mandating that your gas taxes be used to build his courthouse. He later said he hadn't meant to use gas money, but an aide was quoted as saying that the senator's objective "is to make sure that the space problem at the Brooklyn courthouse is fixed, no matter how he has to do it."

Of course, one reason the GSA may not have had the money to accommodate Moynihan was because of all the other buildings they're told to put up. Bob Byrd was getting two new courthouses, for instance, and Cardinal Ed Roybal, who heads the subcommittee that funds these things, was getting the Edward R. Roybal Federal Building in Los Angeles. There was also what's known around Washington as the billion-dollar boondoggle, a giant federal office complex called the Federal Triangle under construction on Pennsylvania Avenue just down from the White House. At a time when Washington is drowning in private office space and the federal government is supposed to be shrinking, the government is building the biggest structure since the Pentagon.

The man behind that plan? None other than Daniel Patrick Moynihan.

**CHARITY PORK.** Anyone who sticks his nose into this pot runs the risk of having it lopped off on a charge of insensitivity. Here you find the projects that on their face sound unchallengeable: good government doing good deeds.

The new budget had things like $2.5 million to build a dormitory at St. Joseph's School for the Blind in Jersey City and $3 million for a training center for the blind in Lafayette, Louisiana; a detoxification center for the homeless in San Francisco; advanced care for the elderly in Boston; and "job retention of agricultural workers at two sugarcane mills on Hawaii's Hilo-Hamakua coast."

One would have to be possessed of a pretty suspicious mind to question endeavors such as these. But let's try.

Why, for instance, are so many of these projects only in the districts of the appropriators? There are blind people throughout America, but New Jersey and Louisiana got the money because Bennett Johnston and Frank Lautenberg sit on the HUD subcommittee that gave it out. Few of these grants go through any kind of review process; they're just issued on the word of a congressman. Why do Hawaiian sugar workers deserve a handout any more than Florida sugar workers or Chicago steelworkers? Then there's the issue that all these needs are already supposed to be serviced by a flotilla of government agencies. There was, for instance, housing for the Navajo Indians sneaked into the HUD bill, which seems like a worthy cause until you realize that there's an entire Bureau of Indian Affairs and about a hundred programs designed to help Indians with housing and other problems.

The ultimate question is, What's the real cost of letting one of the cardinals feel good about himself, and who's being cheated in the process?

**TROPHY PORK.** This is money that would have been spent anyway but gets steered in special directions based on who you are and whom you know. Some of it's relatively harmless stuff, the consequence of a congressman who can't resist hanging the trophy on his own wall. Thus Arkansas State Highway 71 is now the John Paul Hammerschmidt Highway. The Joseph Ralph Sasser Boat Ramp on the Mississippi River in Tennessee came courtesy of his son, Senator Jim. And Bennett Johnston, the chivalrous old southern gentleman, rewarded retiring House colleague Lindy Boggs for her undying support of his good works by naming a new lock and dam on the Red River Waterway after her.

But the best example was in the highway bill, a five-year transportation package that was paid for by the federal gasoline tax. The money was going to be spent on roads and rails, but whose roads and rails?

The bill was pork driven from the start, with prime sponsor Bob Roe actually asking House members for their shopping list of special projects before he put it together. After he divvied them up, he then told members that anyone who quibbled about the bill would have his projects slashed out. When it finally passed, there were almost five hundred projects worth at least $5 billion and by some estimates as much as $11 billion over five years. And the big winner? Surprise! *Come on down, Bob Roe!* You've got a whole new transportation system for your state!

Other big winners were Hammerschmidt, the ranking Republican on Roe's very bipartisan committee, and the two fellows who drafted the bill, Norm Mineta of California and Bud Shuster of Pennsylvania. Along with all kinds of road expansion, some of which might actually have been useful, there were the usual university research centers and oddball projects to build experimental timber bridges, purchase buses and ferryboats, build bike paths and fix up shopping malls. There was even a new category called "smart pork," which involves research into high-tech highways. The idea is to use satellites, cameras and buried sensors to move traffic along, and while there must be merit to this research, that merit was tainted by the fact that New Jersey and New York, which have most of the power, got most of the money.

All this, and it only costs an extra fourteen cents a gallon every time you fill up.

**PERPETUAL PORK.** These are the programs that, once started, will never die. Many date back to the New Deal and others to Lyndon Johnson's Great Society. For instance, the Tennessee Valley Authority was started in the 1930s to bring civilization to the folks living around the Tennessee River and its tributaries by building dams and providing cheap electric power. A resounding success, TVA is now a large, profitable corporation that pays its own way—as intended. But TVA still takes $135 million of federal money as it invents make-work projects that are touted by a variety of congressmen. The principle is similar to what happened to the Rural Electrification Administration, another well-intentioned New Deal program that brought electricity to practically every farm in the country. But since REA needs a reason for existence, it's now redefining itself to bring subsidized telephones and cable television to those same homes—at a cost this year of $270 million. The good news is that its generous low-interest loans are rarely in default, because they're made to large, profitable telecommunications companies that don't need the money.

Less successful was the Appalachian Regional Commission, once a keystone of the war on poverty but now the private preserve of a few congressmen. More than half of its $190 million budget will go to building roads in just three states: Alabama (where Tom Bevill lives), Mississippi (home of Jamie Whitten) and West Virginia (Bob Byrd's state).

But at least these agencies can claim some accomplishments. The Johnson-era Economic Development Administration was intended to help depressed rural areas, but "depressed" and "rural" quickly got defined to include 80 percent of the congressional districts in the country. EDA became a little piggy bank for weird projects including a twenty-acre "water theme" amusement park in Beaumont, Texas, and grants to companies in New London, Connecticut. Mostly the agency gives out loans, up to 40 percent of which aren't repaid. But every president since Richard Nixon has tried without success to take the piggy bank away. And although it topped Dick Darman's hit list this year, EDA turned out to be one of the big winners, with a hefty boost in funding to $250 million.

Another big winner was the woefully mismanaged Small Business Administration, which also traces its lineage to the New Deal and has been denounced by critics as diverse as David Stockman ("a billion-dollar rathole") and *Common Cause* magazine ("an empty paean to the free enterprise system"). Despite a few notable successes—it supposedly gave Federal Express and Apple Computer their seed money—the agency has been a mire of scandal, patronage and waste with no mission other than what its congressional masters decide they want doled out in a given year. SBA lends money to shaky businesses based on congressional clout, and the default rate for some programs is a hefty, but not surprising, 30 percent. Living off the SBA fat, according to Common Cause, was that high-flying hustler of the corporate world, Neil Bush, the president's son, who had a huge SBA-related loan. But the 1992 bottom line for this agency, which doesn't understand the bottom line: an 80 percent budget hike to $837 million.

Then there's the National Endowment for Democracy, typical of many little fiefdoms squirreled away in odd places. The fund is supposed to promote democracy around the world, but mostly promotes nice trips for congressmen and their friends. *Congressional Quarterly* discovered that despite a "devastating report" by the General Accounting Office saying that money had been "misused, mismanaged or not effectively accounted for," the fund got $27.5 million for the year.

**PRESIDENTIAL PORK.** George Bush's kid isn't the only one who benefits from the pork process. The old man's no slouch either. Despite his high-pitched bluster directed at "little carping liberal Democrats" and their "pork-barrel bonanzas," Bush had plenty of his own in the 1992 budget. He also managed to cut none out. When the final tally was in, all of Darman's targets for pork had been missed. But as one Appropriations Committee staffer noted, "How could he try to cut anything with a straight face when he was putting his own in?"

And the president's pork was often double-edged: to get his, he had to let others get theirs. Consider the space station, which was arguably its own boondoggle but also opened the floodgates to outrageous projects throughout the HUD/VA appropriations bill. The same thing happened with the superconducting supercollider, a project that makes Bush's Texas cronies happy as rancheros at a pig pull but also cost a bundle of other water projects to buy the silence of such crafty gents as J. Bennett Johnston and Tom Bevill.

The highway bill provided an interesting case study in this president's prerogative to change his mind. Luckily for him, he never actually said, "Read my lips: no new pork." When the bill was introduced, Transportation Secretary Sam Skinner gagged at the almost five hundred pork projects—perhaps an all-time record for a single bill. They were to be paid for by a sly increase in the federal gas tax—actually an extension of the boost already put into place by the budget deal. With White House approval, Skinner went on the warpath and told Congress it was heading for Veto City. That is, until Bush started dropping in the popularity polls and he finally got the point that the economy was in the toilet. Suddenly Bush started thinking just like Jamie Whitten: any spending is good spending. Skinner, a pragmatist like Bush, got the message quickly and shut up. The tax passed, the bill passed and the next time anyone heard from Skinner was when he went to Texas where Bush was signing it in a hokey ceremony. Now the president's chief of staff, Skinner put his arm around some construction workers in a truck stop and told them that this president is going to do the right thing and put some greenbacks into their jeans. What are you gagging on now, Sam?

Not much later, as his slide in the polls steepened and the primary season heated up, George "I will do whatever it takes to win" Bush trekked to New Hampshire to talk up all the projects of local interest he'd brought to the state including a new courthouse. Pork had suddenly become a very important service to be provided by the Bush administration.

And Bush had petty things, too. Like the Thousand Points of Light Foundation, an agency intended to keep alive the unfulfilled vision of his campaign speechwriter who saw an America where slogans and volunteerism would solve all problems. Bush saw it as a way to keep alive his campaign themes in an election year. The cardinals saw it as a way to twit the president. He wanted $10 million, which they at first sliced out completely. Then, like schoolyard bullies who'd taken his lunch money, they gave him back half after they'd had their fun.

Makes it a little hard to take him seriously.

**ACADEMIC PORK.** If you thought that universities are above the degrading business of begging for federal favors, you thought wrong. Pork tied to research grants is one of the fastest-growing types, soaring from practically nothing ten years ago to about a billion dollars this year. Most commonly, it comes as earmarked funds in which the appropriations bill says, "$84,800,000 will be available only for the Institute for Micromanufacturing, Louisiana Tech University; the Ambulatory Research and Education Building, Oregon Health Sciences University . . ." The earmarks usually leap out because the schools that get this stuff tend to be small, obscure colleges in strategically placed locations—that is, the congressional districts of people with clout. The grants are issued by fiat, without any competition or review by other academics who might be able to evaluate the best place to study a given problem. The standard argument of the porkers is that the big schools— Harvard, Stanford, Michigan—would get all the big federal money, and earmarks are just a way to spread it around.

And spread they do. Academic pork pops up in the strangest places, including the energy bill, the defense bill, the agriculture bill and even the education bill.

The Pentagon in particular gets robbed each year. And Sam Nunn, who heads the Senate Armed Services Committee and sees himself as a serious-minded guardian of national defense, goes crazy. He was particularly outraged after the post–budget deal bender that ended up with Congress billing the Pentagon for everything but its laundry. Nunn was all set to hold up the entire defense budget, but at the last minute he relented in return for a written promise that the porkers wouldn't do it again this year. But boys will be boys, and sure enough, just as Nunn was about to kick the football, they yanked it away and he landed on his duff. The 1992 bill has more than $100 million of research earmarks of questionable value, including funds to put a submarine into an Oregon museum and to breed fish in Hawaii. Nunn must almost feel like a taxpayer.

"Evidently these projects are of such questionable value to the Department of Defense that the bill has to exempt these projects from any form of competition or merit review in order to assure their funding," Nunn whined in that nasal drawl. "This is not the way the process is supposed to work." And this from a man who's been in the Senate for twenty years?

But he shouldn't feel singled out. For instance, the Forest Service was told it has to spend $3.3 million—much of it at West Virginia University—to take us back to the nineteenth century by learning new ways to build bridges out of timber. One imagines the hand of Robert Byrd, who has been accused of having nineteenth-century sensibilities, behind this. While NASA saw its entire research budget cut to the bone to pay for the controversial manned space station, the Senate still managed to find $8.25 million to construct something called the "classroom of the future" at that noted citadel of higher education, Wheeling Jesuit College in— well, look at this!—West Virginia.

The broader question seems to be whether any of these grants is worth the money. In the same week appropriators were loading up their favorite schools, a group of colleges were sheepishly admitting to another congressional committee that, yes, they had used quite a bit of the federal handouts for things that, if you were to quibble about it, might not *technically* be considered the pursuit of knowledge. Things like, oh, well, $7,000 worth of Porthault sheets for the bed of Donald Kennedy, the sophisticatedly sleazy president of Stanford, an antique commode for his house, expenses on the school's seventy-two foot yacht, a retreat for the board in Lake Tahoe and expenses at a shopping center owned by the university. That sort of thing. Probably only an extra $400 million or so over the last decade. And that was just Stanford. Lots of schools like Yale, MIT, the University of Chicago and Rutgers have been doing the same thing, costing the government an extra billion since 1980, according to congressional investigators. All of which goes to prove what your father always told you when you asked for a raise in your allowance: "If you don't have to work for it, you won't appreciate it"—a lesson that might apply to much of what the government gives out.

**SNEAKY PORK.** These are usually small, annoying bits that get stuffed into bills totally unrelated to the matter at hand. The best example is the Stuttgart, Arkansas, catfish farm. A perennial favorite that's starting to cost some real money, it's the godchild of Arkansas Senator Dale "Catfish" Bumpers, a cardinal-in-waiting, who got the freshwater farm another $600,000 from the National Oceanographic and Atmospheric Administration, which, as its name suggests, is supposed to study saltwater fish.

Not so obvious was zebra mussel research, which sounds strange but actually may be a legitimate problem. The little bivalves were recently introduced into the Great Lakes and found the climate so hospitable that they've been multiplying a billion at a clip. They collect in colonies like barnacles and are apparently a nuisance to shipping. But if they're such a genuine problem, why does the patron saint of the research, Cardinal Bob Traxler, have to sneak it into at least four different places: $500,000 in the Department of Transportation; $250,000 in the Environmental Protection Agency; $980,000 in one Commerce Department account, and $3 million in another?

The Energy Department bill contained lots of things having nothing to do with energy, such as $10 million for a center to train math and science teachers at Bridgewater State College in Massachusetts, thanks to Joe Moakley, an honorary cardinal who runs the House Rules Committee and can be a good friend to have. That bill's conference committee made no bones about the fact that the center had little to do with energy or education, noting that its benefit "to the economic development of this particularly hard-hit area of Southeastern Massachusetts would be tremendous."

Cardinal Neal Smith continued to fund his eccentric plan to have the Small Business Administration provide $105 million over the next few years to plant trees, a job that the Forest Service seems to handle just fine—although with all the work they need to do for Bob Byrd in West Virginia and Mark Hatfield in Oregon, perhaps they're too busy.

But the best sneaky pork was some of the items in the squealing VA/HUD bill, you know, the bill that funds urban development. Yet here were things like a "rural health care clinic" in McDowell County, West Virginia, which is about as rural as you get; a rural health education center in Nebraska; and $850,000 for "rural development assistance demonstration activities" in Utah.

**CULTURE PORK.** Perhaps the purpose is to court the favor of fat-cat contributors, or perhaps congressmen are more aesthetically inclined than they appear, but funds for the finer things in life have long been a staple of the pork barrel. The fundamental question is, Why is the government, especially a strapped government, engaged in the business of funding art? You might start by wondering why the National Park Service spent $23 million to fund the Kennedy Center for the Performing Arts in Washington. Few ordinary citizens will ever go there, though many congressmen will. And while it certainly looks nice, perched there in its marble splendor alongside the Potomac River, the center is mostly used as a set for television specials that feature professionally patriotic country-western artists singing "I'm Proud to Be an American" while

George and Barbara beam away in the presidential box. They ought to pay for it out of his reelection fund.

Hard-nosed conservatives like to throw the Corporation for Public Broadcasting and its $275 million subsidy into this tank and wonder why the government is in the television business. Then there's the whole National Endowment for the Arts, which, Jesse Helms, nude paintings and Christ in a jar of wee-wee aside, still raises the question of what is the point of government-sponsored art?

Then there's culture in the provinces, such as the Victory Park Auditorium, which the Department of Housing and Urban Development built out of an old gymnasium in North Miami Beach so the rich pensioners of that community wouldn't have to travel downtown to enjoy the road show of *Cats.* The town was doubly blessed this year with the good news that everyone who needs housing assistance from the federal government must be getting it because HUD was also instructed to spend $2.5 million to expand the North Miami Center for Contemporary Art. And if that wasn't enough, residents will soon be able to ride their mountain bikes to the museum because the Department of Transportation will be building them new bike paths. All of this comes courtesy of that former used-car salesman and very aesthetic guy, Bill Lehman.

**SUBSIDY PORK.** Rarely considered in the pork roundups, subsidies are an enormous font of federal favoritism that contain many hidden costs. Sometimes the cost is in actual dollars laid out; sometimes it's in dollars not collected; and sometimes it's in additional funds that consumers must spend because the government is regulating the market by doing things like setting prices. Like most government programs, once they're enacted they develop rabid constituencies and are hard to ferret out. They also tend to be supported by blocks of congressmen rather than lone wolves.

The Bureau of Reclamation provides cheap water to farmers in the West, a program that was once intended to help out the mythical rugged, lone American taming his piece of the frontier but has now become a sop for giant agribusinesses that are adept at finding loopholes in the law. In fact, according to Congressmen Richard Armey and others, a large part of the billions in farm-related subsidies is going to very rich folks. Congressman Harris Fawell has estimated that just cutting out subsidies for farmers earning over $100,000 a year would save a billion dollars a year.

The same principle applies to grazing lands, timber forests and mining. By some estimates, the Mining Law alone restricts the government to leases that are $1 billion below what it could get on the open market. And none of this takes into consideration the environmental costs that occur when you undersell a public asset.

Electricity rates in the Northwest are 40 percent below those in the rest of the nation, thanks to hydroelectric dams built with everyone's money. Yet the Western Area Power Administration still got $306 million for expansion. And in a ploy that would seem to tip the hand of inequity, the appropriators this year stuck in a provision that expressly prohibits the federal government from even *studying* whether rates are too low.

One of the most perverse types of subsidy is the Maritime Administration, which is responsible for regulating the nation's merchant marine fleet. Since George Washington decreed that the nation should ship cargo on its own boats, a dense web of subsidies costing as much as $5 billion a year has grown up around shipping and turned it into one of the country's largest welfare recipients.

Gosh, those burly sailors don't *look* like welfare queens buying vodka with their food stamps, but the new budget had $272 million just to subsidize their jobs, or about $120,000 per. That'd buy you a whole block of welfare queens in Bed-Sty, Brooklyn. Then there are various requirements that ships be built in the United States and certain kinds of cargo be carried only on U.S.-built and -manned vessels.

All this is preserved by the House Merchant Marine Committee, a whole committee established just to oversee this one area of special interest and a committee that not surprisingly has gone into the tank for its clients. Propping up the committee is an aggressive lobby that greases the members, most from port areas, with campaign contributions early and often. And sometimes with more than contributions: four of the last five chairmen have been investigated for criminal ties to the industry, and two have gone to jail.

The purpose of all these handouts is supposedly to keep a strong cargo fleet ready in case of war. Since the Jones Act of 1920, few in Congress have dared challenge this premise. But the irony of the subsidies is that not only are they expensive, they're apparently worthless. The fleet has dwindled, and the Pentagon doesn't want to use it.

"The laws were meant to protect the shipping industry, but they're killing it," said Rob Quartel, a maritime commissioner who thinks the agency he oversees is crazy. During the Persian Gulf War, he discovered that only six of sixty subsidized ships were used to move military cargo. Almost all war cargo was sent on foreign-owned ships chartered through regular shipping companies.

"This explodes the myth," he said. "The subsidies are a corporate and labor welfare program thinly disguised as a national security project."

And this irony-rich realm offers one more lesson about pork. Because all domestic shipping must be done with American-made ships, the cost is so high that it no longer makes sense to use water to move something from Boston to Florida. Or, say, to use a spanking-new inland waterway like the Tennessee-Tombigbee. Thus the failure of that infamous canal, and others, can be attributed to a little-known trait of hogs: left untended, they're cannibals. Big pork will be eaten by bigger pork.

But the biggest pork of all was in the world of agriculture. The domain of Mr. Whitten was subsidy heaven. Start with the fact that this year the Commodity Credit Corporation got a whopping $3.25 billion increase in its budget, a 50 percent boost, and you've got to be suspicious of what's coming. The CCC is Whitten's private bank, allowing him to regulate the many crop subsidy programs.

The favored ones include sugar, wool, honey, wheat, cotton and rice. In simple terms—and there is nothing simple about ag subsidies—the government sets a guaranteed target price, and if the market price drops below this, the taxpayer makes up the difference. The wonderland quality of this system is that it encourages farmers to overproduce, which further drives prices down and forces the government to buy more of the crops. Which encourages the farmers to overproduce . . .

One way off the merry-go-round, as long as you're not the one paying for the ride, is to give the farmer money *not* to grow crops. This has worked well. According to Congressman Harris Fawell, by 1990 the government had paid to shut down about 60 million acres, about the size of three midwestern states.

The result is billions of dollars in higher food prices to go along with the billions of tax dollars paid out directly to farmers.

Take the case of peanuts, which have been protected since World War II. Supply is restricted by allowing goobers to be grown only by those who had licenses in 1941 and by sending out squads of peanut police to make damn sure that's the way it stays. Imports are also curtailed and prices guaranteed. Needless to say, many peanut farmers are wealthy men. But consumers, Fawell says, pay an extra forty cents on a $1.79 jar of peanut butter.

Or consider another World War II legacy, the temporary honey program, which was started to encourage production of honey as a sugar substitute and create a supply of beeswax to use in water-proofing combat equipment. After the war, there was a glut of honey and the simple solution would have been to let the market weed out the inefficient producers. But congressmen with bee-keeping constituents made the case that lots and lots of bees were needed because they pollinate other food crops. How crops had become pollinated in the many centuries of organized agriculture prior to this is unclear, but the subsidy program was continued. Now, forty-six years after the end of the war, honey soaks up almost $200 million in subsidies.

One of the most egregious subsidy programs is for sugar, which costs consumers an extra $3 billion a year. Here prices are kept high by restricting imports. There are lots of parts of the world that grow sugar—under their own subsidy programs—and would dearly love to sell it to us. But Uncle Sugar says no—despite the fact that those that benefit from the subsidy are almost all giant corporate farms.

Typical of the bizarre geometry that emerges in these complex subsidy arrangements is the role of Archer Daniels Midland, a huge food processor based in Illinois. ADM produces no sugar, yet it lobbies hard on sugar's behalf, including running a series of television commercials in praise of our wonderful sugar program, the envy of the world. The reason is that ADM processes corn, which is used to make the increasingly popular sugar *substitute* called high-fructose corn syrup. The higher the price of sugar, the higher the price ADM can charge for corn sweetener. And the consumer pays for it all when he buys a can of Coke.

Finally there's milk, the Rubik's Cube of subsidies, which is so complicated that the rules are laid out in a three-volume set that apparently no more than six people in this country understand. Among the insanities this promotes is the production of much more milk than we need and the maintenance of perhaps twice as many dairy farmers as there should be. Thanks to the government, farm-ers know they can always make a profit milking cows, which is why many farmers have some and why, in the mid-1980s, the govern-ment had to pay farmers a billion dollars to kill the excess animals. The cost to the consumer is simpler to calculate: up to $2 billion a year. But even that's not enough. Dairy farmers tried all year to get a boost in their subsidies. They failed, but they'll be back.

Whitten argues that this is the way God made farming to be. But as agriculture critic James Bovard points out, most crops don't come out of the ground with subsidies attached. Pecans aren't much different than peanuts, but they seem to do fine on their own; corn gets billions, but soybeans get none. We know about milk, but chickens are on their own, as is—ain't life amazing?— pork. What's the common denominator? It's not who you know, but who you elected.

**BYRD PORK.** The Pontiff of Pork has become his own category, his own subgovernment, almost. The year brought no great new initiatives to his state but featured continuing expenditures on existing projects. Harpers Ferry remained on its path to becoming the nerve center of the Fish and Wildlife Service and a vast tourist mecca, the Bureau of Public Debt was told to pack its files and head for Parkersburg, the IRS was given funds to move a research operation to Beckley. Another $48 million went for the FBI's new fingerprint system to go inside the new fingerprint center Byrd had scored the year before, and a $12 million down payment was made on a new road to get to the place.

In highway funds alone, West Virginia got about $200 million in addition to those it would normally receive. West Virginia University was once again one of the best-funded schools in the country, as was Wheeling Jesuit College, which was starting to be known on the Hill as "the Harvard of the Ohio River Valley." Floodwaters would soon touch no part of the Mountaineer State, thanks to another $100 million in locks and dams. And now that the Cold War was over, the military finally began to pay attention to the state that had been just too hilly and inaccessible in the past. Bases and training facilities worth about $50 million would soon be going up.

The damage? It was about a half-billion-dollar year for the man they need to start calling Two-Billion-Dollar Bobby.

**TAX PORK.** If there was one reassuring development in 1991, it was that there wasn't any tax pork. There weren't any deals to give breaks to individual companies and whole industries. The reason was that there weren't any tax bills.

Which is not to say that there wasn't ongoing tax pork. Deals cut in previous years continued to come home to roost, draining billions that would otherwise be going into the Treasury. But the lions of the tax committees were largely silent.

Still, there was hope for them. As the session closed, there was serious talk of a new tax cut bill. And anytime you open up the tax code, you unleash not only the hogs of Congress but their very crafty fellow travelers in the lobbying business.


**DEFENSE PORK.** Gee, we had to hold up that peace dividend again this year. You know, the one the country was supposed to get for hanging tough and winning the war on communism? A few other projects came up that people just *had* to have. We're going to have to get back to you on that one. First we've got to save the Pentagon from democracy.

Not many things Congress did that fall were more ludicrous or wasteful than the 1992 defense budget. Amid its hundreds of pages of retina-boiling acronyms like JSTARS and CHAMPUS and its hundreds of billions of dollars in spending was a sad, simple tale. Here we were, having just won a war against a bunch of Third World cheeseballs while using a tiny amount of all the wonderfully expensive stuff we'd bought over the last twenty years. At the same time the leaders of the Evil Empire we built the stuff to fight in the first place were wandering around like old rummies. And yet for some reason, we were STILL BUILDING A BIGGER ARMY!

Admittedly, the process had begun earlier in the year and had been well along before the Soviet Union collapsed entirely and ceased to be a military threat. But the Soviets had lost most of their claws a lot sooner, and the need for us to maintain the largest military machine in the history of the world should have been outdated a few years ago. But the White House stuck to a plan of taking mouse nibbles from the larder and calling it "meaningful reduction." Then Congress went it one better by ensuring that what was left would be fat and tasty rather than lean and mean. The result was an obscenity. But *whose* obscenity?

That a grotesque defense spending bill passed that fall was not at issue. By its very nature, defense spending is always grotesque and wasteful. The only question was, Where does misguided waste stop and willful pork begin? The Pentagon calculus was always a tricky one, with interservice rivalries, powerful contractors and Congress members of every ideological stripe playing a role in the political architecture of the thousand-plus-page bill. And in the recent past, you had to assume that everyone in Washington was milking the bill for his own purposes.

But of all years, wouldn't you be inclined to give the Pentagon a break this year? In the wake of Desert Storm, one of the most remarkable military victories in history, wouldn't you think that maybe these guys knew what they were doing, that maybe they had a pretty good idea of the kind of weapons they might have to take into battle against the next second-rate army to come along? The Pentagon was actually trying to be reasonable and asking Congress to make some real cuts. But old habits die hard.

Congress talks about cutting military spending incessantly, but when it comes to actually doing it the members say, "Good God, man! Don't take me literally! Take your hands off that! Those are jobs there!" So a whole barn full of weapons and ve-*hic*-les the Pentagon brass wanted to ditch got forced on them. There were M-1 tanks, Bradley Fighting Vehicles, OH-58B helicopters. And that was just existing weapons. The new weapons in the budget included an air-cushioned amphibious landing craft and the Osprey, a $25-million-a-copy whiz-bang combination helicopter-plane that the marines apparently want but the Pentagon had been trying to kill for three years.

In fact, the Pentagon didn't want any of this, old or new. It had plenty. For instance, remember the impressive array of aircraft in the war with Iraq? For the whole war the United States used only ten of its fifty-seven fighter wings. We could have bombed the hell out of five more countries at the same time. The war showed the clearest proof possible that we don't need any more weapons. But more got bought because some combination of Congress members wanted them and deals were cut. You buy mine, I'll buy yours. The Ohio and Michigan guys wanted the M-1; Pennsylvania coveted the Osprey; and so on.

Not that the administration was blameless. It wanted to keep the B-2. (And at $865 million a copy, Congress also needs to keep it as a benchmark just so Appropriations Committee staffers can say things like "Hell, the pork in that bill isn't half the cost of a single stealth bomber." Oh, right. I feel better now.) The B-2 was also worth 40,000 jobs in California, which means nothing for national defense but a lot for electoral votes. The White House also wanted a new model F-18 fighter (the old one seemed to work pretty well in Iraq), an even newer superjet, the Advanced Tactical Fighter (to fight, one assumes, armies from the planet Zoltan); the latest generation of flying cost overruns known as the C-17A transport plane; and the Seawolf, a billion-dollar attack submarine to hunt all the high-tech subs in the world's oceans that don't belong to the Russian Navy—of which there are none.

But maybe there's an argument that the United States has to keep spending on a small, selected number of these systems to keep its high-tech edge on the rest of the world. If you don't spend now, you won't have it five years from now when the next Saddam Hussein acts up. What seemed indefensible was the thousands of niggling items weaseled in by Congress that had nothing to do with grand strategy and everything to do with parochial interests.

The secretary of defense, Dick Cheney, was telling anyone who would listen that he really was going to cut spending sharply—he had a plan right here, he said—but that Congress was making it awfully tough. You could almost believe him. "The choices we're making aren't about jobs back home in the district," he complained in one speech. "It's not about how much pork a congressman's able to deliver on election day. It's preparation for the next time we go to war." That's what he thinks.

The primest pork of the year went to the National Guard. Congress not only blocked the Pentagon from cutting the size of the force but also built dozens of new armories and other facilities because every member of Congress wants to ride at the front of the parade with a three-star reserve general. In some cases, the Pentagon had planned to eliminate entire active-duty divisions, but Congress refused to allow it to cut the reserve units attached to them, leaving the possibility of renegade reserve armies roaming the country in search of a general. Guard-related slop probably added $2 billion in extra spending, thanks in large part to Sonny Montgomery of Mississippi and John Murtha, who considers the Guard his private army. Murtha got a new $30 million reserve facility in his district and also got Guard commanders a few more of the executive jets he's been giving away as door prizes. There was so much Guard money going around that even the lowlier vassals of Congress were getting theirs. Albert Bustamante of San Antonio shoved six new San Antonio–made C-26 cargo planes into the bill, planes that Les Aspin, head of the House Armed Services Committee, called "the worst pork in the business."

Military construction, which has its own spending bill—and a rich one at that—actually increased for the year. And while no one's arguing that the military shouldn't keep up its facilities, doesn't it make you just a wee bit suspicious that so much of the money goes to a few states—and not those states with the most bases? The big winners in military construction were Hawaii, Alaska, West Virginia, Tennessee and Alabama—each and every one represented by powerful members of the appropriations committees. The National Guard was also a big winner here, with about $700 million in new facilities spread among a hundred congressional districts.

Then there was the kind of silly stuff that drove Sam Nunn up the wall. *The New York Times* reported his assertion that the bill had an astonishing $3.3 billion in non-military projects put in by the appropriators to fund things like museums at closed military bases and grants to universities to research things that had nothing to do with defense—or nothing to do with research. When he asked Byrd what the hell was going on, Byrd blamed those rascals in the House and said the senators just couldn't talk them out of it. Nunn, sounding like the class valedictorian who'd just had his homework stolen by someone on the football team, sniffed, "I do not believe there has been a very vigorous effort." Lighten up, Sam, it's not your money.

Reassuringly, there were many of the perpetual standbys as well: the military would be buying anchor chain, canvas and, of course, coal from American companies, and God help the colonel who tries to put oil heat into any European barracks.

Finally, there was this truly startling fact about the Pentagon budget reported by *Congressional Quarterly:* $37.8 billion in funds that had been authorized in past years *hadn't* been spent. All that money, more than most other departments in the government would spend in a whole year, $150 for every person in America, is just sitting in a bank account while someone figures out what to do with it.

## 17

# HOW MUCH IS THAT PIGGY IN THE WINDOW?

*Waiter! Check please.*

*Yes, sir. You had the pork? That's, let me see, ninety-seven billion dollars.*

*Ho, that's a little more than I thought. Can I put this on a card?*

*Of course, sir. We only take credit.*

*Uh, if it wouldn't be too much trouble, could you itemize this for me?*

*Well, ordinarily we don't like to . . . but if you insist . . .*

Ninety-seven billion dollars. That's the cost of pork for 1992. Give or take a few billion here and a few billion there. Whatever, you're talking about real money.

The evaluation of pork is not a science, and much depends on your definition—which probably depends on your politics.

But putting aside for a moment the question of whether pork is good or bad and just focusing on the notion that pork is money given to a specific area or group of people—federal spending with a Zip code attached—it's actually possible to tote up the $97 billion figure.

A number this large is way out of line with the conventional wisdom of Washington—which portrays pork as crass but petty items that add up to a minor amount in the grand scheme of fiscal policy. For instance, *The Washington Post*, in an exhaustive series on the appropriations process several years ago, came up with a pork-induced total of $1 billion. That number would only seem to cover the rottenest of Rotten Pork, but it became the word of God in Washington—the *Post* having an annoying habit of being received that way. Other estimates usually put the number under $10 billion—significant, they say, but hardly profound when compared to a $1.4 trillion budget.

Those lower numbers come, however, only from those line items in the budget with questionable parentage or purpose. There's another—and more accurate—way to do the pork accounting.

A close, skeptical view of the 1992 budget finds that the pure domestic discretionary spending that could be called pork totaled $14.5 billion. This figure covers Bobby Byrd's roads and Joe McDade's Steamtown and Bennett Johnston's waterway and all the other thousands of projects that found their way into an appropriations bill for the sole reason that one member of Congress wanted it there. It's a conservative estimate.

The highway bill adds an average of $1.5 billion in pork each year.

A very kind reading of the defense budget finds $15 billion, including the Christmas presents showered on the National Guard, new M-1 tanks, new submarines and the like.

The subsidy side of the ledger—which combines money paid out, money not coming in and higher prices paid by consumers—is $13 billion. This is everything from favors to sugar producers to cheap electricity for the residents of Seattle.

Tax pork, all of which was put in during previous years but which clearly affects each subsequent budget, has been estimated by a variety of sources to cost $20 billion. These are the special breaks for Oregon wine growers and Kansas airplane builders and Texas oilmen. This, too, is money not coming into the Treasury rather than cash going out.

Finally, there's a category of pork-driven decisions. These are things the government is prevented from doing by Congress because they would affect local districts. The most examples are in the Pentagon—bases not closed, Guard units not disbanded, weapons systems not canceled—but plenty can be found in other areas.

Unnecessary Veterans Administration hospitals and regional offices of everything from the Army Corps of Engineers to the Environmental Protection Agency fall into this category. Essentially these are expenses you wouldn't incur if you didn't have Congress micromanaging over your shoulder. A conservative total here is $33 billion.

Grand total: $97 billion, tip included.

So is this a big deal? That, too, depends. It depends on what you think the federal government is supposed to do for you and everyone else in the country. And it depends on whether you think the deficit matters. Evaluating pork requires you to ask some fundamental questions: Should the federal government *really* be doing this? Should *another* part of the government be doing it? Just because a project or program sounds like a good idea, can we *afford* to do it? Just because it doesn't seem to cost me anything, is it *really* free? Is it *worth* borrowing money to do this?

To take just one example the average person might not ordinarily think about, is it a good thing for the government to fund Amtrak? Railroads are energy efficient, all right, and they may reduce crowding at airports. But they serve only a very small part of the population, and no matter how popular they become, they make sense for only certain areas of the country. *Who should pay?* That's a profound question that draws into the debate all sorts of issues about the meaning of a federal system of government and the responsibilities of the states. The experiences of two hundred years of trying to fine-tune a fragile democracy hang over that very question. Given such weight, when the senator from New Jersey takes it upon himself to decide how Amtrak gets funded, does that become a gross violation of the public trust? That's how you have to think about pork.

Certainly pork needs to be seen as something much broader than the sneering little projects that members stick in to earn a cheap press release for the folks back home. Pork is not a sideshow on Capitol Hill. It's the main event. What matters is the culture of pork, the porkland mentality that has gradually come to govern Congress and even the White House. It's becoming more, not less, pervasive. The numbers tell that.

In 1987, the highway bill had 152 pure pork projects costing $1.3 billion; in 1992, 480 projects costing $5.4 billion. In the defense budget, earmarks increased from 82 in 1970 to 807 in 1987, while line-item adjustments made by the appropriations committees went from 830 to 3,422. Earmarked academic pork went from almost nothing a decade ago to a billion dollars a year. The entire 1991 budget was a pork bonanza; 1992 built on that base and added some more. The budget deal is supposed to start clamping down on spending any day now, but no one believes the deal will hold together. There will have to be a new deal with the same old pressure to spend more money. And when that new deal is negotiated, the key cardinals of the appropriations committees are sure to play a major role. They've consolidated more power than at any time in the past two decades and are primed to expand their turf.

Pork is real money—and it's growing. It's a significant part of what the government spends each year and it's a significant part of the deficit.

A favorite tactic of those who dismiss pork as merely a nuisance is to hold it up against the total $1.4 trillion federal budget. With such numbers, they will say, $10 billion or even $20 billion is no big deal. Of course, as shown above, those numbers are much too low. And $1.4 trillion is too high. Included in that total budget figure is about $500 billion for Social Security, Medicare and some other entitlement programs, all of which are funded with separate tax deductions, and interest on the national debt. Take those out and you're left with less than $700 billion—so $97 billion worth of pork seems like a very substantial number.

Or go the other way. Use a more conservative definition. Cut the pork estimate in half. Call it $50 billion, which is approaching 10 percent of what you might call the government's operating budget. Even a few percentage points becomes significant in something as massive as the federal budget. There are several realistic plans floating around in the world of think tanks that show how the federal budget could be balanced in five years just by holding the *increase* in spending to around 4 percent. Just take the really excessive stuff out, hold spending to a reasonable level, and you could balance the budget and eliminate the deficit.

At ten *or* a hundred billion, pork matters.

True, pork isn't everything. There's more waste in government than you could ever fit into the pork barrel. To keep a sense of perspective about all this, you've got to consider some other areas. The bureaucracy itself is no doubt a sty of its own when it comes to overstaffing and inefficient use of resources. The Grace commission, for instance, found several billion dollars' worth of savings that could be wrung out. Aside from the pork in the Pentagon budget, it's also been well documented that there's all kinds of excess, waste and inefficiency throughout the military. Does it seem at all out of line to assume that the $300 billion behemoth headquartered on the south bank of the Potomac River could be deporked and streamlined to $200 billion and still be the most powerful army in the history of the world?

And then there's something else.

"It would be a fraud to make people think that if you cut all the waste and pork you've solved the deficit problem," said one Hill staffer with many pork-fighting scars. "There's a lot of that budget that we can't even touch."

That part is called entitlements, or mandatory spending. Some call it Everyone's Pork.

"We spend all this time worrying about the little deals, and this giant thing called mandatory spending just rolls on and on," a White House staffer said one day, shaking his head.

When you bring up the subject to anyone on the Hill, they roll their eyes and say, "Now *that's* a whole other problem. You're right. Absolutely. That has to be dealt with. *Next year.*"

Entitlements are the pork mentality spread like a Hong Kong B flu virus. *Where's mine?* becomes the battle cry not just in the committee rooms of Congress but on the lips of every American citizen. Ask not what you can do for your country but what your country can do for you.

Government money has crept into everyone's life in such a way that no one can bear to see it go. Each program has a fierce, skilled lobby—from the American Association of Retired Persons to the American Medical Association—and no one has any interest in showing the least bit of self-restraint.

Entitlements have come to mean "This is what the government owes me, and nobody better try to take a penny of it away."

Thus the Bush administration can't even succeed in its modest attempt to cut back farm subsidies for those farmers earning more than $100,000 or raise Medicare premiums on those senior citizens earning more than $150,000. And make no mistake, an old codger taking in $150,000 a year is a very rich person indeed.

*But don't even talk about changing this, or we'll rip your head off!*

"One of the biggest flaws of the 1990 budget deal was that it allowed us to turn our backs on entitlements," said Bill Frenzel, the former congressman who was involved in negotiating the deal.

"To say this middle-class welfare is untouchable is amazing. It's more than fifty percent of the budget."

Entitlements are federal programs that give money to people because they fall into a certain group. If you're over age sixty-five, for instance, you get Medicare health insurance benefits. You're *entitled* to those benefits, not because you necessarily need them, but because of your age. The same principle applies to farm subsidies, unemployment benefits, school lunches.

Some are for the poor—welfare, Medicaid, housing and nutrition programs—and they approach $150 billion.

Some are for the middle and upper classes: school loans and less obvious subsidy programs like the tax deduction on home mortgage interest payments, worth an estimated $40 billion.

Then there are mandatory payouts like veterans' pensions ($15 billion), federal workers' pensions ($35 billion) and everyone's favorite mistake, the savings-and-loan bailout, totaling more than $200 billion by 1992.

In all, entitlements and interest on the national debt made up 65 percent of the federal budget for 1992 and are expected to climb from there. There are few if any checks on this spending; it often grows automatically. Congress made these programs mandatory so they wouldn't have to battle for funding each year. And now no one controls them.

Unless Congress and the White House come up with a way to reign in these costs—or pay for them—there seems to be no hope of substantially reducing the deficit.

But if you could deal with pork and waste and the Pentagon and entitlements and not view them in isolation and not say they're hopeless so why bother, then maybe you could get somewhere.

Until then, the size of government will remain vastly larger than anyone imagined it would ever be. The pig becomes the symbol of so much more than a little political favor trading. And the greatest question of politics becomes, How do we divide the check?

*Okay, who had the chops?*

## 18

# WAXING WELK

**S**OME HAD THOUGHT THE STRUGGLE OVER THE BUDGET FOR 1992 might turn into the Great Pork War, a titanic contest for the soul of America between the forces of spending and the forces of thrift. But when the smoke had cleared and the last of the wounded were carted from the battlefield, the Great Pork Barbecue was more like it. Aside from some cases of indigestion, there were few casualties. As the year came to a close, the guests were fat, smiling and picking their teeth. The only fatality: Lawrence Welk's museum. The fiasco that had started it all, ended it all—with nothing changed in between.

The reasons were plentiful: the cardinals of the appropriations committees had amassed more power than ever; largely because of the recession, nobody really had the stomach to cut spending; the budget deal created a pool of protected money that was going to be spent no matter what; and George Bush, with his own pork barreling and deal making for petty goals, proved that he was part of the problem, not part of the solution.

Dissidents of Congress managed a few stray victories. A stunning upset came when Cardinal Dan Inouye persisted in his attempt to score $50 million for his alma mater, George Washington University, which hoped to expand its hospital. He based his argument on the theory that since doctors there had saved Ronald Reagan's life when John Hinckley, Jr., decided to take a shot at him, taxpayers would be grateful to hand over a ton of cash. The Senate, of course, agreed. No telling when someone would take a shot at one of them. But the House staged an open revolt and routed the item by a vote of 405 to 0. One explanation was that House members are less recognizable and are rarely, if ever, shot at by crazed constituents. Another was that the lower chamber just got fed up to their nose hairs with the imperious ways of their elders and resented the manner in which the stately senators were increasingly pushing their snouts into the trough. A final, less plausible, explanation was that the item really was wasteful.

Some people won minor concessions. Jim Slattery, the man who had started the Welk bandwagon and nearly got run over by it, came up with a new philosophy of life. The little projects, he said, had proved too troublesome to attack—and too damn dangerous. Congress seemed to echo the famous maxim of university politics: the smaller the stakes, the fiercer the fight. Slattery wanted to concentrate on big-ticket waste. And he actually had some success, pulling together a coalition of fiscal tightwads and guardians of the urban poor that almost killed the B-2 bomber program and, in the end, got its funding cut back.

The role of Mr. Small Change went to Dan Burton, the former insurance salesman from Indiana who chased every pork item like a new client lead. In the process, he made himself one of the most annoying people in the House, popping up from his seat with a snarl whenever a spending bill was on the table.

"Mr. Speaker," he'd say with that flat midwestern twang. "There's pork in this bill!"

Other members rolled their eyes. But nobody said pork hunting was easy duty. Along with Harris Fawell, Bob Walker, Tim Penny and a few others, Burton stuck to his calling and at least kept the cardinals on edge. His biggest win came when he singled out a curious grant to a university in West Virginia to conduct research into the nature of wood. It didn't take a bloodhound to smell the presence of Byrd and, late in the year, Burton turned it into a rallying cry.

"He doesn't just want to bring home the bacon!" he told his colleagues. "He wants the whole hog!"

Some people were getting a little sick of Byrd by this point. Even by the standards of Capitol Hill, his appetite had become grotesque. Wood research got the ax.

The victory proved significant because it laid the groundwork for the most important win of the year. In a possible portent of reforms to come—though don't hold your breath—Byrd was stopped in his most audacious ploy yet.

He was planning to steal nothing less than the Central Intelligence Agency right out from under the noses of Congress and the White House. With all the brass of a jewel thief robbing an occupied hotel room, Byrd had conspired to move a substantial part of the spook factory to Jefferson County, West Virginia. Even though the agency had just gotten a new wing on its campuslike Langley, Virginia, headquarters, the spy masters—including director William Webster—were complaining that they still didn't have enough space and were forced to house people in leased offices around Washington. Reading the Washington wall posters with more acuity than they did those in China, the spooks could also see that with the defusing of the Soviet menace and defense cutbacks in general, cloak-and-dagger work would be a declining industry. So rather than wait to get gnawed and nibbled to death by cost cutters, they decided to move boldly and snatch a new facility while no one was looking.

The operation was better planned and executed than much of what the CIA has been able to accomplish in its day job. It was swift, secret, deceptive and brutal. Everything we pay the agency to be—in someone *else's* country.

And like all good spy gambits, it had a mercenary—a cold-hearted SOB motivated by money. He was code-named "Byrd."

The sly senator was the middleman who could deliver the goods. He had the power to summarily give the CIA a new headquarters—just like that, red tape cut, cash in the budget, no questions asked. One condition only: it had to be built in West Virginia.

Of course, the plot had a twist. The CIA had hired a top real estate consultant to find the best sites, and after thousands had been reviewed and sorted, none of the finalists was in West Virginia. Not even close. But after all, this is the CIA we're talking about. Things could be made to disappear.

And things did. Suddenly West Virginia was the winner of the site selection. Days later, Webster went to Capitol Hill for a meeting with Byrd and Senator John Warner of Virginia, who needed to be bought off because his state was going to lose about three thousand jobs. In the sort of compromise that happens only on the Hill, Warner got a *second* new CIA site in Virginia. Total cost: a billion-three and change, the most expensive government move ever. The deal was sealed; everyone was happy.

Except, apparently, a bunch of CIA employees who were about as anxious to move to West Virginia as the weekend warriors from *Deliverance* were to take another trip down the Chattahoochee River. They did what any American would do when oppressed by the forces of government: they called their congressman.

In a series of whispered calls from pay phones in drugstores and pancake houses throughout northern Virginia—this was, after all, the CIA—Congressman Frank Wolf learned of the scheme and realized he had a lot of unhappy constituents who were either going to have to move to another world or commute about four hours a day.

Wolf was angry. A family man, he said he was moved by the pleas of parents who feared they'd never see their kids. He was also peeved by the small matter of Webster having used some trade craft on him. When he first had gotten wind of the move, Wolf had gone to meet with the director, who assured him that a decision was far off. Nine days later, the deal was done in secret.

Wolf said that when he tried to find out what was going on, Webster's aide Rae Huffstutler told him, "Byrd can get us the money. Can you?"

"I've never seen such outrageous behavior," said Wolf.

He began a counterintelligence operation, crafting an intricate coalition to stop Byrd. His key break came when he alerted the members of the House Intelligence Committee to the deal and suggested that they'd been hoodwinked. Normally, the folks who oversee the CIA might expect to be consulted on a subject like moving more than half the agency's employees. Chairman Dave McCurdy held an unusual public hearing during which he and his colleagues roasted Webster and his aides over a slow fire.

"If this wasn't so pathetic, it would be funny," said one member.

Wolf had another important constituency as well. He was a member of the House Appropriations Committee—in fact, the ranking Republican monsignor on the Treasury Subcommittee. There'd never been any great affection between House cardinals and Senate cardinals, and Byrd's voracious ways had made the situation worse. Wolf enlisted several key members, particularly those with military ties, to say that while it would be bad form to lobby against Byrd, they wouldn't oppose Wolf. Rank-and-file members of the House took note.

Then Wolf and McCurdy peppered the full membership with "Dear Colleague" letters laying out the scheme and followed up with many hours of one-on-one lobbying—discovering in the process that general resentment toward Byrd and the heavy-handed ways of the Senate was bubbling up. It worked. By a vote of 388 to 32, the House essentially said it wanted the CIA move knocked out of the appropriations bill. Recognizing a losing hand when he saw one, Byrd agreed that the time had come for "further study." The item magically disappeared from the defense bill.

Whether the vote has broader significance or was just a rare moment remains to be seen. The win came because, like an eclipse, some very important factors aligned at the right time. Still, the vote demonstrated hope. Byrd could be beaten; Congress could find in its heart the courage to kill projects that made no sense.

Of course, "kill" suggests a finality that rarely applies in the land of it-ain't-over-till-it's-over. Byrd conceded nothing; he merely beat a strategic retreat to plot his next move. By year-end, he was telling people in West Virginia, "Don't worry. We'll get it."

So that left the hapless folks of Strasburg, North Dakota, and their fond memories of the Champagne Music Maker to bear the brunt of the Pork War of 1991.

They became the pork equivalent of Grenada. The might of an angry White House descended on them like a regiment of airborne rangers. They didn't have a chance. Somewhere one imagines the president of the United States reading of the $500,000 Welk museum and boiling, the veins on his neck standing out in relief, his jaw tensing as he fixes his glare on a trembling Dick Darman and says with grim determination, "This . . . will . . . not . . . stand."

And . . . it . . . did . . . not. Darman put top men on the case who sent word to the Agriculture Department that the disgusting lapdog obeisance they'd shown to Congress for a hundred years was going to stop right here. At least for a few minutes.

The department, which normally would have rolled over and put up its hind legs for an old dog trainer like Cardinal Quentin Burdick, suddenly decided to bite the hand that fed it. Word went from Agriculture Secretary Edward Madigan to LaVerne Ausman, head of the Farmer's Home Administration, who then sent a stern letter to Burdick expressing amazement that anyone had ever dreamed that such an ill-considered proposal as the Welk museum would get by him.

Even though earlier in the year Burdick had assured the people of Strasburg that everything would be okay, he couldn't work his usual magic on this one. By late fall, Welk was still radioactive. In October, one year after he'd first put it into the appropriations bill, Burdick conceded defeat.

Nobody bothered to tell the folks in Strasburg. They heard about it on the radio. They weren't happy.

"I think we've been treated really badly," said Sharon Eiseman, one of the first people to get it into her head that a Welk museum would be a good idea.

And she had a point.

Folks in Strasburg didn't see this as any great struggle over fiscal philosophy, and they didn't see what was wrong with Lawrence Welk.

"We didn't realize that providing twenty years of wholesome entertainment was something to make fun of," said Gary Satern, the project's director.

Like a lot of pork, when you saw the meat firsthand, it didn't seem as bad as portrayed. Surely there was worse. These Welk lovers were good people with good reasons. But after the issue reached a certain critical mass of national publicity, the details no longer mattered. The residents of Strasburg were like passengers in a bus accident. They hadn't asked for it, but there they were, dazed and bleeding on the side of the road.

Strasburg sits in the middle of the Great Plains, an hour below Bismarck in the south-central part of the state. The land there rolls like a choppy sea of dry yellow grass down to the banks of the Missouri River, across to the Sioux Indian reservation where Sitting Bull is buried and on to a horizon that seems a thousand miles away. Wind-scoured tables of rock push from the soil, and huge square blocks of hay stand among the empty fields like primitive icons. You can drive for thirty minutes and not see a human, a cow or a car.

This is hard western country, the scene of legend and movies, not to mention Marlboro commercials. Out here beyond the smoking cities, some historians argue, the mystic pull of the frontier forged the American character. Conquering this land over and over is how we see ourselves as a nation, they say. We're all rugged, independent, resourceful people—in our minds.

The buffalo, the Indians and the cavalry were gone a few years by the time homesteading farmers like Christina and Ludwig Welk rolled up in their wooden wagon about 1890. They got off the train at Eureka, bought a wagon for $100, a mule team for $20 and a hundred pounds of flour for a dollar, then headed west. They claimed the 160 acres they were allowed under the Homestead Act a couple of miles outside the rail stop called Strasburg, after the Russian town from which they and so many others had come when the American railroad offered free land. Over the years, they built a tiny main house, a barn and three outbuildings on a gentle rise overlooking a now-dry pond bed and the dusty prairie beyond.

Many years later, one warm fall day, Rosemary Schaefbauer stood in front of the peeling red barn, ignoring a steady breeze that hinted at the fury of seventy-below north winds to come, and explained that nobody in Strasburg was trying to pull a fast one on anybody.

"We wanted to show our children how we lived," she said as the wind whistled through a nearby screen door. "The idea started during the state's bicentennial. We wanted to preserve the heritage of the German-Russians who came here. Lawrence Welk was the most famous, so we decided to use his house."

And she was right. This was no garish temple of star worship. No Graceland for Elvis necrophiliacs, or Dollywood, or sleazy Nashville museum-cum-souvenir-sales-shop dedicated to the glory and further profits of Barbara Mandrell or Hank Williams, Jr. The Welk homestead was an accurately restored small, tidy farm of plain construction. There was a white clapboard summer kitchen where the field hands had eaten lunch; a smithy; an outhouse; the small main house, built of mud brick and covered with boards, with an exterior set of stairs to the attic where Lawrence slept; and a decaying barn.

Inside was the rough-hewn furniture and simple tools of the era, including a washboard and tub, butter churn, cabbage shredder, potato masher, icebox and wood stove, all laid out neatly enough to meet the approval of any German housewife. In fact, there were so few bits of Welk memorabilia that it could have been any of a few hundred thousand farms of the times. Except, of course, for the life-size cardboard cutout of Welk in white tie and tails with the words "Keep a song in your heart" written across his middle, standing amid his mother's furniture in the tiny living room.

But no Welk key chains for sale, no videos, T-shirts, child-size accordions, locks of his hair in Lucite, signed photos with the president or sweat-stained band jackets in display cases. This was really just a farm.

"Not an easy life," noted Rosemary Schaefbauer, picking up a battered bread pan. Not a particularly interesting one, either. At least not interesting enough to merit a half-million-dollar museum. You didn't doubt for a moment the authenticity of the project. This had to be an accurate picture of the hard, isolated and simple life of turn-of-the-century prairie farmers, and it left the unmistakable impression that Welk had done the prudent thing by leaving as soon as he could.

But the most notable thing about the farm was that, except for the barn, the restoration had been finished and it was open for business. "We raised about two hundred thousand dollars on our own," Schaefbauer explained, with half coming from Welk's private foundation.

"We got six thousand three hundred visitors last summer," she said proudly.

So what was the point of the federal money?

"Well, we did hope to do over the barn. First we were going to put a German-Russian museum in there, but the government people said that would seem too commercial. So we planned to build the museum on Main Street in town. The rest of the money was going to be for rural economic development. We wanted to set up a loan fund to start some businesses related to tourism. It would have been for people who wanted out of farming. It was not a handout."

What could be wrong with that?

You could safely assume that Rosemary Schaefbauer's never conned anyone. For thirty-three years she's milked five dozen cows twice a day, whatever the temperature, raised seven kids and taught school. She's lived through a lot of hard times, not the least of which was the current three-year drought, which she pronounced "drowth" and which had cut the harvest in half. If she says the Lawrence Welk project had never been intended to be some gaudy souvenir pit stop, you probably ought to believe her.

And you probably ought to fear for the fate of the Republic when she says, not angrily but wistfully, "I have an idea now how politics works. It's kind of sad."

But then she added a remark that suggested there was more to the Welk project than some quaint community spruce-up.

"Whether it's from the government or not, I'm not going to give up raising money," she said, "because I don't want to see my town become a ghost town."

If you pressed the point, you found that she and others in Strasburg saw the stakes in the Welk project as not far from life and death. Tucked just off U.S. Highway 83, Strasburg isn't a ghost town yet, but it's looking a little pale. A tidy square of a few hundred houses, a magnificent red-brick Catholic church and a business street ending in a new grain elevator, it seems no better or worse than thousands of other towns in America. The people who live here have their Chevy trucks and their color TVs and VCRs. The kids go to school. The shrubs are trimmed. You wouldn't call it prosperous—several storefronts are empty and the Time Out Tavern, Horner's Lounge "Home of the Blue Room," and the Pin Palace bowling alley–café are all for sale—but then, as anyone who's done much traveling around this country recently could tell you, there aren't many places that look very flush. Whether it's the farms, the mines, the forests, the steel mills or the car factories, everybody's living in the shadow of something that isn't what it once was. So why does Strasburg, North Dakota, deserve some kind of a special break?

Al Kramer, owner of the Pin Palace, agreed. Sitting in a window booth looking onto a deserted Main Street, he said in the same faintly German accent as Welk's, "People criticize us and, sure, maybe it's a handout. Okay, so maybe we shouldn't be so eager to take it. We're not usually like that here."

Not that they couldn't use the help if it came along. Take him, for instance. At sixty-five, he was ready to pack it in. He'd been trying to sell his place for a couple of years, but there were no takers. It was worse for the farmers.

"These're hard times. The young farmers, all they got to go on are the government loans. They're deep in debt. The better farmers and older ones don't do that. Once you get the government money, it's hard to get out. Seems like these days, milking's about the best you can do."

"Why's that?"

"Government keeps the milk price up. It's the best of the subsidy programs."

Overall, the state ranked eighth in the country in receipt of federal funds, with $4,800 per person. That would mean Emmons County's 5,600 people got roughly $27 million, mostly in agriculture subsidies and not including what it cost consumers in higher prices to keep the farms operating.

"These are proud people," Gary Satern had said. "They're hurting, but they don't go around with their hand out."

They don't have to. The government comes to them.

One aspect of the Welk controversy touched on nothing less than the future of farming in America. Farming in the Great Plains is a dying business. Some would say it has been since the Depression. North Dakota has fewer people today than it did in 1920; South Dakota, Nebraska and even Kansas are all losing population in their rural communities. There are several reasons for the decline, but much has to do with the greater efficiency of large corporate farms in more fertile places such as California. The drought of recent years has just accentuated the same fundamentally dry conditions that once produced the Dust Bowl.

Those who favor minimal government would say, "If people enjoy the life-style and want to farm in the semi-desert of the plains, fine, but why should we pay for it?" Other people, for instance, might enjoy making turquoise belt buckles in the remote mountains of New Mexico or might like to hunker down in the arid beaches of Florida's west coast to, say, write books. Do they deserve subsidies as well?

On the other hand, do you just cast off a part of the country and tell it to fend for itself?

People in Strasburg saw the Welk project as a way out of farm subsidies because it was supposed to be a way out of farms.

"Tourism is the future," said Kramer. "Not many people can farm anymore. So what do you do, send them all away?"

There it was: a sound rationale for a project that seemed from a distance to be one of the most wasteful imaginable. But if the concept made sense, there was still a problem in the execution. Despite what they said, the people of Strasburg were still looking for a lump of extra government money that they'd use as they saw fit.

"It wasn't for Welk," said Kramer. "No kidding. It was always for the German-Russian center." He was a charter member of the German-Russian Society, begun in 1972. ("People were afraid to make too much of being German before then," he added. "The war and all.")

But the center was going to cost less than $100,000. What about the rest?

"I don't know what they wanted to do with that," Kramer shrugged. "Build a road to Lawrence's house, maybe? They talked about a bed-and-breakfast. People had mentioned interest in several kinds of businesses. I'm sure over a few years they could have spent it."

Surely. These were resourceful people. They'd find a way.

Thousands of other farmers had. The program that Strasburg wanted the money from was the Farmer's Home Administration, widely believed to be one of the worst-managed government giveaways ever. Whatever you think of the philosophical arguments of saving farms or not saving farms, the way the government goes about it is a disaster for everyone concerned. As James Bovard wrote in *The Farm Fiasco*, "The FmHA is a welfare agency that routinely destroys its clients' lives."

The agency, one of several that extends credit to farmers under various programs, had, by the time of the Welk museum, already written off about $50 billion in bad loans, most made since the mid-1970s, when a drop in crop prices and a generous government turned many farmers into credit junkies. Although the national farm crisis had eased, FmHA still showed $11 billion in delinquent loans—about half the loans it made. In repeated studies, the General Accounting Office had found FmHA an incomprehensible mess.

But blame belonged on more than the bureaucrats. As loan problems increased, the ag staters in Congress kept changing the rules, eventually turning many of the loans into straight grants. They were just following the theory of farm management pioneered by Jamie Whitten and others: no farmer, however inept, should ever be allowed to fail.

The Welk project, however noble in intent, didn't even meet FmHA's historically horrendous guidelines. And maybe that was the simplest explanation for why it deserved to be cut. Forget agonizing over the future of the farm economy and the government's role in preserving dying regions. The Welk project couldn't make the grade on merit, but it got stuffed into a bill anyway—in the purest sort of pork-barrel power play. And the result was not harmless, because if Strasburg bent the rules to get the money, then somebody else who might have a better case would go without.

Al Kramer didn't know anything about FmHA's problems or wheeling and dealing on Capitol Hill. But he wanted to make clear that whatever had happened, Strasburg's money would have been well spent. He was surprised anyone could suggest otherwise.

"Now, wait a minute. This isn't anything like a lot of the stuff I hear goes on in Washington, D.C., there."

He jabbed at the ice cubes in his glass of Diet Pepsi with a swizzle stick.

"You know what burns me up? What really burns me up?"

He said *birnse*, the way Welk would.

"All that pork-barrel stuff I hear about. You know what I'm talking about? That, you know, study the fish, and how come people fall in love and the sex life of bees. Now *that's* bad. What do they want to spend money on that for?"

It was suggested to him that some people actually considered the Welk grant to be just such a pork-barrel project.

"*No?*" he said with genuine surprise. "That's crazy!"

Then he drained his soda, fending off the swizzle stick with a forefinger so it wouldn't stab him in the eye, and banged the glass back on the table with a satisfied whack that sounded like a gavel ending a hearing.

Al Kramer, who is a very nice man, just didn't get it. But then, hardly anyone does.

## 19

# THE POLITICS OF GREED

**W**HY WASHINGTON CAN'T STOP SPENDING MONEY HAS ONLY been debated by about a million fairly smart people for the last two hundred years. They may have come up with *answers* to the question, but they've never come close to *solving* the problem. Someone would have to be about as arrogant as Robert C. Byrd to suggest that in a year spent rummaging through the closets of the Money Congress he'd magically discovered the key that everyone else has been missing. However, a close look at the various and varied adventures in Porkland does make one smarter about a few crucial things.

Pork is not a simple subject. It goes straight to the heart of the matter—and that matter is that the government's system of spending money these days is seriously, awfully, grotesquely screwed up. This may not come as news to some people, but the shocker here is just how badly screwed up it all is. The closer one gets to the core of the system, the more it becomes apparent that the problem is beyond anyone's worst expectations. Following the pork trail is like looking for a stray mouse in your basement and coming upon a colony of foaming rats in residence.

One other find: there's a reason things are screwed up and it has to do with specific flesh-and-bone people with names and addresses. When you pry into the process, government spending becomes not some abstract event or uncontrollable force of nature like El Niño, but a bunch of individuals, often with conflicting intentions, who once a year make decisions on a thing called a budget. Money is spent—or misspent—the way these people *say* it should be spent.

What guides their decisions is not pork, precisely, but the "pork mentality." This can be defined as the belief that all politics is about me getting mine and to hell with you.

After holding newborn budgets heavier than newborn children, turning thousands of pages filled with blurring words and numbers, cross-referencing paragraphs in a half-dozen documents like a cryptologist just to find out who got fat on a line that read "In lieu of the sum proposed by said amendment insert $17,700,000 . . . ," sitting through stupefying hearings just to see who kissed whose ring and seeing more pork in one year than anyone other than an Iowa farmer, one finds it difficult—no, nearly impossible—to see politics as it's played in this country today as *anything* other than competing interests grabbing for the main course with both hands. The central motivation of American politics is greed. The question that starts the day is, How do I get all I can? Just like Wall Street in the 1980s, Capitol Hill has become a rigged market controlled by the strongest and the most unscrupulous. The only difference is that little of what happens in Washington is illegal—which is not surprising because Washington writes the laws. But is the wholesale heisting of billions of dollars of taxpayers' money by a handful of legislators any less criminal than what Mike Milken or Ivan Boesky did?

Like capitalism, our political system is based on a certain amount of self-interest. Competing factions are supposed to vie for what they can get. But something's gone wrong. The self-interest has become total, from the iron triangles like the Pentagon–defense contractor–congressional committee wedge, to the behemoth interest groups like the American Association of Retired Persons, to individual congressmen madly protecting their seats, to voters who want an endless free lunch. And maybe, too, that's the way the system was supposed to be. But it *wasn't* supposed to be $4 trillion in the red.

To conclude that there's a major problem here shouldn't be a question of whether one's politics are liberal or conservative. The issue was framed long ago by one of the great liberals of history,

Franklin Roosevelt, who said, "We have always known that heedless self-interest was bad morals. We know now that it is bad economics."

Pork is heedless self-interest.

And it's getting worse all the time. Looking at budgets over the last five years, one can see that the trend is clearly toward more and more pork. Just the *pure* pork barreling is getting out of hand. As Dan Burton said of Byrd in what could have been the slogan of the 102nd Congress, "He doesn't just want to bring home the bacon! He wants the whole hog!"

Again, there are reasons for this. Some are perpetual, some unique to these times.

The appropriators, for instance, are at a peak of power. Partly because of the budget deal of 1990, partly because of Byrd's energy and stealth, partly because of the disarray in the rest of Congress, the cardinals are the strongest, most unified force on the Hill. The budget committees in the House and Senate, which supposedly act as the check on appropriations, were carved into eunuchs by the terms of the last budget deal. Combine this with the weakness of Bush on spending matters and the suspicion that Dick Darman's affection for the cardinals may extend to cross-dressing in clerical garb, and you have a formula for fiscal disaster.

All this comes against the permanent culture of the Hill—which embraces spending with the energy of Ted Kennedy on a date. Every year the emissaries of the special-interest groups and the bureaucracy troop up the slopes to plead for more money because *even though we know how tight funds are, we feel we are the one special exception that should be made all year.* Rarely does anyone ever argue the opposite case.

The individual member of Congress is predisposed to listen to pleas for spending because, these days, that's how he sees himself earning his living. The perception held by just about every member of Congress, whether it's true or not, is that he lives or dies by what he brings home.

Undergirding the lone member's inclination toward self-preservation, there is still an old-style liberal Democratic philosophy that may be changing elsewhere in the country, but continues to govern Congress with the notion that all spending is good spending. Except for small, possibly growing, pockets of rebels, the idea that we have to spend smarter, not larger, hasn't made it up the gentle incline of Capitol Hill.

Which isn't to let conservatives off the hook, because many of them are the worst part of the problem. The Democrats at least stab taxpayers in the front; the Republicans stab you in the back. Their hypocrisy can be astounding. From the early days of Ronald Reagan and his misfired "supply side" canon, rhetoric and action have more often than not opposed each other. George "Read My Voodoo Economics" Bush has taken the ruse to a new level. And disciples of them both, like Warren Rudman and Bob Dole, abound on the Hill.

Finally, there's the pork-is-business-as-usual attitude which says, We've done this for two hundred years, what makes you good-government morons think there's any reason to change?

Set all this against the runaway costs of health care, the savings-and-loan debacle and the legacy of the defense buildup, and you've got a foul-smelling pen full of beasts who are just about to knock their way through the kitchen door.

So the question becomes, Can the hog be tamed? Can he be trimmed back down to cuddly size?

Maybe.

It depends on whether the folks who own the farm want it done. This pig belongs to everyone in the United States, and if the Communist Party can be tossed from the Kremlin onto the ash heap of history, it's not out of the question that democracy could take hold on Capitol Hill. But change won't happen on its own.

The absolute first solution to consider is that great old American political remedy: *throwing the bastards out.*

It's simple, direct and effective. One man, one vote, one politician on the street. Just as the founding fathers intended.

Voting out senators, congressmen, local representatives and even presidents would make the point that the job was being botched. It's the American way. Let some new folks take a run at it. They can't do much worse. And if they go in with a mandate that says "The politicians have been screwing up this economy by allowing too much waste and allowing us to walk away without paying for the government we're getting," then maybe they could do a whole lot better.

Stop the pork. Go kosher. Be tough. Pretend it's your own money. These are not complicated messages. They will be received.

Listen to former Congressman Bill Frenzel: "Congress will begin to restrain its spending the day its constituents say, 'Stop spending or we're going to take away your favorite toy: your seat in Congress.' Until then, they will spend because it profits them."

Or current Congressman Dick Armey: "The politics of greed is always wrapped in the language of love. The spenders say they're spending to help people, but they're really helping themselves. That's called self-interest, and that's what they'll do until somebody votes them out."

Ah, but as H. L. Mencken said, "Every complex problem has a solution which is simple, and wrong." Even here, he may be right.

Short of throwing the bastards out, there are all kinds of more complicated schemes to tinker with the process that could produce genuine results.

Among the most logical would be an amendment to the Constitution, or even a rule in Congress, to balance the budget starting right away. The single best answer to the question of why members of Congress can't balance the budget is "Because they don't have to." *Make them!* No more red ink. Every year, by September 30, either the spending matches the income or lawmakers start going to jail. A total of forty-nine states now require a balanced budget so the process can't be too difficult. Of course there are still ways to weasel out of it—and Congress will find them—but it's a starting point on the road to budgetary weight loss.

One tool to help enforce a balanced budget is the line-item veto. The governors of forty-three states have it, and every president asks Congress for it every year. The line-item veto would allow the president to knock out a single expense, say, a monument to Li'l Abner wedged into the defense bill, and leave the other quarter-of-a-trillion dollars alone. Congress would then be forced to demonstrate its deep desire to have this particular item by coming up with a two-thirds majority to override the veto. As it is now—and as insane as it may sound—to go after a small project the president has to veto the entire bill! Some years Congress even wraps the whole budget into a single bill. Try slamming down a veto on $1.5 trillion in spending just to ferret out a few things. A president—especially one running for reelection—could look mighty reckless. And once the inevitable scare stories started to come out with headlines like "President's Veto Jeopardizes Funds for Sick Old People, Including Your Grandmother," he could look mighty callous as well. So presidents almost always view pork hunting as more trouble than it's worth. "You can't say 'no,' so let me be the one to say it," presidents have argued much of this century in support of the line-item veto. It's not outside the realm of possibility that if a president got it, he might even use it wisely and save some money. But precisely because it's an effective tool, there's little chance that Congress will hand it over—unless there's a voter revolt.

Short of demanding a balanced budget, there are other ways to limit the growth of federal spending. Tim Penny, a Democrat who understands numbers, has a plan to restrict spending to the growth of personal income. That means the government can't grow any faster than your paycheck, which seems fair enough for starters. Scott Hodge of the Heritage Foundation takes to heart the cynically intended quote of Everett Dirksen, "A billion here and a billion there, and pretty soon you're talking about real money." Hodge thinks you could come close to shutting the budget gap in less than five years if you could cut out the pork, manage the good programs tightly and hold down entitlement increases. Overall, it means keeping all government spending to an annual growth rate of 4 percent. "We're not talking about cutting," he explained, "but the little things that everyone seems to dismiss these days *do* matter. Pork matters, waste matters, efficiencies matter. Because if you take care of the so-called little things, the numbers will start to fall in line."

Then there's the radical notion of truth-in-budgeting. Tell the people exactly what they're spending their money on. Despite what they say about laws and sausage, the truth is that however gruesome the process, you can't afford *not* to watch. History tells us it's more brutal if you don't.

Certainly there's a case for eliminating baseline budgeting, the wonderland accounting method that allows you to say you're saving when you're really only spending less than you said you were going to spend. "We continue to bamboozle the public with this," says former Budget Director Jim Miller. "They don't seem to catch on, and it's just an outrage." The premise would be that every dollar out of a taxpayer's pocket is a real dollar. It's not an inflation-adjusted dollar, the COLA-adjusted dollar, a decrease-from-the-increase-that-had-already-been-projected dollar. It's just a dollar that he or she can't spend on something else. Every taxpayer ought to know that.

In fact, why not go all the way? Why not require that the government tell people in an easy-to-read annual report where their money is going? Or even a monthly statement? Of course, it would have to be done by the same sort of independent, trustworthy people who count the results of the Oscars and put them into sealed envelopes. And there would be harsh penalties for fudging the numbers the way every president in recent memory has done. But imagine the result.

After all, *35 percent of the income of an average family goes to taxes, including state and local.* Shouldn't they be able to see the parts? Such as $2,000 a year to service the national debt (on a monthly invoice, that would be $167). What would happen if people started to think of the national debt as a second car payment? Same thing with the defense bill, about $275 a month (of course, it *could* have a little note in there from the secretary of defense about how they're saving you money by, say, turning down the thermostat in the barracks). There's already a separate paycheck deduction for Social Security, though it would be nice to have an annual explanation of where the money goes. Then you could have the domestic spending bill, with so much for charity, so much for savings-and-loan thieves, maybe with a Bob Byrd surcharge thrown in. A few dollars a month for West Virginia? Perhaps people would gladly pay it, and that's fine.

This isn't crazy, entirely. Sane, sober people have said the same thing. The economist Norman Ture said, "We have to reform the process in such a way that people see the true cost of government. Make sure that all of us are aware of the cost and approve spending only if we think it's worthwhile." Dick Armey said as much by making the opposition's point: "The key to spending is *always* to make sure that the clients don't get the bill for the service."

There's another whole school of thought that says that the problem of pork comes from the way Congress is rewarded. Members are rewarded for *spending,* whether by reelection or extraordinary perks. They've got to be given a carrot or a stick based on whether they *save.*

The biggest stick is term limits, which, to anyone who believes in the marketplace, seems like a pretty brutal restriction to place on the process. There's a powerful argument to be made that freely electing your representatives means just that. Still, the idea has clearly struck fear into the hearts of elected officials across America.

Congress could reform its own incentive structure if it wanted to. Both houses have the power to put into place all sorts of rules that would make pork barreling difficult and unpleasant. They could even, all by themselves, create a structure to produce a budget that was close to being in balance. If they wanted to.

Then there's the role of the president. He's got to lead. As most members of Congress will tell you, it's not the role of Congress to whip itself into line and deal with these problems. And, discounting for a certain amount of self-serving rationalization, they're probably correct. By one theory, the institution is supposed to be a disorganized rabble of children yelling for attention. The president is supposed to be the stern parent who sets the weekly allowance. While the appropriators and the tax committees have proved that the children are smarter than they let on, the president still has a vast amount of power to get what he wants. Even without the line-item veto, for instance, a president has other tools, including the regular veto, that he could use to attack pork. Some presidents—George Bush comes to mind—haven't been hesitant to use that power to go after seemingly small matters such as the use of tiny amounts of federal money to fund abortions. Bush has routinely sent bills worth hundreds of billions of dollars back to Congress's drawing board over that one issue. Why not the same stand over a piece of pork?

Or maybe it's time for more radical approaches. This would be the course for those who doubt whether our whole system of government is able to handle the kind of budget problems facing it today. Did the penurious old Puritan ancestors who wrote the Constitution really imagine a day when the country was going to be borrowing almost one dollar for every three it spent? Even Richard Darman, who's part of the problem and not part of the solution, appreciates this. He once said, "Representative democracy is good for ordinary, incremental approaches to problems. We are not so good at handling large shifts. The deficit is not an ordinary problem. It is an extraordinary problem."

Maybe we don't need an appropriations committee. The Constitution says only that Congress has to appropriate the money in a law; it doesn't specify the process. Putting the appropriators in charge of spending is like putting your children in charge of grocery shopping. They just can't help themselves, and you shouldn't be surprised when you find yourself eating Twinkies for dinner. Time for the adults to step in.

Maybe the budget mess should be dealt with by some sort of super commission, some blue-ribbon panel of czars, the fiscal equivalent of the God Squad that was set up to decide for the

Interior Department which animal species were to be considered endangered and which were fair game. It could be something like the Defense Base Closing and Realignment Commission—which would save Congress and the entire political process from itself by making rational spending choices and permitting a mechanism to review them sanely.

Whatever, the point is that there are lots of approaches no one has tried. There are ideas and there are solutions, they just won't be pretty or easy. As David Stockman said, "A true economic policy revolution means risky and mortal political combat with all the mass constituencies of Washington's largesse—Social Security recipients, veterans, farmers, educators, state and local officials, the housing industry and many more."

Yet Stockman didn't fight that fight and concluded that the failure of his own ideas came from "a false belief that in a capitalist democracy we can peer deep into the veil of the future and chain the ship of state to an exacting blueprint. It can't be done. It shouldn't have been tried."

Which is, of course, the ultimate Washington-wimp conclusion: It's not my fault. The system's too mighty.

But it *was* Stockman's fault. And Reagan's and Bush's and Carter's and Ford's and Nixon's and Byrd's and O'Neill's and Wright's and Mitchell's and all of ours. And the cowboy way would be to accept the blame and get up and do something about it. There are ideas, and there are remedies to try. The problem isn't immovable, it's only lacking the political will—or the political courage.

Which is why the first reform probably ought to be to bring in a lot of new folks into government. Not that it would ever happen, but imagine the message it would send to the nation if the voters of West Virginia said, "Thanks for all your good intentions, Bob, but as long as the national economy is screwed up, West Virginia's going to be screwed up. So how about you step aside and we put in some new folks who take a look at the bigger picture?" Less implausible is that the whole Congress, one seat at a time, will acquire a critical mass of new thinkers who'll say, "Bob, knock off those greasy pork games and get serious. We've got some big problems to work out here." If no one's afraid of him, he has no power.

Of course, none of this will happen unless people get angry and start demanding it.

We've got to start asking ourselves, Are these the kind of people we want to represent us? Grasping little bagmen whose horizon is the next press release?

Maybe we could have put up with all this bullshit before, when the deficit wasn't out of sight and our children's children weren't going to have to pay for every latest boondoggle with their payroll deductions forty years from now. If they played games with our money, wasted it, spent it to their benefit, we could tolerate it because there was so much to go around. But now it's outrageous. It *has* to stop. This isn't free money, we know that. The guys who are giving us back our own money and making us thankful for it are con men who need to be tossed onto the street. The old rules have to go, and so does the old guard.

Yes, there are many valid spending needs, as Byrd and others point out endlessly, but the greedheads, led by the example of Byrd, ruin the system by making it irresponsible and irrational. They violate the pact between leaders and followers. If we have such an overwhelming need for education spending, as Byrd says, why are we spending extra hundreds of millions to move half the CIA into West Virginia at a time when we should be moving half the CIA into retirement? If we need bridges repaired so badly, why do most of them have to be in the home state of Bob Roe and his cronies? Why do all the critical water projects happen to be in the states of those on the Water Appropriations Committee? Or are these projects really so critical? And why even in the best of times do we need a suspended monorail in Altoona, Pennsylvania? All this pork, and a thousand other examples, makes a joke of the system and perverts the legitimate needs. Do as we say, Byrd and the other leaders tell the members, not as we do.

That said, you've got to concede that the problem of federal spending is breathtakingly complicated. And it's unfair to slam all of the members of Congress with the same two-by-four. Anyone who spent time watching the ways of Capitol Hill closely would come away surprisingly impressed with the seriousness and honesty of many members—though more depressed about the system in which they operate. Most members of Congress aren't clowns. Many are well-meaning people who find themselves in an incredible struggle to make hard choices in a system of divided government—and with a public that says, "Give me more, but cut my taxes."

Noble as their intentions may be, they're presiding over a process that borders on lunacy. By the standards that apply to most businesses and individuals, this is a bankrupt government. It keeps piling on debt with no intention of ever repaying it. It should be run by a receiver, the way they do with belly-up real estate moguls. Imagine some grim old white-haired judge who'd haul guys like Byrd into court and come down on them like the wrath of God. "You're planning to spend money on *what?* You better think again unless you want this court to hold you in contempt and show you a nice quiet cell. You won't be building any swimming pools in your backyard until you straighten out that income statement, Mr. Byrd."

But none of that will happen until the simple part of the problem is addressed. Namely, the voters have to say it's time for a change. Ultimately, the blame and the responsibility for the system belong on all of us. Under the category "Democracy in Action," the Final Jeopardy answer is "Because you won't let them." And the winning question is: "Why can't Washington stop spending your money?" Or, in the famous words of Joseph de Maistre, "Every country has the government it deserves."

If we deserve better, we've got to say "stop" somewhere, sometime. Why not start with pork? It's easy to give up. There are many painful aspects to bringing the budget under control, but every piece of pork—all $97 billion, by this count, from Byrd's highways to Bush's space station—could be lopped out and the welfare of the nation would be unaffected. The country would be defended, the old folks would get their checks, the poor would have a safety net. That's because trimming pork isn't about taking away, it's merely about not giving in the first place.

Okay, so it's not $97 billion. Use somebody else's definition and cut it in half. It's only a $50 billion annual saving. The simplest point of sweating out the pork isn't the dollars but the principle. Pork is the first cigarette, the first drink, the first hot fudge sundae. The only way to diet is to say no at some point and change the way you live. Common sense says we've got to stop expecting that the people we elect will bring us a catered hot lunch every day of the week and never hand us a bill. We can't keep saying, "I'll give up my pork if you give up yours—but you go first."

It's our pig, and it's best to remember that a pig will eat anything that comes into its path. Including the farmer.

## EPILOGUE

# THE PORK GOES ON

JUST LIKE BASEBALL, ANOTHER GREAT AMERICAN SPORT, ONE season of pork barreling was hardly over when a new one was on top of us.

As usual, the president took the lead with a State of the Union speech in late January that was studied by Washington insiders like a farm team scouting report. Not that anyone expected to do what the president said, but his words, his tone, his emphasis would set the agenda for the year. How much room for maneuver was he allowing? Where would the fights be? Was he going to dredge up some hoary old spending cuts? Did he have costly new initiatives that would drain funds from existing projects?

In an exceedingly sly budget, George Bush proposed all sorts of strange gimcracks and doohickeys that would take weeks to fully digest. But toward the end of the speech, he did take a moment to focus on pork in general and the Lawrence Welk Museum in particular.

"I call upon Congress to adopt a measure that will help put an end to the annual ritual of filling the budget with pork-barrel appropriations," he said with a hawkish frown. "Every year the press has a field day making fun of outrageous examples, a Lawrence Welk Museum, a research grant for Belgian endive. We all know how these things get into the budget . . ."

He sounded tough. He sounded like he knew what he was talking about. But those who make it their business to spend the taxpayers' money were chuckling in their seats. They knew that this was the absurd spectacle of a man crowing over the corpse of a fresh-killed fly. In Bush's case, it was *all* he could crow over. Welk was the only pork he'd managed to knock out all year. And now he was swaggering around like Clint Eastwood on a battleground of dead desperados?

In reality he was still Porky George, the man who said, "I will do whatever it takes to be reelected" and set about to prove the point with a shameless display of goodie-goosing on the campaign trail. As the year progressed, it would only get worse—as anyone could tell who heard him cackling to the people of New Hampshire or Florida about all the road and sewer projects he was bringing their way. He was raiding the larder, and he hadn't even begun to deal with the appropriators yet. The cardinals must have been rolling their eyes to the heavens in gratitude.

Step two came the next day. Once again, Richard Darman would unveil his . . . uh . . . the president's budget in the auditorium of the Old Executive Office Building in front of the economics press.

Standing under the hot lights, bad haircut and all, he seemed to have become fatter and, well, pinker. Like . . . no . . . it *couldn't* be.

He was loose and laughing, not showing any of the usual tautness. As he talked about one scheme or another that he was proposing in his oh-so-complicated budget, his eyes lit up. He laid out the mechanics of government the way he'd like to see it, scurrying from the podium to charts so filled with type they were unreadable to anyone farther away than Darman. He jousted with questioners and allowed himself a smile or two when he got off a subtly witty line. He loved this stuff, and it was a joy to watch someone happy in his work. Until he got to the deficit.

What effect, a reporter asked, would all these tax changes and new programs have on the deficit?

"There could be a modest adverse impact on the deficit," Darman said with the same casualness as if he'd been asked what he had for breakfast.

Just what is the current deficit?

"Oh, let me see, heh, heh, the last time I was quoted on that . . . Let's see, a few weeks ago. That would be $399.6 billion." And he quickly went to a chart with five different deficit lines, or "scenarios," that purported to show all variety of economic assumptions, some of them ending in truly frightening figures like $800 billion of red ink by the end of the decade. Darman's wishful-thinking course showed a high number for the next two years, then "a decline in the out years"—starting in 1995. For four years this had been the Darman game: conceding a rise in the next year's deficit, but insisting it was only in return for savings down the road. Right.

But wait a minute. What was that *current figure?* The deficit for 1992?

$399.6 billion.

*Ding-ding-ding-ding!* We have a winner!

Dick Darman, you've got the highest deficit since World War II!

By any standard, you're a winner! You've topped Dave Stockman's record in 1983, when it hit the highest percentage of GNP in peacetime. And that actual number—*could it really be $399.6, like some kind of K Mart shoppers' blue light special? Nah, you know he's fudging that, too, just to make it look good*—was the biggest deficit in the history of deficits anywhere on the planet!

So why was he acting so happy? He was grinning and shrugging and gliding around the stage in his little loafers like a man with nothing more important on his mind than lunch. But how could this be?

There could be only one answer. He'd finally gone mad. He was slaphappy. The numbers, the pressure, the constant harping by Congress, the deal making, the subtle lies, the deceit, the burden of being the only one who really knew what was going on, and finally, the need to obey those imperious cardinals and spend money their way, even though he knew in his heart it was wrong, had all caught up with him.

Think of it: he'd been living in a personal hell-on-earth for a decade, ever since he and Stockman had made their bargain with the Devil and let the deficit soar. As punishment, Darman had been condemned to be budget director for a thousand years, during which time nothing would change. You could see it in that year's budget, which was just like one of Stockman's old ones: the same futile attempts to cut the Economic Development Administration and a couple hundred other programs, the same ranting about how entitlements were eating up the country, the same shifty gimmicks like "the magic asterisk," which you put anyplace the numbers didn't balance, and tax revenue estimates that bore absolutely no relation to reality. But he was supposed to take this and step in front of the public and say with a straight face that here was a good budget.

Like a lot of good Americans, Darman finally couldn't take it anymore. One of the smartest men to serve in government had gone completely out of his mind. The evidence was there. After all, Darman had misestimated the size of the deficit by $900 billion in four years—*and he was chuckling about it!* Dick Darman had become the Dr. Strangelove of economic policy. Now he was about to lose it right here in the war room of economic policy.

That was the only explanation that made sense. Any psychiatrist watching this giddy, reckless performance would have to conclude that Darman had become a threat to himself and others. Grounds for immediate hospitalization.

Surely more responsible officials like Nicholas Brady, the nation's rich uncle, would step to the microphone and say, "Mr. Darman did not mean to suggest that the largest deficit in modern history is a trivial matter. We want to reassure the American people that we are well aware of the significance of this, and we are in control of the situation."

Or what about Mike Boskin, the president's top economic adviser? True, he seems a little wacky himself—after all he keeps talking about economics as a science—but he's a professor from Stanford, for God's sake. He must know this is insanity.

But no one moved. People are sometimes like that when a loved one behaves dementedly. The natural reaction is to ignore him and hope he stops, though clinicians often favor an immediate, positive response, such as hugging.

Brady's eyes darted nervously around the room. Boskin looked at his shoes. Marlin Fitzwater ended the press conference uncomfortably. The economics reports dutifully lugged their seven-pound copies of the budget back to their offices, still trying to figure out the point of what they'd witnessed. Being sober professionals, they'd first file straight page-one stories about what the budget contained. Then, a week or so later, many of them would write prickly analysis pieces, buried deep in the paper, which would say, in essence, "This budget stinks like a dead possum."

Meanwhile, over on the Hill, the cardinals waited. The president's budget, demented though it might have been, was just the dinner bell. Now it was their turn. But all indications, there would be a Pork War in 1992 as well. Only this time it would be a holy war with the cardinals taking the offensive. Bush was incredibly vulnerable to them now. His puny attempts to satiate their lusts would not stand. These were the men who were really in control. The Money Congress. The hog had been brought to the table and the cardinals were sharpening their knives. An observer of the ritual might recall the famous words of Ronald Reagan, who said with a chuckle, not long before he stuck taxpayers with an earlier check, "There you go again . . ."

# ACKNOWLEDGMENTS

Though much of the route through Porkland was uncharted territory, a number of people offered valuable cautions, suggestions and encouragement that helped me navigate my way. Among them:

Sandra Fine, a great researcher, and Margaret Hill, a great pork hunter. Jeffrey Birnbaum, Larry Haas, Mike Binstein, Bill Hogan, Mary Hager, Rich Thomas—all first-rate journalists who understand how Washington works.

Ann McDaniel, Evan Thomas, Mark London, Brian Sexton and Bill Regardie, who listened to half-baked ideas, came up with suggestions, plodded through early drafts and never winced.

There are a number of Capitol Hill staffers who best remain anonymous, but who were nonetheless generous with their time and patience. Several books were also essential: James Bovard's *The Farm Fiasco* is ground-breaking journalism about all sorts of spending, *Congressional Quarterly*'s special edition, "Where the Money Goes," is a remarkable collection of reporting, and David Stockman's *The Triumph of Politics* is amazing in its insights—if only he could run an economy as well as he could write, we'd all be home free.

My editor, Peter Gethers, believed in this project from the first moment he heard of it; his associate editor, Stephanie Long, made the trains run on a very tight deadline.

Rafe Sagalyn is such a great agent, he not only sold the book, he came up with the idea.

And Patti Kelly, my best friend and best editor, put up with a case of temporary insanity.

# INDEX

## ABOUT THE AUTHOR

BRIAN KELLY is the former editor of *Regardie's Magazine* and a former political reporter for the Chicago *Sun-Times*. He is co-author with Mark London of *Amazon* and *The Four Little Dragons*. Currently an editor with *The Washington Post*, he lives in Washington, D.C., with his wife and two children.